THE GOOD LIFE

EDWARD F. FISCHER

The Good Life

Aspiration, Dignity, and the Anthropology of Wellbeing

*With best wishes for
your good life,

Edward F.*

STANFORD UNIVERSITY PRESS

STANFORD, CALIFORNIA

Stanford University Press
Stanford, California

Printed in the United States of America on acid-free, archival-quality paper

Library of Congress Cataloging-in-Publication Data

Fischer, Edward F., 1966- author.
 The good life : aspiration, dignity, and the anthropology of wellbeing /
Edward F. Fischer.
 pages cm
 Includes bibliographical references and index.
 ISBN 978-0-8047-9096-3 (cloth : alk. paper) —
 ISBN 978-0-8047-9253-0 (pbk. : alk. paper)
 1. Well-being—Cross-cultural studies. 2. Quality of life—Cross-cultural studies. 3. Economic anthropology—Cross-cultural studies. I. Title.
 HN25.F57 2014
 306—dc23

  ISBN 978-0-8047-9261-5 (electronic)

Typeset by Bruce Lundquist in 10/14 Janson

For Mareike, Johannes, and Rebecca

Contents

Preface

The genesis of this project, as with so many ethnographic endeavors, began with a chance encounter: in this instance, a reproachful look from the owner of a small cinema. I was in Hamburg with my family over the Christmas holidays, and my 7-year-old son desperately wanted to go see the recently released Harry Potter movie. We had come to Germany to visit family but also to take a breather from the frenetic commercial pace of stateside holidays. Still, Johannes had cheerfully attended all of the *gemütliche* feasts and gatherings, and so we felt that we could hardly deny him such a simple, easy pleasure. Thus, on the *zweiten Weihnachtstag* (the second day of Christmas, December 26, a public holiday), we looked up the schedule in the newspaper and discovered that a neighborhood cinema had a showing at 5:30 that evening. With good German punctuality, and led by my good German wife, we arrived a few minutes after 5:00, only to find a long line already stretching from the ticket window. We took our place at the end of the queue and arrived at the window just in time to buy three of the four remaining tickets, much to the dismay of the family behind us.* As the woman counted our

---

* The little cinema neatly captures some stereotypical German traits: an usher takes one to assigned seats; there is a shelf for drinks and snacks; of course, beer is sold at the concession stand. The Harry Potter movie was subtitled, although most foreign fare on television and at the movies is dubbed, and the German dubbing industry is renowned. Some dubbing voice performers have become wellknown celebrities in their own right, complete with fan clubs. The dubbers work to make the German fit the mouth movements of the English or Swedish or Russian or whatever language is being spoken. A long way from the kung fu movies I watched as a kid, it is difficult to tell that the best German work is dubbed at all—you look closely to catch the occasional gap between what you see and what you hear. It is a minor point of national pride.

money, I asked why she did not offer earlier matinees since there was obviously a demand. She looked at me over half-rim glasses—pausing for a moment as if she did not know where to start—and replied reproachfully that during the holidays kids should not be inside watching movies; rather, they should be at home with their families or playing in the park. She was pleased with my surprise—it seemed to be the effect she was going for—that a small-business owner would voluntarily support a notion of common good at the expense her own material gain, a moral position at odds with the rational expectations of much economic theory and a stance that would be foreign to many American entrepreneurs.

This was one of those a-ha moments of participant observation and ethnographic fieldwork that Willis and Trondman (2000) write about, when a pervasive yet subtle pattern crystallizes for a moment in a concrete interaction. The cinema incident reminded me of experiences from my years of fieldwork in Guatemala, those many economic anomalies (and yet cultural consistencies) in which social concerns trumped self-interested rationality. Once while living in the Kaqchikel Maya town of Tecpán, some friends from there (who had studied abroad and secured good jobs working for international organizations in Guatemala City) came home for a visit. My wife and I were pleased to see them and gladly accepted when they invited us to go with them to the land they kept in one of the surrounding hamlets. Getting to their fields was a trek—we drove about five kilometers and then hiked over a small mountain. I had thought we were just going to check out the land and maybe clean up a little bit, but as it turned out we worked all day—with a break to eat tamale-like *chuchas* heated over a fire for lunch—to harvest the remains of what was missed when the hired hands gathered the crop. In the end, we wound up with a few paltry net loads of maize (which is often carried in large nets on one's back). I was surprised, and frankly a little irritated, at having worked so hard for such a small reward, and that my friends would take time off from their relatively high-paying jobs since, in economic terms, the maize we harvested that day was not worth nearly what their time could garner in wages. Given the opportunity costs, spending our time this way did not make economic sense. I said as much to our friends, and they replied that it was not just about the money, the monetary value of the maize, but the fact that *this* maize came from their ancestral plots; that the maize from there tastes different, better; and that, in any case, it is *xajan* (taboo) to waste maize (one is taught as a child not to drop it or step over it). Most important, they stressed, are these affective ties to the land, a connection with the collective weight of history and the generations of relatives who had worked this land, a value that could be measured in financial terms. Here land and its produce embody familial and social values that coexist with, and sometimes trump, their value as an economic asset.

A final introductory example comes from closer to home, from a cab driver who picked me up at the airport in Washington, D.C., a few years back, just before the city switched to a dashboard meter system. Arman owned the Lincoln Town Car that he drove, and he had it arranged like a car service car, with the front seats moved all the way forward to give more leg room in the back and a newspaper tucked into the seat-back pocket. He obviously took pride in his vehicle, and when I asked him about it he said that he could drive an old beat-up taxi and charge the same fares, but that he liked the professional style. He went on to say that he studied maps and monitored traffic so that he would always know the best route around the city. When I asked him about the switch to meters, he said he was opposed. I protested that the zone fare was such an opaque system for visitors, and that I always had the vague feeling that I overpaid for cab rides. He said that he never overcharged—but when his passenger seemed to him to have money, he charged the normal full fare; for needier passengers he often reduced the zone price to give them a break. He would work out, in the blink of an eye, a complex algorithm, taking into account all the subtle signals of dress and speech that a passenger conveyed, to come up with what he judged to be a fair and just fare. He took great pride in achieving excellence in his trade and he stressed the value of having a sense of control over his life that meters would partly take away.

In each of these stories we find folks motivated by culturally embedded conceptions of "the good life." They envision particular sorts of futures for themselves and the world—the agency to control their own destiny, the meaningful obligations of family and friends, the delicate balance between private interests and common goods. We see individuals giving meaning to their economic activities, each seeking the good life each in his or her own way, and often in ways that run counter to their immediate material interests.

Amartya Sen (1997: 3–4) observes that, "first, there is the broadly ethical question 'How should one live?' To emphasize this connection is not the same as asserting that people will always act in ways they will themselves morally defend, but only to recognize that ethical deliberations cannot be totally inconsequential to actual human behavior." The examples above, and the many that follow, show individuals making decisions based on culturally particular and deeply held values: valuing—materially—things beyond narrowly defined self-interest. These are economic decisions embedded in larger projects, actions motivated by particular conceptions of the good life. Our understandings of economics, commerce, public policy, development programs, and, indeed, of our own quotidian ways of being and doing, can benefit from taking into account these different value systems. What follows is my effort to move in that direction, looking for best practices and cautionary tales across cultures to develop a positive anthropology of wellbeing.

THE GOOD LIFE

Introduction

The Good Life: Values, Markets, and Wellbeing

This book explores what the good life means for people living in very different places and circumstances. I report on ethnographic fieldwork among urban German shoppers and among rural Maya farmers, looking at how people engage the market to pursue their own visions of wellbeing. By the last chapter, I hope to have convinced you that there are lessons to be learned from different understandings of wellbeing across cultures, lessons for how we organize our own lives and societies.

I begin with a simple proposition: that we should understand the ends of economics, as well as politics, to be provisioning the good life as widely as possible for people as they themselves conceive it. This normative assertion then raises the empirical questions: Just what are different people's visions of the good life? And how do they engage markets in pursuit of wellbeing as they conceive it? In this book I document the well-established importance of material conditions (income, health, security) but show that most people's views of wellbeing—across cultures—cannot be reduced to material conditions alone. People are more than self-interested agents concerned only with material gains, even if we do fit that stereotype at times. Here I focus on key non-material qualities that define the good life: aspiration and opportunity, dignity and fairness, and commitments to larger purposes. Recognizing such elements of the good life in other cultures allows us to see our own social structures, markets, and political systems in a critical light, and to evaluate market forces and regulatory systems as mechanisms to promote not only material wealth, but greater overall wellbeing.[1]

We often use "happiness" as shorthand for wellbeing, but there are at least two types of happiness. There is the "hedonic" happiness of everyday contentment (and the cheeriness the term calls to mind in common American usage). Then there is a broader sense of "life satisfaction," judged by the criteria of "wellbeing" and "the good life."[2] Some might call this second condition simply "happiness" as well, but it is more in line with the Aristotelian ideal of a fulfilled life, *eudaimonia*. The Greek roots of eudaimonia aptly carry the connotation of benevolent power over one's destiny, the power to construct a life that one values.

If wellbeing is more than just being well, then perhaps the good life is not a state to be obtained but an ongoing aspiration for something better that gives meaning to life's pursuits. In this view, striving for the good life involves the arduous work of becoming, of trying to live a life that one deems worthy, becoming the sort of person that one desires. As such, the good life is not made up of simple happiness. It requires trade-offs, and often forgoing hedonistic pleasure. Robert Nozick (1974) asks if it would be preferable to live in an "experience machine" that could give one any experience desired (indistinguishable from real life) or to live one's real up-and-down life. Nozick argues that most folks would choose real life, that the pleasures and pains of real experience and struggle give value to the ends enjoyed, and that individuals are driven to be certain sorts of people (not indeterminate blobs). Similarly, in the film *The Matrix*, Neo is faced with a blue pill/red pill dilemma, and clearly the scary reality of the red pill is the right, and virtuous, path to take, even though it is the antithesis of the blue pill's blissful ignorance.

These two sorts of happiness—hedonic and eudaimonic—can well be at odds with each other, a tension familiar to most from daily life and one crucial to understanding economic behavior. In this book I examine wellbeing and the good life by looking at how different sorts of values (cultural, moral, material) inform economic relations. We look to German supermarket shoppers, who overwhelmingly say they prefer organic and free-range eggs, but as often as not actually buy cheaper alternatives. A complicated and imprecise calculus is at work here, translating moral values into hard prices at the level of individual choice. More broadly, such concerns inform public policy, as we see in Germany's "social market economy" and its model of co-determination. In the second half of the book I turn to a very different case: Maya farmers in Guatemala growing high-end coffee for the global market. Here too we find values congealing around market relations. In a context of material scarcity and limited opportunities, smallholding rural famers actively engage new market demands for specialty high-altitude coffee, seeing them as an imperfect path to the *algo más* (something better) they envision.

Germany, Guatemala, and the United States

Germany and Guatemala may seem like an odd pair for comparison, sharing little beyond their alliterative quality. In fact, they have a number of striking similarities. In both countries there is a strong attachment to place of birth and much less mobility than in the United States; marked regional ethnic and linguistic variation; and a preference for using cash in daily transactions.* Both places are defined in fundamental ways by histories of genocidal state violence: the German Holocaust and Guatemala's *violencia*. Germany and Guatemala are also bound by intertwined histories of migration and coffee exports. All the same, those coincidences are less relevant for our present purpose than the lessons we can learn about wellbeing from a close examination of vastly different social, political, and economic contexts.

In both places we find broadly similar concerns around aspirations and agency, the ability and opportunity to effectively pursue one's vision of the future; around dignity and fairness; and around the moral projects that impart a sense of larger purpose to one's life. These similarities emerge from very different political economies. According to the United Nations Development Programme's Human Development Index (HDI), and by almost any measure, Germany ranks in the top tier of highly developed countries. While gross national income per head is much lower in Germany than in

* A more extensive list of Guatemala/Germany similarities may be found on my blog at www.tedfischer.org.

the United States, for example, Germany gets high marks in health, education, and security.* Much derided during the 1990s and early 2000s for its rigidity and perpetually high unemployment, the German model emerged from the 2008 financial crisis as an example to be emulated, lauded in remarks from the World Economic Forum in Davos to the pages of the *Wall Street Journal* and the *New York Times*. In contrast, Guatemala is more often held up as a cautionary tale. In terms of national income per capita, it ranks toward the bottom of "middle-income" countries, although this masks very high levels of inequality. By any measure, the Maya (who make up half the population) suffer the highest rates of poverty and exclusion in the country. In the 2011 HDI rankings, Guatemala ranks 131 (out of 187 countries), following Botswana (118), Vietnam (128), and just ahead of Iraq (132); for comparison, Brazil ranks 84 on the HDI and Mozambique is at 184. In the 2000s, Guatemala became a key spot in the international cocaine trade, and traffickers effectively control large swaths of the country. The violent death rate is among the highest in the world, and impunity largely reigns with a murder conviction rate that hovers around nil. In these and many ways, Guatemala and Germany could hardly be more different.

Economic and Social Indicators for Germany, Guatemala, and the United States

	2011 Human Development Index Rank	Gross National Income per Capita ($US)	Life Expectancy (years)	Gini Index of Inequality[a]	Murder Rate (per 100,000)
Guatemala	131	4,167	71.2	55.1	39
Germany	9	34,854	80.4	27	0.84
United States	4	43,017	78.5	45	4.8

SOURCE: *UNDP World Development Report* (2011); *CIA World Fact Book* (2012).
[a] 0 = perfect equality, and 100 = perfect inequality (both extremes are hypothetical, of course).

Elements of the Good Life

Looking at how wellbeing is conceived in Germany and Guatemala, we see people engaging their circumstances as both producers and consumers to pursue their own visions of the good life. In both cases, the concept of wellbeing is morally laden—replete with ideas about value, worth, virtue, what is good

* Gross national product (GNP) and gross national income (GNI) are roughly similar measures of national economic activity; I use them interchangeably here, depending on the source.

or bad, right or wrong. We find people who give moral meanings to their many market interactions, and take moral meanings from them as well. This is true not only in exotic Guatemala and distant Germany, but also in our own culture. Think of the moralities around consumption—the overtly ethical component of trade in Fair Trade and organic goods, but also the ways consumption embodies meanings around thrift and generosity, family obligations and social relations, and a whole host of other personal and cultural values.

To understand the good life, wherever it may be found, we must take seriously not only material conditions but also people's desires, aspirations, and imaginations—the hopes, fears, and other subjective factors that drive their engagement with the world. Such motivations are resistant to simple quantification and often dismissed or overlooked in the economic and development literature (Miller 1998; Biehl 2007; Laidlaw 2007). Anthropology provides the possibility of another approach, valuing what people say the good life should look like and building an understanding of wellbeing from the ground up through the dialectic engagement of fieldwork. Arjun Appadurai (2013: 292) observes that "the missing piece here has been a systematic effort to understand how cultural systems, as combinations of norms, dispositions, practices, and histories, frame the good life as a landscape of discernable ends and of practical paths to the achievement of these ends."

Toward that end, this book presents a systematic comparison of conceptions of wellbeing and the good life in very different places, focusing on commonalities as well as differences.[3] In line with other research, I find that **adequate material resources** ("adequate" being relatively defined), **physical health and safety**, and **family and social relations** are all core and necessary elements of wellbeing. Yet alone they are insufficient. The research I report on here points to the importance of three more subjective domains:

- **aspiration and opportunity**
- **dignity and fairness**
- **commitment to a larger purpose**

In what follows, I show how these qualities are expressed by German consumers and Maya farmers, what they mean for *their* visions of the good life, and what they can tell *us* about wellbeing.

Wellbeing requires a capacity for **aspiration** as well as the agency and opportunity to make realizing aspirations seem viable. Appadurai (2013: 187–

89) distinguishes specific *aspirations* (which "form parts of wider ethical and metaphysical ideas that derive from larger cultural norms") from *the capacity to aspire*, conceived as a navigational capability ("nurtured by the possibility of real-world conjectures and refutations"), mapping the steps from here to there as oriented by cultural and ethical visions of the future. This perspective recognizes the strategic element of choice, often overlooked in studies of poor and marginalized peoples, and the substantive basis for what is broadly glossed in the development literature as "empowerment" (control over one's destiny). It also has the virtue of embracing a subjective sense of desire and the role of imagination in determinations of value (Fischer and Benson 2006; Beckert 2011; Moore 2011; Nelson 2013).

Michael Jackson (2011:xi) writes that ideas about wellbeing "are grounded in the mystery of existential discontent" (an inevitable "sense of insufficiency and loss") that leads to hope, "that sense that one may become other or more than one presently is or was fated to be." Living up to the expectations of particular values is in many ways the stock and trade of human existence; and it is this forward-looking, aspirational quality that gives meaning to much of what we do, affluent and impoverished alike.[4]

Notions of the good life orient the aspirations of agency and provide a dynamic framework with which to interpret one's own actions and those of others, all the while bound by the realm of what is seen as possible. The market is a key venue through which to pursue the good life, and, as we will see, a sizable percentage of German middle-class supermarket shoppers explicitly link their buying choices to their support for particular ecological and social ideals. Similarly, we find Maya farmers actively engaging and changing the coffee market in Guatemala in pursuit of their particular aspirations for the good life.

Yet the effectiveness of aspiration and agency is often limited by available **opportunity structures** (the social norms, legal regulations, and market entry mechanisms that delimit, or facilitate, certain behaviors and aspirations). The *will* is important, but there also has to be a *way*. Opportunity structures encompass not only market relations but also formal and informal social norms; ethnic, gender, and other systematic distinctions; the principles and practice of legal rights; and the whole range of institutional factors that define the space of the possible. Individual agency acts on choices, but those choices are structured through political-economic processes that transcend the individual (Ferguson 1999; Tsing 2004; Li 2007; Thin 2012).

In situations where agency far exceeds available opportunity structures, we find "frustrated freedom."[5]

Wellbeing also builds on cultural valuations of **fairness and dignity**. On the one hand, these include basic rights such as freedom from discrimination and exclusion. In a more expansive sense, they also entail the positive value of respect, a sense of being treated fairly. What is considered "fair" varies across cultures, but wherever one draws the line, the respect of others is crucial to subjective wellbeing. Our reaction to what we perceive to be unfair inequalities is almost visceral (de Waal 2009), and this may be magnified by the relational and symbolic values of positional goods (Frank 2010). To the extent that fairness overlaps with greater material equality, it is associated with better health, security, and education (Wilkinson and Pickett 2009). Among Maya coffee growers in Guatemala, dignity is associated with control over land and productive resources, as well as strong social norms that define what is considered fair and just. In Germany, a different sort of dignity is expressed through discourses around the notion of "solidarity" and through the regulatory structures of co-determination.

Many German shoppers say they buy free-range eggs to support the environment and good working conditions, a project they articulate as showing "solidarity." Maya farmers are explicitly working toward a different future and a better life for their children. In both cases, we see people building meaningful life projects oriented around visions of the good life. Having such **larger purpose** and being part of meaningful projects that go beyond narrow self-interest are central to wellbeing among both the affluent and the poor. What constitutes "meaningful" is defined through cultural values and a sense of purpose based on what matters most in life. This idea overlaps with Alasdair MacIntyre's (1984) definition of virtue—excellence at a given practice that can range from mastery of a particular skill (a commitment to the trade of carpentry or plumbing, for example) to caring for one's family to any number of the life projects we use to define ourselves and our character. Nor do meaningful projects need to be what we might consider positive: they encompass hate-group ideology as well as religious fervor, the mastery of a video game as much as mastery of a vocation. Larger purposes have to be meaningful, but their meanings are not determined by any absolute code and span the range of political and social leanings. A Pew Center study reports that extremists on both sides of the political spectrum (hard-core ideologues) express much greater life satisfaction than do moderates (Brooks 2012); I suggest that this is due to their commitment to a project that gives meaning to their life, regardless of their efforts' success. In pursuing larger purposes and life projects, we improvise, adapt, and even sometimes act against our own better judgment, betraying values we have earlier proclaimed. Yet believing in these projects gives meaning and direction to life.

Dimensions of Happiness

Since the late 1990s there has been a boom of research around issues of wellbeing. In the United States, Germany, and the developed world, this usually falls under the rubric of *happiness studies* and builds on innovative work coming from psychology and economics. For the developing world, a parallel field has emerged through *multidimensional approaches to poverty* and Amartya Sen's influential capabilities perspective on development. While it is telling that we use two different terms to study wellbeing in the developed world and the global South, the overlap in their general findings is most significant.

Happiness studies and multidimensional measures of poverty show that income is crucially important for one's ability to achieve a good life, but alone it is not enough. That is to say that income, wealth, and material resources are necessary but insufficient prerequisites for wellbeing. In fact, increases in happiness level off dramatically after people reach a relatively low income threshold. People need financial and material resources, but not in the proportion we might first imagine. Daniel Kahneman (2011: 397) observes that although being poor usually makes one miserable, being rich does not ensure experienced wellbeing. People who feel they contribute importantly to a larger project, those that possess the agency and power to effect change, are more satisfied with their lives.[6]

Wealthier people are on average happier than poor ones, but there is no neat linear relationship between income and happiness. The Easterlin Paradox holds that in international comparisons average happiness does not rise with average income, although within a single country the wealthier tend to be happier than the poor (Easterlin 2001). Richard Easterlin's findings have been challenged by Stevenson and Wolfers (2008),[7] but it still seems that, at least above a certain point, income is valued relative to the income of one's peer group and others.[8] Richard Layard (2005: 44) writes that "income is much more than a means to buy things. We also use our income, compared to others', as a measure of how we are valued and (if we are not careful) a measure of how we value ourselves" (see also Gilbert 2005; Veenhoven 2000). Robert Frank (1999) has argued that the ways the affluent tend to spend additional income (on positional goods and conspicuous consumption) adds little to collective happiness. On the other hand, José Juan Vázquez (2013: 1) finds that garbage collectors in León, Nicaragua, "state that they are happy, have optimistic expectations regarding their future, and show a lack of any relationship between overall happiness and income."

Perhaps there is a hedonic treadmill of adapting quickly to upward mobility. (Although, as the recent financial crisis reminds us, adaptation can occur either by adjusting aspirations upward or by adjusting them downward.) This would explain the curvilinear relationship between income and happiness: more income produces proportionate advances in happiness up to a given point. Kahneman (2011: 397) reports that, in households with incomes of $75,000 and above in high-cost areas in the United States, experienced wellbeing does not increase along with rising income. Kahneman and Angus Deaton (2010) argue that although hedonic happiness is not tightly associated with income, broader measures of life satisfaction do have a linear relationship. Carol Graham (2011) suggests that instability and uncertainty significantly decrease happiness (at a national level in economies undergoing rapid transition, and individually with life changes). But people also adapt more quickly than they think they will to even catastrophic disabilities (such as becoming paraplegic) and great good fortune (such as winning the lottery) (Brickman, Coates, Janoff-Bulman 1978).

Development, Income, and the Good Life

Inspired by the work of Nobel laureate Amartya Sen (1979), a capabilities approach sees the goal of economic development as substantive freedom: the capability of individuals to pursue the life that they themselves value. This pursuit requires income, but (as with the relatively affluent subjects of happiness studies) also agency, the capability to act with intention, to envision and make changes in one's life, to aspire.[9] In this vein, James Foster et al. (2013: 1) define poverty as "the absence of acceptable choices across a broad range of important life decisions" that results in "a severe lack of freedom to be or do what one wants."

Income can be a useful measurement of development, and we have long ranked countries by average GNP per head. But such averages are at best imperfect measures of wellbeing. As in Guatemala, they may hide inequality: a country can have a relatively high GNP per capita with the vast majority living in poverty. (In the same vein, if Bill Gates walked into a soup kitchen in Seattle, the average annual income of people there would skyrocket—but that would not tell us much about the distribution of wellbeing among individuals.) In response to the shortcomings of national income measures, and inspired by the work of Sen, in 1990 the UNDP introduced its now widely used Human Development Index (HDI), which incorporates measures of health and education as well as income to measure a more holistic "human development."*

The idea of looking at wellbeing in addition to economic metrics to measure the success of public policies has taken hold in Latin America, Africa, and the developing world, as well as in Asia and Europe. The concept of *buen vivir* explicitly informs policy in Bolivia and Ecuador (Gudynas 2011; Fatheuer 2011). China's overarching policy goal of promoting a "harmonious" society melds Confucian principles with multidimensional measures of wellbeing. Bhutan famously has adopted a gross national happiness index to orient public policy and measure the country's development in terms of wellbeing. France and Britain too have explored ways to move beyond GNP as a measure of economic and political success (see Stiglitz, Sen, and Fitoussi 2010; and Dolan, Layard, and Metcalfe 2011).

The HDI and other multidimensional measures are a big improvement over GNP rankings, but they remain very blunt measures for overall wellbeing, *eudaimonia*. The Oxford Poverty and Human Development Initiative (OPHI), led by Sabina Alkire, has introduced more holistic measures, focused on what they term the "missing dimensions" of poverty (adapted from www.ophi.org.uk): *Employment* is the main source of income for most households globally; having a good and decent job is usually associated with being out of poverty, however poverty is defined. In addition, employment can give

---

* The World Bank defines two categories of poverty in absolute terms: extreme poverty is living on less than $1.25 a day (in purchasing power parity terms) and moderate poverty at less than $2 a day (see Ravallion 1994, 2008; Ravallion and Chen 2008).

one a sense of self-respect and a fulfilling life, and low employment quality is a fundamental aspect of individual deprivation. *The ability to go about without shame* addresses the painful effects of discrimination and humiliation cited by poor people and communities as painful components of their deprivation. Shame and humiliation can result in isolation, thereby corroding social relations. *Agency* denotes the freedom to act on behalf of what one values and has reason to value. The opposite of a person with agency is someone who is coerced, oppressed, or passive. Agency recurs as a variable that is of intrinsic and instrumental importance to impoverished communities. *Psychological and subjective wellbeing* are key components of the other dimensions, as well as an end result of their attainment. Moreover, they contribute a richer perspective to our understanding of human experience and values, and particularly the importance of their non-material components. Finally, *Physical safety* is fundamental to ensuring the viability of development gains achieved in areas such as education, health, employment, income generation, and infrastructure provision (see Alkire 2005, 2008; Alkire and Foster 2011; Alkire and Santos 2010; Alkire, Qizilbash, and Comim 2008).

The OPHI missing dimensions are not meant to be an exhaustive list of the conditions of poverty, but they do a good job of covering key areas and possess the great virtue of being practical: these are items that can actually be measured with surveys and available data. While I focus on more subjective qualities, the elements of wellbeing I find in the cases discussed here significantly overlap with the OPHI list. For example, what I label fairness and dignity includes employment conditions and the ability to go about without shame; what OPHI calls agency, I have broken down into aspiration, agency, and opportunity structures.

Robert Skidelsky and Edward Skidelsky (2012) identify seven "basic goods" necessary for the good life. They begin with health, security, and respect, which clearly overlap with the OPHI dimensions; they continue with personality, which maps closely to my dimension of aspiration and agency; and they round out their list with friendship, leisure, and harmony with nature. The Legatum Institute's Prosperity Index includes eight distinct composite variables, from social capital and personal freedom to governance and the economy (www.prosperity.com). Martha Nussbaum (2011: 20) offers a more expansive list of what she considers to be the ten central capabilities required for the good life ("not just abilities residing inside a person but also the freedoms or opportunities created by a combination of personal abilities and the political, social, and economic environment"). Intended as an open and revisable list, Nussbaum's dimensions extend the scope of wellbeing to include emotions, practical reason, play, and imagination. While harder to operationalize, Nussbaum's concern with the subjective experience speaks to my focus here on desires, aspirations, and ethnographic conceptions of the good life.

No matter how long the particular list, accounting for the more subjective dimensions of poverty and wellbeing allows us to find correlations we would miss from income and material conditions data alone.

But here is the rub: We may all want to live the good life, but we also differ widely on just what that entails, on what the good life might look like and the best means to get there. Conceptions of the good life are laden with deeply held moral valuations, the various meanings behind a "meaningful life." Such conceptions are culturally specific and even idiosyncratic, but they share a common concern with *values* (what is *really* important in life) and an orientation toward the future that is not necessarily, or at least not easily, quantifiable.

Values, Virtues, and Wellbeing

For Aristotle, fulfillment comes from pursuing ends for their own sake (not as an instrumental means toward other ends); he argues that there is virtue in the purity and sincerity of such pursuit.[10] For example, it is virtuous of me to write this book because I have a desire to do so (a desire to develop thoughts and express them), but not because I want to make some money (and that is a good thing, too, given the state of academic publishing). Aristotle recognized that we have to have the material resources to enjoy such virtuous pursuits (and this is a very big condition indeed), but his contribution comes from stressing the values that go beyond just material resources. Significantly, he also saw virtue as a disposition of habit, what we might term cultural.

While words like "morals" and "virtues" are often used in popular discourse to denote timeless, essential cultural prescriptions, I use them in a more ethnographic and descriptive sense to refer to those cultural (and psychological/ethical) processes that deal with valuations of what is considered good and bad, better and worse (see also Laidlaw 2002; Sayer 2011). I see moral projects as the product of ongoing processes of socially situated negotiation, continually enacted through the dialectic of everyday social life and yet strongly conditioned by path dependencies and the weight of history and tradition (Fischer 2001). I draw on the work of Alasdair MacIntyre (1984) and his view of virtue as excellence within the domain of a given "practice," a perspective that moves away from the universalizing tendencies of cardinal virtues and allows for greater cultural latitude.[11] In such a practice, one finds meaning in larger projects, and culturally salient virtues reference visions and valuations of what the good life could and should be.

The Kichwa concept of *sumac kawsay* (usually translated into Spanish as *buen vivir*), for example, bases its holistic view of wellbeing on the values of "fullness of life in a community" (Gudynas 2011: 442). These are understood to include health, shelter, food, education, and community participation, with an emphasis on environmental harmony and the rights of *Pachamama* (Mother Earth).

The Dismal Science and the Good Life

Moral values inform economic behavior. On its face, this is an unassailable proposition. Think of the often spiritual appeal of consumer goods or the value-laden stakes of upward or downward mobility. Think about the central role that moral questions regarding poverty, access to health care, the tax code, property and land rights, and corruption play in the shaping of modern governments, societies, and social movements. The moral aspects of the marketplace have never been so contentious or consequential (Fischer 2014).

Despite this, the realm of economics is often treated as a world unto itself, a domain where human behavior is guided not by emotions, beliefs, moralities, or the passions but by the hard calculus of rational choices. The fiction that "it's not personal, it's just business" is taken as unquestioned fact (Hart 2005). Many economists recognize "the limits of the self-interested, rational actor as a proxy for human decision making" (Goodenough 2008: 228), and the 2008 financial crisis led even true believers such as Richard Posner and Alan Greenspan to question some of their axiomatic principles. Daniel McFadden (a recipient of the Nobel Prize in economics, no less),[*]

---

[*] Formally, the economics prize is the SverigesRiksbank Prize in Economic Sciences in Memory of Alfred Nobel, and not one of the prizes endowed by Alfred Nobel, despite being widely known as the Nobel Prize in economics.

writes that, "The neoclassical model of the individualistic utility-maximizing consumer that forms the basis of most economic analysis is largely a finished subject" (2013: 1). But, as Deirdre McCloskey (2002) points out, in economics classrooms, public policy debates and popular discourse, a simplified view of *Homo economicus* and the nature of "free markets" has come to dominate, with explanations of why humans behave as they do focusing on rational, self-interested, utility-maximizing individuals.

There are ethical and political consequences to such models of economic behavior. If humans are assumed to be unwaveringly driven by self-interest, then the economy is best managed by isolating moral questions and concerns. Judging economic behavior and public policy is not a question of good or bad, but rather efficient or inefficient, of how to best maximize utilities (Becker 1996; Becker and Becker 1996; Samuelson 1976). In this view, trade restrictions, national borders, political corruption, religious values, and other such issues are seen as barriers to and distortions of a fluid marketplace. Efficiency is championed as the ultimate moral practice—producing the most goods for the most people (even if distribution is seen to be handled by the fundamental fairness of a "free" market).[12]

·   ·   ·

The attraction of the neoclassical approach rests in its parsimony, translating the chaos of everyday life into a metric system of numbers and models. Applying scientific rigor to behavior, economics has come to rely on mathematical modeling based on assumptions about equilibrium and maximization as expressed through utility functions. Textbooks liken the workings of markets to natural forces, distancing the field's historical roots in philosophy and ethics. Popular books like *Freakonomics, Discover Your Inner Economist*, and *The Undercover Economist* convey a message of ethical agnosticism about human behavior (just letting the facts speak for themselves) and fuel the conceit of a brand of economics most closely associated with Milton Friedman, Gary Becker, and the Chicago School.

This trend tragically popularizes a certain variety of economics as the field's public face at the very moment that economics is witnessing a proliferation of new and innovative behavioral and empirical approaches that not only recognize but embrace the classical model's anomalies.[13] In fact, economics has a good deal to offer anthropology and the other social sciences, especially in its sophisticated models of preferences and utility maximization, and these new directions in the field open the possibility of a more complicated picture of subjective components of economic behavior, especially moral values, that have long been bracketed in utility functions (see Hart, Laville, and Cattani 2010; Gudeman 2008; Chibnik 2011).

If Adam Smith is the unwitting patron saint of neoclassical free-market economics and *The Wealth of Nations* its Ur-text, his other great work, *Theory of Moral Sentiments*, gives equal weight to the role of morals. McCloskey (2006: 306) sees Smith as a "virtue ethicist for a commercial age." While he famously claimed that there is a human "propensity to truck, barter, and exchange," he also saw sympathy as an original part of human nature for both "the civilized and the brutish."* Smith was contemptuous of self-love, and saw sympathy (or "fellow-feeling"), the ability to identify with others, as both a fundamental part of human nature and what keeps in check self-love (if, perhaps, only because injury to another causes sympathetic pain in oneself); his is a moral stance built up from fellow-feeling.[14]

Of course, the flip side of virtue is vice, and greed (or avarice) is one of the West's deadly sins; for St. Paul and Aquinas it is the root of all evil. Albert O. Hirschman (1977) shows how Smith and other 18th-century philosophers transmogrified the passion and vice of "greed" into the rationality of "interests." Hirschman (1977: 43–44) writes that "interest was seen to partake in effect of the better nature of each, as the passion of self-love upgraded and contained by reason, and as reason given direction and force by passion. The resulting hybrid form of human action was considered exempt from both the destructiveness of passion and the ineffectuality of reason."

Shared moral values undergird economic systems, including, and perhaps even especially, anonymous market exchange. As Kenneth Arrow (1974), among others, has shown, trust, loyalty, and honesty have clear economic value and are essential to the efficiency of the economy. Indeed, pursuit of the intrinsic rewards of a value-based system (virtues) is necessary for the workings of free and fair exchange. Businesses would crash if employees only did what they were explicitly told to do (or were explicitly paid to do);

---

* Smith also saw a desire to better one's condition as a human universal that "comes with us from the womb, and never leaves us till we go into the grave." As with utility, the rub is that there is great variation in what "something better" might mean (see Fischer and Benson 2006).

work-to-rule strikes can virtually stop production when workers simply start following rules to the letter. Economic systems built simply on the enticement of extrinsic rewards often fail in the long run.

Values may also stand in opposition to market relations. Debra Satz (2010) looks at "why some things should not be for sale," arguing that markets should be organized around explicit principles of justice as well as efficiency. Most folks accept that the prohibitions on selling human organs, sex, and freedom are just and fair incursions on the free market. Richard M. Titmuss (1970) found that paying for blood instead of relying on donations actually decreased the quantity and quality of blood, indicating that people have a deep preference to give rather than sell certain items. And Michael Sandel (2012) points out that often what is most important in life is precisely what money cannot buy. Still, markets are increasingly involved in our lives, even in areas once considered anathema to market logics. Markets are certainly important venues for expressing all sorts of values (from frugality to ecoconsciousness to nationalism), but they also help shape those very same values through the suggestions of advertising and the framing of choices.

To reduce moral and cultural values to an individualistic and monetary "utility" is to miss an opportunity to understand the fundamentally social and contextual dimensions of human behavior. That morality matters in ordinary people's economic decisions and attitudes, and that values and norms are historically particular, is contradicted by market fundamentalists who view moralities and moral beliefs as superfluous, as nothing more than secondary explanations that detract from an objective account of natural laws: "morality represents the way we would like the world to work and economics represents how it actually does work" (Levitt and Dubner 2005: 50).

In fact, how we want the world to work is just as important as how it actually does work in understanding what drives us toward a particular future and what informs visions of the good life.

Moral Economies

Moral and cultural assumptions about what is good and bad, right and wrong, fair and just are inherent in all economic institutions and systems.[15] Most closely associated with the work of James Scott (1977, 1985), "moral economy" often refers to cultural traditions that are subversive to capitalist relations, such as moral values about fair prices and economic practices (Thompson 1971; Hann 2010).

For present purposes, I follow Andrew Sayer's (2000, 2004) expansive understanding of moral economy. For Sayer, morals are not external to the market, but internal to all economic orders. This is to say that all economies are "moral" in the sense that they embody and reproduce values. Economic systems are built on assumptions—often taken-for-granted and naturalized assumptions—about what is good, desirable, worthy, ethical, and just. These assumptions are culturally informed and historically particular, even though some actors (say, policymakers, neoclassical economists, or human rights advocates) struggle to codify certain values as "universal."

Put another way, economic systems aggressively promote moral values. Economies are evolving historical systems, and moral values are part and parcel of their normal functioning.[16] Competing values of self-interest and public good are worked out through moral frameworks, often involving the translation of different sorts of values.[17]

Anthropological approaches treat the market as a system shaped from cultural and institutional legacies, treating capitalism as a vernacular phenomenon that must be understood in terms of how economic processes are "embedded" in social networks, local cultures, or political systems (Polanyi 1944; Sahlins 1972; Wilk 1996; Gudeman 2008; Chibnik 2011). The ethics of the economy are formed from the ground up in an ongoing creative process, and market values are tightly linked to identity politics and moral discourses around fairness and dignity. While moral values reflect the accumulation of historical experience, they also orient people to the future, shape a sense of how things ought to be, and define what "better" means. As Appadurai (2013: 293) observes, "it is only through some sort of politics of hope that any society or group can envisage a journey to desirable change in the state of things."

This Book and a Positive Anthropology

The chapters that follow document key components of wellbeing in different cultural contexts. I have divided the book into two parts, the first focusing on Germany and the second on Guatemala, and I begin each with an extended ethnographic example.

Part I ("German Eggs, Cars, and Values") starts with a look at the odd case of egg purchases in a Hannover supermarket. Because of the prominent labeling regime there (organic, free-range, caged, etc.), consumers are forced to make an ethical choice about social values with each egg purchase, and one with clear material costs. In Chapter 1 we see what Hannover shoppers say about their egg choices, the meanings they embody, and what these say about the good life. Then, in Chapter 2, we look at what consumers actually buy, which is not always the same as what they say they prefer. Doing so allows us to critically analyze the economic distinction between stated and revealed preferences, and to see how stated preferences are attuned to core values and reflect the long-term, pro-social ends so important to wellbeing. Where our goods come from has particular cultural meaning, and Chapter 3 turns to the role of provenance in our valuation of things, focusing on moral provenance and notions of the good life. Pulling back from the ethnographic particulars to how institutional constraints and cultural values play into the formation of uniquely German forms of markets, in Chapter 4 we look at the structural framework of German capitalism—finance, labor relations, and consumer regulations—as well as the ways individuals engage the market economy in pursuit of the good life.

The second half of the book ("Guatemalan Coffee, Cocaine, and Capabilities") turns first to Maya coffee farmers in highland Guatemala. Working on remote, high-altitude plots, these smallholding farmers have benefited from a global boom in high-end coffee. In Chapter 5, we examine their visions of the good life and how market interactions feed into their sense of wellbeing. These farmers want something more out of life, and they see coffee production as an imperfect but useful vehicle for their aspirations. In Chapter 6, we look at the interaction between their aspirations for the future and the opportunity structures with which they are presented, calling on a capabilities approach to human development. Reporting on the results of economic experiments a colleague and I conducted in two Maya communities, Chapter 7 examines the role of fairness and dignity in economic rationalities. In Chapter 8 I pull back the lens, as I did for Germany in Chapter 4, to give the reader a look at the larger institutional context, examining the role of drug trafficking and endemic violence and their impacts on wellbeing.

Finally, documenting stated preferences and visions of what the good life might look like opens the door onto a "positive anthropology." In the conclusion, I explore this way of combining cultural critique with non-prescriptive, ethnographically informed positive alternatives that engage public policy debates. If the ends of economies and politics are to have folks live more meaningful and fulfilled lives—and not just increase income and consumption—then we should look to ways to help people realize their longer-term goals and an affluence that is seen in all of its multiple dimensions.

Arjun Appadurai observes a tension between "the ethics of possibility" (of hope, aspiration, desire) and the "ethics of probability" (of systematized rationalities, risk management, and costs/benefits). He calls for a renewed commitment to an ethics of possibility "grounded in the view that a genuinely democratic politics cannot be based on the avalanche of numbers—about population, poverty, profit, and predation—that threaten to kill all street-level optimism about life and the world. [This ethics of possibility should] offer a more inclusive platform for improving the planetary quality of life and can accommodate a plurality of visions of the good life" (2013: 299–300).

.   .   .

The approach I take here advocates for studies of economic behavior that work between the "is" and the "ought" of David Hume's distinction, between how the world can be empirically shown to work (the "is") and how the competing and diverse value systems that anthropological research documents can be linked to moral reflection about things might be different (the "ought"). In this light, ethnographic understandings of different values—what is the good life, what is the balance of private gain and public good—are a crucial corollary to the study of economics. What counts as a "conclusion" to an ethnographically grounded empirical study of economic behavior can be expanded to include both relevant research findings and more conjectural discussion with an eye toward the future.

PART ONE

German Eggs, Cars, and Values

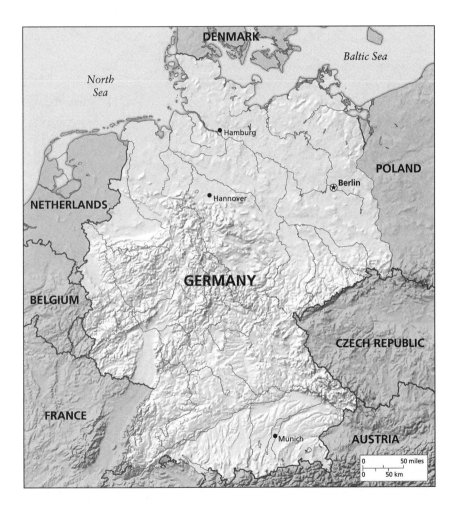

CHAPTER I

Values and Prices

The Case of German Eggs

What price are we willing to pay to be virtuous? Can we put a dollars-and-cents price on specific acts of virtue? Are these two realms even compatible—or fungible, as they say in economics? Are folks willing to pay a premium to do the right thing? Or does material self-interest prevail when we are asked to put our money where our morals are? What does all of this mean for the good life?

Let's start with buying eggs. That might seem an odd place to begin a discussion of the good life, but a lot of wellbeing is linked to such small moments that fill our days. Buying eggs may be something most of us do without much thought beyond occasionally comparing prices. But egg shopping in Germany compels one to make an explicit moral decision with every purchase, to lay bare the price one puts on certain values. This presents us with an ideal natural experiment to answer the question, What price are German shoppers willing to pay to be virtuous?

Since 2004 the European Union (EU) has required all eggs (the packages and the individual eggs) to carry a numeric code. (This could be a set-up for one of the commonly heard jokes about the more absurd and intrusive EU regulations, such as the specifications for cucumber curvature.) The first in the string of digits denotes how the chicken was raised, followed by a two-letter code for the country of origin (DE for Deutschland), and then a unique identifying number for the farm and packing company. The designations for how the eggs were handled are 0 (organic and free-range), 1 (free-range), 2 (cage-free), and 3 (coop-raised, also sometimes pejoratively termed "KZ," or concentration camp, eggs—a strong analogy indeed for Germans, who tend not to joke about the Holocaust). These designations are posted over display shelves, putting front-and-center details on the conditions of production and forcing a morally laden decision about how much to pay for the social values embodied in different sorts of eggs. There is a price to pay for perceived virtue, and it is a decision one has to make every time one buys eggs.

In this chapter, I look at middle-class supermarket shoppers in the Südstadt neighborhood of Hannover, Germany, focusing on the eggs they buy and the reasons they give for their selections. Shoppers express a broad concern with the provenance of eggs, which is facilitated by the mandatory labeling. They often explain their choices in terms of a salient cultural notion of social "solidarity" and a broad commitment to environmental stewardship. Our focus here is on how such moral values affect even in mundane supermarket purchases.

In the chapters that follow I return to the example of shopping for eggs in Germany to illustrate the concept of moral provenance in value chains and to argue for a new way of looking at consumer desires and preferences. Chapter 2 looks at what German egg choices tell us about the difference between "stated" preferences (what people say they want) and "revealed" preferences (what people actually do). In the consumer realm, stated preferences are more likely to be concerned with what I call in Chapter 3 the "moral provenance" of goods—positive and negative externalities, the impact of commodity chains on the environment, social relations, and our views of a just world. Chapter 4 then shows how these themes relate to the larger structure of German political economy and the pursuit of the good life.

Economic choices are always laden with moral consequences. And as much as we may try to segregate the study of economic science from moral philosophy, the two are intimately interwoven in practice. Adam Smith and

Karl Marx, to name but two, saw themselves as moral philosophers as much as economic observers. Today the dominant model of economics is more about math than philosophy, and the allure of mathematical precision can easily divert us from the moral ambiguities of real life. At the same time, as consumers we are increasingly faced with explicit moral choices—whether to buy Fair Trade coffee, whether to shop at the corner grocery or the Walmart Super Center, whether to go local or global.

Prices are often assumed to condense all other values into a single number, but of course it is not that simple. Price certainly does signal an important aspect of value, but as Patrik Aspers and Jens Beckert (2011) point out, we rely on many cultural (and contextual) value systems in determining worth. Prices are important, but they are not everything: recall Oscar Wilde's quip about the sort who knows the price of everything and the value of nothing. The case of German eggs is especially revealing because it explicitly brings different value frameworks—material thrift and social solidarity—into play.

Südstadt, Hannover

To the casual visitor, Hannover in many ways looks like an unexceptional German city. With a 2006 population of 520,000 (and 1.1 million in the metropolitan area), it is about the same size as my home town of Nashville, Tennessee. Indeed, I often describe Hannover as being a lot like Nashville in that both are pretty typical cities in their countries. Still, there are more churches in Nashville, and there is more overt religiosity; in Hannover, 37 percent of taxpayers are registered as Protestant (predominately Lutheran) and 14 percent as Catholic; the rest claim no religious affiliation.[1]

Hannover also has a longer history. The Electorate of Hannover (and then the Kingdom of Hannover) played an important role in 18th- and 19th-century regional politics, and starting with George I in 1714, the House of Hannover ruled Great Britain and Ireland until 1866, when Hannover was annexed by Prussia. (The Hannoverian line continues to rule the United Kingdom, although it has gone under different names since Queen Victoria's death in 1901). The gardens of the former palace are still a central attraction; the court was home for a while to the composer George Frideric Handel, and the philosopher Gottfried Wilhelm Leibniz served there as bibliographer and counsel. Even though he was always trying to escape the

Plate 1: *Menschenpaar,* 1939

All around Hannover one finds subtle and not-so-subtle reminders of the Third Reich. In the center of town is the Maschsee, a large man-made lake built in 1934–35 as a public works and employment project. After 1937, the Hannover government was solidly Nazi, and over the next few years more than 2,500 Jewish residents were deported to concentration camps.

Today the Maschsee park is a vibrant public space, filled on all but the bleakest days with pedestrians, bikers, skaters, and boaters. Scattered around the park—and the whole city—are statues of sportsmen, Aryan-esque nudes, and other motifs of the period.

This couple neatly captures the contradictory feeling conveyed by such works, their beauty shadowed by the sinister views it embodied. Titled "Menschenpaar" ("Human couple") and dated 1939 (artist: Georg Kolbe), the sculpture presides over a small rest area alongside the lake.

city, Leibniz has become Hannover's favorite son—the Hannover-based Bahlsen food company's most famous products are its Leibniz cookies, and the local university (which started as a technical college) changed its name to the more illustrious Leibniz Universität.

Today Hannover clearly bears the marks of the National Socialism (Nazi) period. A number of buildings reflect the architecture of the time; and the southern part of the city is dominated by the Maschsee, a lake built between 1934 and 1935. After 1937, the Nazis began regularly deporting the city's Jewish inhabitants to concentration camps, leaving just a handful of Jewish families by the time of the Allied liberation. Today, one is reminded of these victims of the Holocaust by the *Stolpersteine* (4″ × 4″ brass "stumbling blocks") placed in the sidewalk in front of former homes of people sent to concentration camps, reading "Here lived . . ."[2]

The city had an important manufacturing base and so was a prime target of British and American bombers during World War II. It was hit especially hard in the last two years of the war (1943–45), with thousands killed and 90 percent of the city razed. It was rebuilt quickly after the war, and today the predominant architectural style reflects an unfortunate postwar infatuation with concrete. Yet postwar public planners were intent on creating a very livable city, at least by the standard of the times, and Hannover is notable for its green space as well as its drab buildings. Close to 50 percent of the city's expanse is undeveloped, and it is possible to bicycle almost everywhere in town, including through forests and greenways, the remnants of royal hunting grounds.*

The current *Land* (state) of Niedersachsen (Lower Saxony) was founded by the British in 1946, uniting the province of Hannover with three surrounding states. In 2006, Niedersachsen's population was 8 million, with a GNP per head slightly lower than the national average. Over 14 percent of the city's population were foreign-born (almost 4 percent Turkish), and at the time I started my fieldwork in 2005 the unemployment rate exceeded 16 percent, just as the national average dropped to around 10 percent. (Since then, unemployment rates have dropped dramatically in Hannover—to 8.4 percent in 2014, and in Germany as a whole to almost 5 percent.)

* Like most German cities, Hannover has an expansive, expensive, and efficient public transport system. With 1,900 U-Bahn, S-Bahn, and bus stops, the system carries 850,000 passengers daily in this city of 1.1m. In Nashville, the public transit system carries fewer than 30,000 passengers daily.

Plate 2: Südstadt, Hannover

The Südstadt neighborhood was built during the 1920s and 1930s, and was spared the worst of the bombing that destroyed much of Hannover during the war (World War II being the inevitable historical benchmark when discussing modern Germany). Südstadt is known for its winding streets, with contiguous rows of reddish-brown brick buildings. Housing mostly apartments and small stores, the buildings circle entire blocks. From the outside, they are charming and well-kept Bauhaus designs, with the occasional whimsical element (such as a gargoyle or a jutting balcony); they also invoke a stark, dark Third Reich minimalism, as in the quaint cheese shop's sign proudly proclaiming "Since 1933."

Inside the apartment blocks are large courtyards, sometimes planted with gardens, sometimes given over to parking. From any apartment, one can see the living and bedroom windows of almost everyone on the whole block. This makes it almost unavoidable to maintain casual surveillance of a fairly large number of neighbors, a panopticonic effect that was perhaps intended. As Michel Foucault observes, "He who is subjected to a field of visibility, and who knows it, assumes responsibility for the constraints of power; he makes them play spontaneously upon himself" (1979: 202). Imagery ©2013 Aero-West, DigitalGlobe, GeoBasis-DE/BKG, GeoContent, Landsat, Map data ©2013 GeoBasis-DE/BKG (©2009), Google.

In rural Niedersachsen, farming reigns, but Hannover is a manufacturing and government city: home to a Volkswagen plant (15,000 employees in their commercial vehicle division, VW Nutzfahrzeuge), Continental tires (with over 25,000 employees), as well as Pelikan (stationery and office supplies), BREE (bags and purses), TUI (tourism and logistics), and the regional bank, Norddeutsche Landesbank (NordLB), among others. Arriving passengers are warmly welcomed at the *Hauptbahnhof* (main railway station) to the Messestadt Hannover, or the Fair City of Hannover—"fair" in this case meaning "market." Hannover has for centuries been home to important commercial fairs, the most famous today being CeBIT, Europe's largest technology exposition, and it hosted the Word's Fair in 2000.

Here, as across Germany, the rate of home ownership (42 percent) is the lowest among member countries of the Organization for Economic Cooperation and Development (OECD). Living in Hannover during the mid-2000s boom years, it struck me as odd that there were few mortgage companies. Much more common were Bausparen, a form of mutual trust to help one save up to buy a house (in cash)—the exact opposite of the mortgage brokers flourishing in the U.S. at the time.

Südstadt is a working-class neighborhood, although it was rapidly gentrifying. One German friend characterizes the area as clearly *kleinbürgerlich* (*petit bourgeois*), but I found it remarkably diverse in socioeconomic terms. There were tradesmen (recognizable by their guild dress, such as the distinctive flared corduroy pants and vests of carpenters) as well as government workers (*Beamter*), doctors, teachers, factory workers, and small-business owners. My family and I lived in the Südstadt section of Hannover in 2005–06 as I conducted the initial fieldwork for this book.

Shopping in Südstadt

It is important to remember that while we often speak of "capitalism" (or "globalization") in the singular, there are in fact multiple capitalisms, or varieties of capitalism. Germany's version—called, variously, the *soziale Marktwirtschaft* (social market economy), the Rhenish model, ordoliberalism, or the stakeholding model—differs in important ways from Anglo-American capitalism (see Streeck 2009; also Becker 2009; Thelen 2001; Turner 1998; Hall and Soskice 2001). The German model tends to be more "coordinated"

Plate 3: Bäckerei am Suttner Platz

The most popular bakery in our Südstadt neighborhood was the small artisanal Bäckerei am Suttner Platz. By the time it opened at 9:00 A.M. on Sunday, there was always already a long line waiting for the fresh rolls and croissants. By 10:30 or 11:00 they were sold out.

The baker is a Master Baker, having gone through the years of training and apprenticeship to obtain that official designation by the national Bakers' Guild. For bakers, as with many trades, an apprenticeship starts for teenagers with half-time theoretical study in school and half-time on-the-job training. To become a Meisterbäcker, they work their way up the ladder through journeyman, having spent several years learning all aspects of the business. These craft professions, with their rigid rules and high standards, often seem constraining to the U.S. observer, an infringement on the freedom to do what one wants. Yet such formal training and recognition of mastery also give rise to a sense of dignity, the virtue of excelling in a practice.

. . .

(Germany has some of the strictest individual privacy laws in the world. Progressive and aggressive in the right of individuals to control personal information in the immediate post–World War II period, they have proven difficult in the digital world. Try to use Google's Street View function for a German city and you will see how limited it is; or the ubiquitous pixelization of published photos. It is not only law but widespread custom and social expectation that one treads lightly and asks permission when representing others.)

than the "liberal" Anglo-Saxon market economies; it is marked by strong unions and workers' rights in corporate governance; and the capital market structure favors long-term horizons (as detailed in Chapter 4).

For shoppers, this means much more regulation, with numerous laws governing store opening hours and the terms of sales. Not only carpenters, plumbers, and other craft tradespeople, but also butchers, bakers, and even clerks in bookstores have to be trained and certified by their trade guilds. That training, apprenticeships, and licensing—as well as high wages—give a sense of professionalism to trade crafts (reinforced by formal forms of address).

In a number of categories, items (such as books) must be sold by law at their suggested retail price, a regulation that favors small operations. Most of the stationery and supply stores in Hannover carry only the sturdy and pricey (German) Hansa brand paper clips (€0.89for a box of 100 small paper clips) rather than the cheap imports I am used to. Typical of the city's districts, our Südstadt neighborhood had three bakeries, a pharmacy, a drug store, a book- store, a bottled drinks store (a *Trinkhalle*, which sells and delivers cases), and a small stationery and school supply store. The subjective experience of neigh- borhood shopping in Südstadt was far removed from my Nashville norms. Most noticeably, there seemed to be less eagerness to sell, almost an aversion to the subservience of waiting on others. One bike shop often refuses to serve customers and has exacting standards for those they will do business with: the purchaser must feel an emotional attachment to the bike she is buying and meet a moral standard that is implicitly acknowledged by the owner and staff.

Our Südstadt neighborhood had two *Reformhäuser** and a small *öko*† super- market, in addition to the growing selection of *bio* and *öko* products (organic, "green," environmentally friendly) in the four regular supermarkets. In Germany the market for bio and öko goods grew at well over 15 percent per year in the early 2000s. In 2007, sales reached €5.45 billion; although this is still only less than 5 percent of the total German food market, it is the larg- est organic market by far in Europe. Reuter and Dienel Consulting found that 10 percent of Germans are "Lohas" (people with a "lifestyle of health

---

* The *Reformhaus* movement began in the early 20th century to promote natural foods; it was consolidated into a national cooperative structure in the 1930s. Today, *Reformhäuser* offer a range of all-natural foodstuffs, herbal supplements, and homeo- pathic treatments.

† The term "*öko*" (eco) is used for a wide variety of organic and "green" products.

and sustainability") who buy products with a "bio" designation for about 25 percent of the items they use regularly. Another 40 percent of consumers are interested in organic but buy more selectively, making decisions more closely linked to price (see also Wilk 2006).

In June and July 2008, assistants and I conducted 114 interviews on the sidewalk in front of an Edeka supermarket on Stefansplatz in Südstadt.[3] The store is located next door to the neighborhood post office and Postbank, which draws a wide range of the area's socioeconomic groups. There is a park half a block away, frequented by groups of unemployed men drinking beer or schnapps, as well as kids playing soccer and scrambling on the monkey bars. On Fridays the park is taken over by the weekly market, with farmers, butchers, and other vendors from the surrounding countryside filling the Stefansplatz. Within a few blocks, there are a public school, a library, businesses, and apartment houses. Our sample reflects the range of standard income categories for Germany, tilted slightly toward the lower end of national averages (a majority of our sample earned less than €21,600 per year).

Respondents were asked to characterize themselves as shoppers, rating a number of traits on a scale of 1 (least important) to 5 (most important). The categories and average rankings are shown in Figure 1.1.

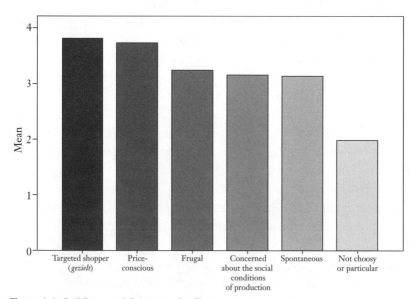

Figure 1.1: Self-Reported Consumer Profiles

(Scale 1–5 = not important–most important)

The top three characterizations—being a targeted shopper, price-conscious, and frugal—likely reinforce one another. Price-conscious consumers tend to be more targeted in their buying, seeking out just what they need. In our survey, it is significant that frugality barely edges out social/ecological consciousness for third place. Germans have a deserved reputation for prudence and frugality ("Frugality is Hot" was one large retailer's successful tagline for a while), and one might expect price-conscious consumers to be frugal. But the German case offers an odd twist predicated on a valuation of quality.

Respondents were also asked to rank the overall importance of several factors in their buying decisions on a 1–5 scale. Average responses are shown in Figure 1.2.

The conventional wisdom of U.S. marketing holds that price, quality, and convenience are the most important elements in consumer decisions (usually in that order). While price and quality remain the top two criteria for consumers, environmental and social considerations now compete with convenience as the third. Significantly, 90 percent of U.S. consumers identify with the label "conscious consumer" according to BBMG's Conscious Consumer Report (Bemporad and Baranowski 2007).

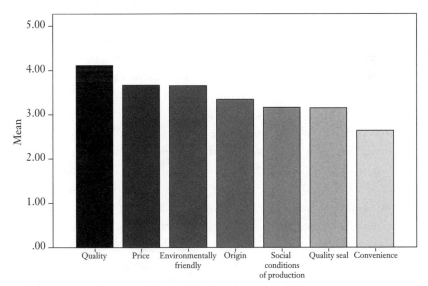

Figure 1.2: Important Factors in Purchasing Decisions

(Scale 1–5 = not important–most important)

For our Hannover sample, quality clearly trumped price;[4] and price only just barely edged out environmental friendliness as the second most important factor. Price is clearly important to many consumers, and decisions usually rest on a delicate and subtle balance among price, quality, and other factors. Nonetheless, the preponderance of preferences for quality over price is remarkable. Furthermore, quality was the single most important factor for all income groups, save those who earned €23,000–€30,000 (who ranked it second). As Wolfgang Streeck (1997: 40) notes, in Germany "price competition is mitigated by socially established preferences for quality." Such a preference for quality may, in fact, be consistent with prudent frugality—as in buying small amounts of high-quality products (e.g., cured meats measured in grams) or investing for the long term (in a BMW, say, which could be expected to last longer than an Opel).

Convenience was not a major factor for our Hannover sample. Indeed, we had difficulty translating "convenience" (as, for example, *Komfort* or *Bequemlichkeit*); there is simply not a salient term in German that means the same thing as American-style "convenience." This is not to say that folks do not take into account factors we would categorize under "convenience." German shoppers do weigh expediency and efficiency in their decisions, but the lack of a neat translation for convenience points to the lack of saliency of the concept as a quick, uncontested justification of first resort. Lotte, a single woman in her early 30s, told us that when she was hungry or in a rush she would go to the Lidl market closest to her apartment, but when she had more time she would visit the Edeka, with its wider selection and more professional employees.

Lotte's comments point to the distinction between different types of supermarkets in Südstadt and the subtle social meanings that attach to different stores. The Lidl is cheaper than Edeka and, to achieve this savings, is much more impersonal. There is an automated machine that accepts empty bottles of water and beer for recycling and spits out a receipt to give to the cashier; there is no meat or cheese counter, just prepackaged portions displayed in coolers; there are fewer employees around, except at the checkout; and goods are often presented in the cartons they came in. At the Edeka, in contrast, one must ring a bell to return empty bottles to an employee, who writes out a receipt by hand; there is a meat counter with a butcher, and an adjacent cheese counter staffed by the cheese clerk; employees work in the aisles cleaning up and restocking shelves. As Lotte notes, there is a very different feel to the two stores, and the Edeka feels much more "professional"; she can have a satisfying business interaction with the workers there, which makes the Edeka a "better" store. But this professionalism is costly, as is reflected in both price and expediency. The Edeka butcher will take his time with a customer, explaining the different cuts of meat, offering sample tastes, and making sure slices are just the right thickness. The cheese mongers likewise. And this takes time. Indeed, a disregard for "convenience" is needed for shopping at stores such as Edeka.

Many consumers in the Hannover sample expressed the opinion that quality was more important than price, invoking a long time horizon and explicit moral projects in their explanations. Joachim, a married insurance salesman in his mid-40s, stated, "We have to change this idea that everything has to be cheap. We are wealthy enough that we can afford to buy more expensive foods. We need for folks to be better informed. With as little income as we spend on food we can pay more. I rarely eat meat, for example, but when I do I buy quality meat. *We can buy less but have better quality*" (emphasis added). This was a common sentiment in our interviews, and not just for grocery products. Germans also expressed a preference for buying a more expensive car and keeping it for a long time.

Discourses around "quality" are also used to convey feelings of national pride, which have long been frowned upon in post–World War II polite society. In our survey, a number of respondents expressed a clear quality preference for specifically German products—and these were often contrasted with "Chinese products" (a phrase that represents cheap goods produced by exploited labor, and a vague fear of China as a threat as it becomes stronger and takes over more of the German export market). Claudia, a woman in her early 30s, explained, "We can see our country like a family, and so it is better to buy German and help the family stay strong." But when pressed, Claudia, and others, backed away from claiming any sort of inherent German superiority, cloaking an incipient nationalism in terms of specific quality attributes and environmental impacts.[5] We look more at such issues of moral provenance in Chapter 3.

So it is with the complexities of moral projects. They may take on many idiosyncratic variations and shades of meaning, from prudence to nationalism. And yet at times they converge, as in the German consumer's concern with quality. Linked to concerns about quality, 60 percent of our sample stated that it was "important" or "very important" to buy organic (and more broadly environmentally friendly, or *bio*) products, and 61 percent said the same about the conceptually linked Fair Trade products.

Fair Trade

Fair Trade started in Germany in the 1950s, and the international umbrella organization for socially conscious labeling (formed in 1997) is the German-based Fairtrade Labelling Organizations International (FLO) (Wilkinson 2007). The FLO seeks to combat the "injustice of low prices" by ensuring that producers and workers are paid a living (fair) wage; the idea is to use a market-based approach to promote social justice. As Torsten Steinrücken and Sebastian Jaenichen (2007: 205) describe, Fair Trade goods comprise "a product bundle" that allows consumers to exercise preferences about the production process "even if it does not affect product quality." Concern with the production process contributes its own utility to the product bundle (a concern with externalities)[6], and Fair Trade products show that consumers are sometimes willing to pay a premium over that merited by functional utility.[7]

The Fair Trade market is currently centered on high-end coffee, cacao, and cotton products but is expanding. For coffee, the Fair Trade premium translates to a $0.24 premium per pound over market rates (in 2007) paid to producers.

Many consumers in our sample expressed a willingness to assume the costs of certain externalities. For example, Barbara, a married woman in her 40s, told us: "I pay more because the price for *bio* is the price that it really costs; sustainability and ecological costs are not included in the price of regular products; I pay more and therefore can have an influence on society and on the next generation." She recognized that there are external effects of her consumption and was willing to pay for it. Barbara's views were not shared by all. Thomas, a man in his 40s who worked for an advertising agency, asserted dismissively that consumption is not a political position ("*Konsum ist keine Politik*")—that political battles should be fought in the political arena and not degraded in the marketplace. Many respondents invoked a moral argument of "solidarity" to justify ethical consumer choices: said one young woman, "I am ready to pay more to help make the world economy more just."

James Carrier (2010) offers an important cautionary lesson in dealing with ethical consumption (and what he calls "ethicality," the inscription of ethical values). While "ethical consumers want things that meet their moral criteria," Carrier writes, their preferences coalesce around certain symbols and cultural categories. This opens the possibility that through "greenwashing," "astroturfing," and other less nefarious-sounding means, producers (and their marketeering allies) may generate symbols of these conceptual categories that themselves come to define moral value independent of real-world relations. In this way, the images and symbols meant to demystify production chains may actually elide the full contexts in order to pander to ethical consumers' moral values. It is all too easy to think one is changing the world by buying Fair Trade–certified coffee, when in fact no one has ever pulled themselves out of poverty growing Fair Trade coffee.

Consumers may purchase certain items for their inherent qualities (their material utility) and, simultaneously, for their promise to promote moral ideals (and the material practice) of social solidarity. A clear majority of consumers in our sample showed a tolerance for higher prices in the service of moral projects linked to notions of "solidarity" as well as for quality.

Eggs and The Different Values They Represent

Nowhere is the effect of moral values on German consumer choices so clear as with eggs. Since 2004, all eggs sold in Germany (except at farmers' markets) carry the 0–3 numeric code designating how the chickens were handled (organic, free-range, cage-free, or battery caged). These designations are clearly posted over display shelves.

In the 2008 surveys we conducted in Hannover, over 60 percent of the supermarket shoppers we interviewed reported buying free-range or organic and free-range eggs. Almost 9 percent bought eggs from a farmer at a local market (also a type of socially conscious purchasing), and 5 percent did not eat eggs (see Table 1.1).

---

* Battery cage systems, used to house egg-laying hens, consist of rows of narrow cells that share divider walls. For many animal rights advocates, they are emblematic of the harsh conditions of industrial food production.

Table 1.1: Egg Purchases and Prices in Hannover

Egg Type	Reported Purchasing	Average Price (per 10 eggs)
0 = organic, free-range	26.5%	3.79€
1 = free-range	33.6%	1.99€
2 = cage-free	12.4%	1.59€
3 = caged	13.3%	1.39€
From farmers in market	8.8%	2.50€

Given the significant price differences, these data are surprising. They reveal an apparent willingness of German consumers to pay a big premium to support their moral preferences—up to €2.40 more (or almost three times as much) for organic than for battery-cage eggs. And this pattern holds true across socioeconomic groups. One shopper, a woman in her 30s who works at a law firm, noted that although there was a big price difference, even so "€3 or €4 isn't so much money, so that may be expensive compared to other eggs, but eggs overall aren't expensive."

This response presents us with that rare natural case in which we can put a price on virtuous behavior. A clear majority of the Südstadt consumers were willing to pay €0.60–€2.40 more for organic or free-range eggs. That is the price of being virtuous.

The egg example captures institutional design as well as the cultural norms and intentions of individual actors. The choice is structured: the alternatives are made explicit and the consumers have to choose among them. To help, the numeric code provides more information than had previously been easily accessible about the provenance of the eggs. And the choices we documented in our Hannover sample reflect a strong concern with moral provenance.

In our Hannover sample, many consumers stressed the quality aspect as well as the positive externalities of öko products. One man reported that öko bread "stays fresh longer and tastes better." Others related quality (and environmental friendliness) to health: "*bio* products are healthier, and this is more important for children and young people. These products taste better, better quality."

With eggs, there are qualitative taste differences. But for many of our respondents this was not the deciding factor: they reported being more motivated by an explicitly ethical stance, a concern for how chickens are treated. (A surprising number of respondents cited a particular television special on industrial chicken production.) One man in his late 30s explained: "When I buy the more expensive—bio—eggs, I feel good about myself because I am eating healthy, and this is important to me. Maybe the bio eggs taste a little better, but that's not really why I buy them."

It is impossible to disentangle the choice here between quality and moral provenance, for both are at work and the discourses around quality converge with those around morality, the commons, and at times a covert form of nationalism.

Most consumers in our sample were able to articulate a conscious balance that they sought between moral values and economic expediency. Overall, consumers tended to explain preferences for bio and *öko* eggs and other such products as a social obligation that contributed to a vague sense of social solidarity (which is often extended to include animals and the environment), a concept frequently invoked in German political discourse.

Gerda, a middle-aged professional woman remarked: "I buy freerange eggs because if the hens' lives are better the eggs taste better. They are more expensive, but more expensive is sometimes worth it because the quality is better. It costs more, but I buy these products. The world is going downhill—not only the environment but humanity as well—so it is important to do what we can." To some extent, these sentiments are wrapped up with self-interested pursuits and self-congratulation: Christian, for example, stated that he "only buys German eggs—in order to be socially responsible, to support good living conditions for everyone; and it makes me as a consumer feel good." Again, we see the complexities and idiosyncrasies of moral projects—here a commitment to a perceived greater good and yet recognizing the vicarious pleasure and self-regard such responsibility may bring.

In Südstadt, we found individuals improvising a multitude of personal moral projects; their buying habits reflected salient themes of solidarity and ecological conscientiousness and served their material self-interest and desire to be frugal. Their attitudes and positions develop through a dialectical engagement with political structures, such as regulations concerning store opening hours, vacation time, and other conditions imposed upon daily life. They also emerge from cultural flows and personal concerns, and are expressed, among other ways, through consumer choices. In our sample of the Hannoverian middle class, the consumers expressed a pronounced preference for "quality" over price, an overt awareness of environmental and social externalities, and concern about moral provenance. These issues evidence stakeholding norms based on a sense of moral community and shared responsibility, a tolerance for higher prices in pursuit of a perceived greater good.

Our sample of supermarket shoppers shows how a non-material preference (such as to support solidarity) can be expressed through market choices—particularly a tolerance for higher prices in pursuit of a perceived greater good; in interview responses, many stressed sympathy and empathy with workers, seen and unseen. This concern for workers is often linked to views on the dignity of working conditions. Benno, a 28-year-old professional man, remarked that he prefers shopping at Edeka rather than discount chains because the customers and employees there are more pleasing to the eye because they are happier about their jobs. He spoke of this in terms of color: at Lidl, a deep-discount supermarket that has been the subject of several scandals over employee treatment, the employees seemed to be "gray," "soulless," and even "almost dead"; he described the Edeka employees and customers as "brighter: they physically look better and this comes from within." Benno was talking about jobs with dignity and the consumer power he has to promote such market relations.

Plenty of folks shop at Lidl, unbothered by the working conditions there. German shoppers are not a type of *Homo communitarius*; individuals are constantly working out a complex and contextually dependent algorithm of costs and benefits. Indeed, German shoppers often pride themselves on being *geizig* (frugal, prudent, "cheap"). Yet, encouraged by institutional structures and the genealogies of power they reflect, their decisions are also formed as part of the ongoing moral projects that constitute their lives.

. . .

The middle-class German supermarket shoppers in Südstadt are among the world's most affluent. Although most would like to earn more, their incomes and material standard of living are more than adequate on a global scale. Unlike in Guatemala and many other places around the world, physical security and health are not significant hindrances to overall wellbeing (speaking in terms of averages, of course, and not individual cases).

What we did find among our Hannover sample were salient, if sometimes vague, notions of the good life and a better possible world, as well as a willingness to pay to promote that eudaimonic vision. People's sense of what the good life should entail orients their aspirations, and the moral projects of individual lives often converge around common themes, sometimes vague ("being a good person") and sometimes with clear behavioral mandates. These themes play out in consumer decisions through what Dan Ariely and Michael Norton (2009) term "conceptual consumption," consuming the idea and moral valences of a product as much as its material utility. Yet the valences are not always clear cut or consistent, for the comfort of "solidarity" entails the exclusion of certain others in an imagined community; and the material virtues of "quality" can convey a sublimated nativism.

CHAPTER 2

Word, Deed, and Preferences

A majority of the Südstadt shoppers we talked to said they buy organic and free range eggs because they support ideas of environmental stewardship, social solidarity, and the common good. Good reasons all, we might agree, and laudable that these consumers voluntarily pay a premium for a common good that they value, to promote their vision of the good life.

Yet what we say is not always what we do. Recognizing this, there is a whole set of folk admonitions about the slippage between word and deed (inevitably privileging the latter: "It's not what you say, but what you do," "All talk, no action," and so on). The gaps between word and deed are not all born of bad intentions and duplicity; rather, they exist because we are very capable of cognitive dissonance, of holding divergent ideas and desires. We sometimes do not know what we want (as marketers understand so well), and our notions about what is best change. Paradoxically, what we (truthfully) say we want may not be what we actually choose. I want a cinnamon roll but I also want to lose weight; what do I *really* want? Sometimes there are difficult trade-offs between short-term hedonic happiness and long-term wellbeing.

Economists distinguish between "stated preferences" (the sometimes crazy things folks say they want) and "revealed preferences" (what they actually do). Revealed preferences are taken to be more authentic: it is thought that when the rubber hits the road and the cash changes hands, one reveals one's *true* preferences. There are also good empirical reasons for focusing on revealed preferences; after all, they are what can actually be measured (and in dollars and cents, no less). Yet I argue in this chapter that we should also take seriously what people say they want; people's stated preferences reveal equally valid desires and are often attuned to long-range and prosocial values. Anthropologists naturally take stated preferences seriously, for we place great value on what people tell us.

Stated preferences imply an intention to enact those preferences at some point in the future. This is to say that stated and revealed preferences are not mutually exclusive; people do often do what they say they prefer. At the same time, less constrained by the exigencies of daily life, stated preferences have the freedom to be more prosocial and to give greater emphasis to long-term goals and moral projects, common goods, and the common good. Revealed preferences also reflect such desires, but they result from a cost/benefit analysis more embedded in market logics of immediate material maximization.

Stated preferences sometimes contradict the deeds of revealed preferences, but it does not automatically follow that revealed preferences are any more real or important. In fact, we must take into account the hopes, desires, and aspirations of stated preferences to understand the pursuit of wellbeing in socially embedded market transactions.

Word and Deed in the Egg Market

With those ideas in mind, let us return to our survey of Hannover supermarket shoppers. More than 60 percent of them reported buying either organic or free-range eggs; nationally, however, just over 30 percent of German eggs sold are organic or free-range.[1] If we take our sample as broadly representative, twice as many people say they buy organic and/or free-range than actually do. So what is their preference? Their revealed preference values price over moral provenance and quality (more caged than cage-free eggs are bought), and yet their stated preferences are just the opposite (organic and free-range eggs). Both tell us something important about consumer values (see Table 2.1).

There is a clear dissonance here between what people say they want and what they actually do. But we should not take their revealed preferences as self-evidently what they *really* want. I suggest that they also really want what they say they want, and this reveals a great deal about their ideals and values: the sort of person they imagine themselves to be and the sort of world they would like to live in. Such aspirational values orient our long-term goals, and yet we often also succumb to short-term gratification at the expense of longer-term ideals.

Behavioral economists such as Richard Thaler (1992) have found a consistent bias in financial decision making: most of us systematically discount the future and overvalue immediate rewards. While this tendency provides immediate utility, it can also erode the welfare of our future self. In preferring $1 now over $5 next month, or eating or drinking too much and regretting it later, we almost unwillingly subvert long-term stated preferences.

Our Hannoverian shoppers want to buy premium eggs, I believe; indeed, because they see themselves as the sorts of people who buy organic eggs, they say they do so even when evidence shows that they do not. We may assume, then, that they *want* to buy the higher-priced eggs because of their moral provenance, but at the moment of the financial decision the 200+ percent premium is too much to bear. This raises an intriguing possibility: that reducing consumer choice might increase overall wellbeing by helping individuals commit to their long-range stated preferences.

Table 2.1: Consumers' Reported and Actual Egg Purchases

Egg Type	Type of Eggs Consumers Reported Purchasing (percent)	Actual National Sales (percent)
0 = organic, free-range	26.5	7
1 = free-range	33.6	23.5
2 = cage-free	12.4	40.2
3 = caged	13.3	29.3
From farmers in market	8.8	

NOTE: National sales figures are from the GfK-Haushaltpanel; see www.animal-health-online.de/lme/2009/09/10/mehr-eier-im-juli-gekauft/3788/.

Preferences and Utilities

The standard neoclassical model of economics rests on a few precepts, such as rationality, optimization, and self-interest, that anthropologists find troubling—not wrong, but incomplete. For the sort of sophisticated mathematical modeling that characterizes the contemporary mainstream discipline, economists are forced to simplify the complexity of real-world decision making, assuming certain traits to be axiomatic of human behavior. These axioms lead to the assumption that human beings, in the aggregate, are rational and self-interested actors who seek to optimize their returns, maximizing utility in pursuit of preferences. Condensing individuals' desires, wants, and goals into "preferences," utility becomes the measure of satisfying those preferences, the aggregate satisfaction that goods bring someone. Mathematical utility functions ($U = f(x_1, x_2, x_3 \ldots)$) have become the stock and trade of most mainstream microeconomics, with an unrelenting focus on what Deirdre McCloskey (2002) terms Max U, or maximum utility.

This approach makes no assumption about the rationality of the goals themselves, just the means: rational choices maximize expected utility. In theory, utility can be found in anything—love, a new phone, orthopedic socks, security—but it is most visible in material objects. But in the final analysis, one's "true" preferences are believed to be revealed through consumption. In reference to consumer behavior, the standard neoclassical model holds that individuals seek to maximize their utilities given budget constraints. In turn, the rule of consumer sovereignty holds that consumers determine what gets produced in an economy through their market choices (revealed preferences). From this perspective, we could explain the German egg anomaly through cost/benefit analyses based on consumer preferences for different sorts of eggs and the utility offered by the different varieties in comparison with the price.

The utilitarian current here goes back to Jeremy Bentham's (and later John Stuart Mill's) idea of measuring utilities ("utils") as the satisfaction or happiness that a basket of goods brings. Despite Bentham's formula ("hedons" minus "dolors" equals utils), the broad notion of utility eludes easy measurement. For this reason, most economists tend to follow Alfred Marshall's proposition:

> Utility is taken to be correlative to Desire or Want. It has been already argued that desires cannot be measured directly, but only indirectly, by the

outward phenomena to which they give rise: and that in those cases with which economics is chiefly concerned the measure is found in the price which a person is willing to pay for the fulfillment or satisfaction of his desire. (Marshall 1920: 78).

Back to our eggs, then. Buying a certain kind of egg reveals a consumer's preference for that product. Given price differences and the differences in egg provenance, we could write a utility function to explain revealed preferences in egg buying. This could be revealing, but it would also miss a lot of what is going on.

Writing against the "secret sins of economics," McCloskey (2002) notes that economists tend to see human behavior (B) as determined by what she calls "P variables" (Prudence, Price, Profit—in short, the structure of the Profane), while anthropologists concern themselves with "S variables" (Solidarity, the Social, the structure of the Sacred). McCloskey concludes that positing either set of variables as determinant is misguided: "To include both P and S is only sensible. It is not wishy-washy or unprincipled. Of course the S variables are the conditions under which the P variables work, and of course the P variables modify the effects of S variables. It is the human dance of the Sacred and Profane" (2002: 25).

Following Marx, Jonathan Friedman (1994), Jens Beckert (2011), and others make a key distinction between symbolic and material utilities. It is often noted that symbolic values (and what Marx termed fictitious capital) have become ever more important in postindustrial economies (see Zak 2008; Frank 2000; Baudrillard 1972; Stehr 2008).

Our German egg shoppers are as concerned about symbolic utilities (which they hope represent material realties somewhere down the chain) as they are about the material use value of the egg. For a significant number of them, buying certain kinds of eggs is part of a larger moral project of identity construction and social obligation (and navigation). These are of greater importance than eggs, and yet the values they represent have to be translated, even if imperfectly, into price in the retail context.

Stated and Revealed Preferences

As noted, economists distinguish between "stated preferences" (those crazy things people say they do, or would like to do) and "true" or "revealed preferences" (what they actually do, usually understood to be the choice revealed when the rubber hits the road and the money changes hands). And, going back to Paul Samuelson's 1938 admonitions, economists tend to privilege revealed preferences (after all, these are what can be observed and measured).

Samuelson (1938, 1948) argues that when a consumer buys product A instead of an alternative, product B, that action reveals A to be better than B for maximizing utility. There are lots of factors that can affect this simple formulation (access to information in making the choice, for example), but in its basic form it has the virtue of being logically rigorous and empirically observable. And certainly, revealed preferences are crucially important to understanding human behavior and choices about values. But Samuelson's commitment to the science led him to be dismissive of other significant elements of the equation. He writes:

> It must be emphasized that the paths along which I as an economic scientist choose to evaluate the man's preference have absolutely nothing to do with the order in which the human guinea-pig *consumes* the goods. I don't know whether he drinks his beer before his whisky or his whisky before his beer; I don't know whether it even makes sense to say that he enjoys his shelter before rather than after he enjoys his food. Note too that in going from A to B the guinea-pig does *not* eat his way along the path, and in going from B to A regurgitate along the same path. Rather we should always regard the budget of goods at A as a steady flow of consumption per unit time, optimally patterned to the consumer's tastes. And the flow of consumption goods at B is again a steady flow long maintained. *The comparison of A and B* (and of intermediate points) *is a case of comparative statics.* We need not invade the privacy of the consumer's castle to concern ourselves with the minutia of his domestic arrangements. (Samuelson 1950: 361)

On the one hand, this is an empirically rigorous approach, as revealed preferences can be seen in documented behavior such as purchases made or votes cast. Faruk Gul and Wolfgang Pesendorfer (2005: 4) argue: "An institution's effectiveness at maximizing the true happiness of its participants cannot justify the persistence of that institution if the criterion for true happiness conflicts with the participants' revealed preferences. After all, only the latter plays a role in behavior."

At the same time, a laser focus on revealed preferences discounts the importance of the cultural and institutional contexts of decisions—the fact that choices are delimited by structural conditions, as in the all-too-common scenario we are faced with in the grocery store aisle and in the voting booth: choosing between the lesser of evils. What if stated preferences are not attended to by the market? What if competition diverts preferences toward goals with less overall utility? In such cases, there may be real value (if not cash) on the table that can only be realized through regulatory structures to collective action problems uncovered ethnographically.

Daniel McFadden also calls on economists to give greater consideration to the realm of stated preferences. He writes:

> The emphasis on characterizing utility solely in terms of the demand behavior it produced became the centerpiece of neoclassical consumer theory, . . . and in its purest statement [formed] the theory of revealed preference. This was a great logical achievement, but the demands of the analysis also narrowed and stiffened the way economists thought about preferences. The cardinal, proto-physiological utility of Bentham and Edgeworth was weakened to an ordinal index of preference. The domain of utility moved from activities or processes to the commodity vectors that were the consequence of choice. Self-interest was defined narrowly to include only personally purchased and consumed goods; reciprocity and altruism were ignored. No allowance was made for ambiguities and uncertainties regarding tastes, budgets, the attributes of goods, or the reliability of transactions. (McFadden 2013: 4)

By their very nature, stated preferences may take a long-term, big-picture view, less constrained by logistics, finances, and collective action problems and more cognizant of both positive and negative externalities (see Wilk 1993). It is not that revealed preferences do not reflect loftier values—they must if we are to ever realize our stated preferences. But at the same time, they are also much more sensitive to the hedonistic impulse and material maximization of immediate, short-term desires. Revealed preferences are more heavily influenced by what Stephen Gudeman (2008) calls calculative reasoning, a drive toward market efficiency and short-term maximization. Stated preferences are also shaped by maximization and material aspirations, but they are more sensitive to prosocial inclinations and mutuality (Trope and Liberman 2010).

Anthropologists are especially attuned to stated preferences, taking seriously what individuals say that they want; this helps us understand their values and ideals, hopes and dreams for the future, the sort of person they want to be, and the sort of world they want to live in. This tells us a lot not only about the way things are, but also about the way things could be, the aspirations that inform life projects.

Revealed preferences capture not just steps toward a long-term vision of the good life; they are also sensitive to myriad hedonistic impulses. In such cases, we might well say that their stated preferences are more "true," that they more fully capture who they want to be. We may then ask if there are cases in which laws, regulations, and social norms that reduce our range of choice and individual freedom might make us better off—not just better off physically or financially, but with a greater self-defined, subjective sense of wellbeing, of being the sort of people we want to be, approaching an Aristotelian eudaimonia.

The nexus of stated and revealed preferences provides a productive site for anthropological analysis. Stated and revealed preferences are not dichotomous frames invoked in discrete contexts. Rather, they are coexisting modalities that variously converge and diverge, informing economic behavior and the construction of moral subjectivity. They represent two different cultural logics at work, both meaningful and important (see Fischer 2001). As Gudeman (2008: 150) remarks, "Everyone is both a socially embedded or conjoint actor who is constituted by social relationships and ideas, and a disjoint chooser with aspirations, hopes, desires, and wants." Such tensions between what is stated and what is revealed point to the often competing pulls of market rationalities of material maximization and the reflexive bonds of mutuality and solidarity.

There are good empirical reasons for the bias of economists toward revealed preferences: revealed preferences, by their very nature, are what we can record with certitude; they are outward demonstrations of a preference. Stated preferences—what individuals *say* they prefer—are harder to capture and less precise in their documentation (see Bertrand and Mullainathan 2001). It is also often assumed that they are, in the final analysis, less important for individuals: if there is a dissonance between stated and revealed preferences, then certainly, it is thought, we should privilege what they do over what they say.

Yet revealed preferences focus on surface manifestations and in so doing often ignore the deeper, equally valid values that stated preferences index.

Stated preferences, in not being bound to the immediate here-and-now (e.g., to choose this or that and walk to the cashier), often take a longer-range view of overall preferences and ideals. Stated preferences are more likely to be concerned with non-material values; these are given more weight in the long-term project of one's life, one's overall wellbeing. Often they are connected to identity. George Akerlof and Rachel Kranton (2010) observe that by focusing on monetary incentives, standard economic price theory systematically ignores important types of motivation, particularly the role of identity. For Akerlof and Kranton, "identity" refers to social category and self-image; they are able to present a model in which "a person's identity describes gains and losses in utility from behavior that conforms or departs from the norms for particular social categories in particular situations" (Akerlof and Kranton 2005: 12). In a similar vein, Robert Frank (1988) documents how economic decisions are informed by a sense of identity and narrative life history.

Akerlof and Kranton's concern with identity recalls Amartya Sen's seminal work on "sympathy" and "commitment" and how these social forces affect preference structures. For Sen, commitment involves counter-preferential choice (going against immediate self-interested material gain) in pursuit of an allegiance to an identity (a cause or religion, an idea of how one should act, a concern for another). Commitment often involves contributions/ investment in common goods and support for notions of "commons."

Sen also points out the tautological aspect of self-interested, rational-choice models, based as they are only on internal consistency: "A person's choices are considered 'rational' in this approach if and only if those choices can all be explained in terms of his choosing 'most preferred' alternatives in all choice situations in terms of some preference relation consistent with the revealed preferences definition" (Sen 1979: 6).

Whereas neoclassical economics has been committed to upholding the sanctity of the sovereign individual as the locus of decision making and rationality, anthropologists have worked with a more complicated understanding of personhood as a social outcome. Rather than the autonomous, self-contained individuals of Western thought, Marilyn Strathern (1988) finds that Melanesian senses of personhood are better regarded in terms of "dividuals," defined by webs of social relations implicated in a given context. While Strathern was writing specifically about Melanesia, the notion that persons are formed in social relations is more broadly applicable. Remem-

Plate 4: Bikes

Hannover, is exceptionally bike-friendly, even by European standards, with hundreds of kilometers of bike lanes on streets, usually with their own stoplights. There are also well-marked and maintained bike paths through the wooded areas, around the lakes and marsh. There are tunnels under train tracks and bridges over highways for bikes. In some places around town, bicycles far outnumber cars.

Across Germany, high petrol taxes discourage driving, and congestion and parking make biking more appealing. But the attraction goes beyond that—the folks I know in Hannover tend to feel a strong connection to their bicycles. Biking heightens their sensory and social connection to the city.

It is not just the bikers that benefit from this extensive and expensive infrastructure, for biking produces any number of positive social and economic externalities. It reduces pollution and eases traffic congestion. It promotes better fitness and health, lowering overall health costs. Bike-friendly cities are more attractive to young, educated, creative-class workers. And beyond that, biking puts one in closer touch with the world, forcing contact with fellow citizens and the natural and manmade environment and subtly reinforcing a sense of community and ownership.

All the same, parking is sometimes a problem.

ber Walt Whitman's rejoinder: "Do I contradict myself? / Very well then I contradict myself, / (I am large, I contain multitudes.)" Such complexities of individual subjectivity belie static models of consistent sets of preferences (see Sen 1979).

Different aspects of persons can have different preference sets and identity goals, and, to complicate things even more, these moments of personhood are constantly changing. There is no doubt that the imagination (including, e.g., aspirations, hopes, dreams, goals) is culturally informed and influenced by mass media (Appadurai 1996). Yet imaginative processes and consciousness are also uniquely personal and situational, shaped by family dynamics, historical conjunctures, illness episodes, and socioeconomic circumstances While a blend of cultural and personal factors underpins a great deal of social behavior, including economic rationalities and activities, the fluidity and construction of identities, subjectivities, and preferences are not without constraints. Cultures have their own logics: these are not hard-and-fast rules but rather dynamic predispositions that inform thought and behavior, idiosyncratically internalized and regenerated through engagement with the material world and social norms (Fischer 2001). And these cultural logics operate in institutional frameworks of political, economic, and social action that delimit the range of what is seen as possible.

Time Horizons and Collective Action Problems

For present purposes, we may identify two key dimensions on which stated and revealed preferences differ: time scale and collective action. Stated preferences, precisely because of their remove from the constraints and contingencies of the here and now, can imagine things as they "should" be, and can encompass a long time frame. This, in turn, allows stated preferences to give greater weight to prosocial behavior. It is easier to promise your time or money or commitment to a collective good next week or next year than it is to do it right now; we discount its cost to us in the future.

Richard Wilk argues that there is a structural relationship between time and the scale of prosocial intentions: we are more likely to narrowly define our self-interest in the present, but when we project out in time, we place more emphasis on other-regarding behaviors. Wilk (1993: 199, 200) observes that "immediate self-interest, the satisfaction of a need or desire felt at the moment of decision, is only one end of a range of self-interested motives. A person can also be interested in maximizing longer-term self-interest, about next week, next year, or a distant retirement." At the far end of the time scale, folks are concerned with the "timeless concepts of value, eternal moral principles of good and bad, right and wrong." It would seem that we are more generous to others when we think about the long run; unconstrained by the immediacies of present circumstances, we exhibit more prosocial attitudes.

In discussing happiness, wellbeing, and the good life, it is useful to distinguish between hedonistic impulses and long-term goals. Recall the distinction between happiness and wellbeing discussed in the Introduction. There is "hedonic" happiness, that everyday contentment; close to the gritty practice of everyday life, such happiness is especially reflected in revealed preferences. But there is also the broader sense of "life satisfaction" or "wellbeing" ("the good life"). I suggest that such overall life satisfaction is most closely aligned with long-term stated preferences. This makes sense: we adjust our daily expectations to what is "reasonable" for us and our circumstances, and adapt our mundane happiness to that norm. But when we look back (or forward) over the broad sweep of possibilities, at what was obtainable and what was not on our life path, we are often more struck by what could have been.[2] Thus stated preferences tend to emphasize long-term ideals and common goods, and imagined futures.

Psychologists Nira Liberman and Yaacov Trope have shown that people's distant future decisions (as compared with choices regarding the near term) are influenced more by desirability than feasibility. Further, future distant decisions tend to be more pro-social and focus on big-picture goals (Liberman and Trope 1998, Trope and Liberman 2010).

Of course, we do often "reveal" our stated preferences. Ethical consumption is but one example. We may also think of saving for the future, where calculative reasoning is (ideally) employed toward long-term, even intergenerational, goals. Or we may give to a charity in order to indulge an immediate feeling of empathy or to enhance our social standing rather than to make a deep commitment to the common good that is being promoted. Daniel Miller (1998) describes a particularly compelling example of the convergence of stated and revealed preferences in his study of a North London supermarket. Miller finds consumption to be a positive form of identity formation in the context of post-Fordism (marked by a shift of investment and consumption toward information and service sectors) . He shows how thrift, a sort of material maximization, is part of a larger moral project of caring and providing for one's family—material maximization in pursuit of mutuality and sociality.

Yet it would seem that we humans are highly predisposed to what behavioral economists call "hyperbolic discounting," taking modest short term-gains over more lucrative long-term rewards (see Thaler 1992). Caitlin Zaloom and Natasha Schüll (2013) show how neuroeconomists map this onto brain functioning, distinguishing between a more emotional and short-sighted beta system (associated with the limbic region) and a more rational delta system that is less apt to discount future returns (corresponding to the executive functions of the neocortex) (see also Camerer 2003). Thaler argues that we can treat delta and beta as two inner selves who negotiate an outcome (in ways that can be modeled using game theory): it seems that through MRIs and PET scans of the brain, econometrics has discovered the multiplicity of selves that Walt Whitman celebrated.

Would you rather I give you $1 right now or $2 in a two weeks? Waiting would produce a 100 percent gain, but most would rather take the money now and run. Most smokers would like to quit and see the long-term gain in health achieved through abstinence, but the pull of immediate pleasure proves too compelling. In preferring $1 now over $5 next month or eating or drinking too much and regretting it later, we almost unwillingly subvert long-term stated preferences. Perhaps, then, these revealed preferences do not capture "true" preferences but rather hedonistic impulse; in such cases, folks would say that their stated preferences are more "true" because they more fully capture who they want to be.

Economists refer to such situations as commitment problems: not doing what we say we want to do, usually involving short-term versus long-term rewards. There are a number of pre-commitment devices that help us stick with our goals. Ulysses, for example, dramatically tied himself to a mast in order to resist the sirens on the way to his ultimate goal; but there are many more mundane devices, such as not keeping snacks around when one is on a diet, or setting up automatic contributions to a retirement fund. It may well also be the case that laws, regulations, and social norms that reduce our range of choice and individual freedom in particular contexts make us better off—not just better off physically or financially, but with a greater self-defined, subjective sense of wellbeing, a sense that we are the sort of people we want to be, approaching an Aristotelian eudaimonia.

In addition to differences in time and scale sensitivities, stated and revealed preferences also differ in how they address collective action problems (situations in which an individual's self-interested incentives are not aligned with the shared goals of the group). Collective action problems occur when, if everyone acted in a rational, individually self-interested way, the outcome would be worse for all. Often at stake are the sorts of common goods that no one individual could effectively support on his or her own (think national defense, public roads, clean air—it does not make sense for one person to contribute to these if no one else does). For example, it is not feasible for one person to pay for the roads she needs, but everyone is better off if we all contribute. And in situations with pronounced positive or negative externalities, such as pollution, a transaction between two parties (such as a chemical plant and its customers) can affect a third party (a neighboring household) not directly involved in the exchange.

Collective action problems give rise to free-rider issues and the situation Garrett Hardin (1968) labeled "the tragedy of the commons." Hardin argued that a common resource (say a community grazing plot) would be abused by individuals because it is in their best interest to get the maximum possible return from it (even if it destroys the common resource). Hardin believed that the tragedy of the commons can only be averted by mutually agreed upon coercion (a Rousseaian view), and indeed much research in free-rider theory has been built on the view that voluntary contributions to the common good are not common. Yet as Elinor Ostrom (1990) has shown, there are a number of situations in which self-organization, cultural norms, and social structure can effectively support common goods and minimize free riders. It seems that a sense of reciprocity is key to solving collective action problems where what is best for the individual is harmful to the whole group (see also Colloredo-Mansfeld 2011).

This idea suggests an ethnographic approach to "the commons," one that focuses on the ideal of a commons and the ideas behind common goods. There are some commons that are so broad—"the environment," for example—that the line between material reality and ideational abstraction becomes blurred. It is this last sort of commons—the idea of broad, abstract, and distant common goods—that comes into play in how German supermarket shoppers' stated and revealed preferences were oriented by time horizons and collective action issues.

Stated Preferences and Meta-Preferences

In this context, it is helpful to call on the concept of "meta-preferences" to link the economic rationality of decision making with neo-Aristotelian views of virtue. Conceiving of the flow of human desire in terms of "preferences" poses a number of problems, not least that individuals may well have competing preferences and that preferences change across time and social contexts. As a way out of this dilemma of categorization, Harry Frankfurt (1971) posits a "meta-ranking" of preferences, in which some preferences are more important or over-arching than others.

The highest level of meta-preferences tend to be oriented around long-term aspirations and goals that require a range of subsidiary preferences and sacrifices and are often tied to identity construction and notions of the good life. Amartya Sen (1979, 1982, 1997), Albert O. Hirschman (1980, 1982), and others suggest a second (or "higher") order of preferences that subsume the first-order preferences of most utility functions and that generally point to larger, longer-range goals, ideals, and questions of identity.

Meta-preferences tend to reflect longer-range life projects and goals oriented around moral values, with the full range of subsidiary preferences implied. Meta-preferences shape proximate first-order preferences, giving them some consistency through an articulation with longer-range life narratives. Meta-preferences also mediate competing preferences and changing preference sets that individuals may hold. Indeed, meta-preferences may be in conflict with first-order, immediate preferences—should one follow a meta-preference to lose weight or give in to the proximate preference to eat that danish? In fact, actors might do things that appear in the short term to be disadvantageous but that make an advance toward larger meta-preferences.

By their nature, meta-preferences tend to be stated, at least to the extent that they concern the future. At the same time, ever implicit is the expectation that they will also be revealed through actions, even if stated preferences are more sensitive to meta-preferences.

This perspective can help account for the powerful role of moral positioning and individual identity construction in the substantive rationality of pursuing immediate or short-term goals that appear to be disadvantageous but that make an advance toward larger meta-preferences. Robert Frank (1988)

Plate 5: The Door Store

Oddly, one does not see cheap doors in Germany. Surely there are some out there, but I never came across one. It is a minor fact, but striking in its pervasiveness—the solidity of every exit, the sort of heft that reminds me of the doors on a 1966 Lincoln Continental.

And it is not just doors: there are paper clips, facial tissues, and a whole range of products for which cheap alternatives are hard to find. German regulations discourage intense price competition, but there is also a greater tolerance—even appetite—for what U.S. consumers would consider to be high prices (if also products of a higher quality).

There is a sort of frugality encoded in these choices that involves time as well as money. Expensive German washing machines use water and energy very efficiently, but a normal cycle may take two hours to complete. Many households hang clothes up to dry. This is changing as dryer sales increase, but the German dryers are as slow as the washing machines. Either way, a serious time commitment is required to do the laundry in this regulated, energy-efficient fashion.

argues that there are real benefits to being a trustworthy person, for example, and that long-term trustworthiness is very hard to fake. Thus to reap the opportunities or benefits that are enabled by such a presentation of self, individuals may need to give up cheating and its short-term gains in pursuit of a long-term meta-preference (and the gains from being, in fact, trustworthy).

Meta-preferences and moral projects are deeply implicated in the process of identity formation—the pursuit of one's desire to be a certain sort of person (and to live in a certain sort of world) and of one's vision of the future (the gap between how one, and one's world, actually "is" and how things "ought" to be).[3]

Meta-preferences may help us understand the anomalies of seemingly irrational economic behaviors. For example, individuals might forgo the pursuit of immediate or short-term goals with a larger ambition in mind or, vice versa, participate in seemingly disadvantageous practices in the short term because they help them advance toward larger meta-preferences and the good life.

Thinking about consumer behavior in terms of moral projects and meta-preferences points us toward the complex, and even contradictory, intentions that underlie the dialectical process of individuals becoming and aspiring while engaged in a larger social world. Moral projects expressed in the corner supermarket invoke not only comparisons of price but also salient themes such as solidarity, fairness, prudence, and nationalism. For example, we have seen how the moral provenance of German eggs turns out to be just as important as price (or even more important) for a majority of Hannoverian shoppers in our sample.

Preferences, Choices, and Happiness

German supermarkets differ from their U.S. counterparts. The carts are smaller, like an overgrown children's wagon; the aisles are narrower; and the selection is dramatically smaller. You would be lucky to find a dozen types of breakfast cereal in a Südstadt grocery; in contrast, the aisles of my Nashville grocer look like Andreas Gursky's photograph "99 cent II Diptychon."

But does more choice make the Nashville shoppers happier? The instinctive American response would likely be yes, but a growing body of literature suggests otherwise. In *The Paradox of Choice*, Barry Schwartz (2004) reviews a range of studies showing that having too many choices actually decreases satisfaction. This is due in large part to "regret aversion," because choosing forecloses the unknown bounty of the paths not taken, and to information overload: there simply are too many variables to consider when choosing a product even as simple as jam or chocolate. One study found that a more extensive array of choices was "simultaneously more enjoyable, more difficult, and more frustrating," and that "the provision of extensive choices, while initially appealing to choice-makers, may nonetheless undermine choosers' subsequent satisfaction and motivation" (Iyengar and Lepper 2000: 1003–04).*

Starting January 1, 2010, new regulations forbid German farmers from selling conventional, cage-produced eggs. (Stores were allowed to continue selling such eggs imported from other EU countries until the end of 2011.) To many Americans, this would seem an unwarranted government intrusion, analogous to EU regulations on banana shapes and sizes. But we have seen that more German consumers *say* they want to buy free-range and organic eggs than actually do—suggesting that the temptation of immediate monetary savings trumps ideal preferences. Perhaps, then, this is a case in which regulation could best help individuals effectively pursue their long-term meta-preferences.†

The German regulations prohibiting certain choices remove the temptation to act against a perceived greater good, and presumably help the majority of our sample to fulfill their stated preferences. Here we should note a new wave of scholarship that questions assumptions about human rationality and points to ways that we might reintroduce moral considerations into our understanding of markets. Several behavioral economists look at how research can influence public policy in such areas. Richard Thaler and Cass Sunstein's (2008) *Nudge*, for example, advocates a form of "choice architecture," framing choices in ways that make the default the most beneficial: organizing school lunch lines so that kids pick more carrots than chips, for example. Such a "paternalistic libertarianism" seeks to

---

* *The Economist* (2010: 124) reports on experiments showing that, unlike Americans, German shoppers are not put off by more choice, something they chalk up to the "sheer dreariness" of Germany grocery stores.

† We might also consider the caring aspect of shopping—the love, devotion, and sacrifice that are expressed through shopping, as Daniel Miller (1998) describes (see also McCloskey 2006 on the role of love in economic rationalities).

protect the freedom of choice while channeling paths of least resistance and the default option.

Lynn Stout (2010) argues for legal structures that help to "cultivate conscience." She describes how the view of humans as merely material maximizers underwrites popular financial incentive models—and how such incentives actually erode the moral value of an occupation. Instead, she envisions laws that explicitly give people incentives to act in conscientious and prosocial ways (not relying simply on financial rewards and punishments).

Robert Frank (2011) moves beyond gentle nudges to propose a "libertarian welfare state." He adopts a libertarian stance—that individual freedom is paramount as long as it does no harm to others, and then it should be regulated in the least coercive manner possible. And following John Stuart Mill, Frank holds that behaviors can be legitimately regulated when they cause harm to others. Frank is able to square this view with the apparent contradiction of a "welfare state" by taking an expansive view of what constitutes "harm to others." Frank deals with some classic "externalities," such as pollution and second-hand smoke, but he also takes into account coordination problems and competition driven by positional goods. (Positional goods value derives in large part from how much they are desired and consumed by others; status symbols are the iconic example.) He looks at, for example, how others' actions influence our decisions—such as how the size of houses in our neighborhood influences what we think we need. He concludes that a highly progressive consumption tax would not only divert resources away from positional goods and toward more productive ends, but would increase the felt utility and wellbeing of those same high-income households. Perhaps the invisible hand works best when it is not flailing about and gesticulating by itself, but when it is firmly in the grip of social norms and legal regulations.

These studies suggest that we would do well to reconsider the value of "top-down" regulations in promoting wellbeing and happiness. Despite its rhetorical taint in much public discourse, such an approach need not lead to socialism and central planning (as Friedrich Hayek warned in 1944 in *The Road to Serfdom*); instead, top-down rules can be built from bottom-up research—taking seriously what people actually want and what they actually do. In the preference models of economists, what is best for someone is what fulfills his or her desires, and more choice would allow us to satisfy more preferences. But individuals are not always good predictors of what

Plate 6: Cereal Selection at Edeka

The supermarkets in Südstadt carried less than 20 percent of the variety of breakfast cereals that we would find in a Nashville grocery. This is true of many consumer products: there simply is not the same breadth of selection as in the United States.

Perhaps this is for the good. Barry Schwartz, in his book *The Paradox of Choice*, shows that in certain contexts, including routine consumer decisions, more choices can actually make us unhappier. Too many paths not taken, it seems, leads to dissatisfaction with our choices. And too many choices can induce what Roy Baumeister calls "ego depletion" and a significant decrease in our willpower and self-control.

Nonetheless, as something of a breakfast cereal aficionado, I thought the shelves looked especially bleak—not quite 1980s East Berlin, but with a similar drab feel.

will make them happy (see Gilbert 2006; Dolan, Layard, and Metcalfe 2011); and even when they know what they want, they may find it difficult to achieve on their own.

The anomaly between stated and revealed preferences speaks to the delicate balance of individual choice and regulatory constraints in promoting wellbeing along multiple dimensions.

Stated Preferences and Wellbeing

Economists make a clear distinction between revealed and stated preferences, privileging the former. Anthropology—ethnography, at least—speaks most directly to stated preferences, taking seriously what people say, their hopes and dreams and aspirations that often ignore the constraints of what is possible. We create the world in which we live, and thus we should take seriously our imaginings of what that world might look like under different circumstances. It is from such desires that the future is forged.

The example of German eggs presents an empirical critique of the concepts of "stated" versus "revealed" preferences. Economic price theory privileges "true" or "revealed" preferences over "stated" preferences. While this is an empirically rigorous approach, it discounts the importance of the cultural and institutional contexts of decision making.

In fact, it is a fundamental axiom of marketing that consumers do not really know what they want. It is their pliability that makes advertisers' jobs possible. Many of our daily economic encounters (in the supermarket, at the shoe store, online) are orchestrated by companies (based on extensive behavioral research) to allow us to "freely" choose in certain ways. This isn't surprising, but it also is not something we actively consider as we make our choices. Of course, we are not completely malleable, and we are not puppets, but we are manipulated all the time in a way that should make us question some of our cherished beliefs about free will.

Thorstein Veblen (1899), writing about the gilded age and its conspicuous consumption, argued that while we think we are satisfying needs, very often we are just practicing emulation. Bringing this perspective into the postwar consumer era, John Kenneth Galbraith argued that:

> If the modern corporation must manufacture not only goods but the desire for the goods it manufactures, the efficiency of the first part of this activity

ceases to be decisive. One could indeed argue that human happiness would be as effectively advanced by inefficiency in want creation as by efficiency in production. Under these circumstances, the relations of the modern corporation to the people it comprises—their chance for dignity, individuality and full development of personality—may be at least as important as its efficiency. These may be worth having even at a higher cost of production. (Galbraith 1998 [1958]: 213–14)

Galbraith raises an intriguing question: does our pursuit of preferences always lead us toward the best life possible? If our commercial system creates demand and fulfills need, what does that mean for consumer choice and autonomy? What does efficiency mean in this context? Some see these as patronizing views of the duped consumer (or at least anti-liberal in the sense of discounting consumer and worker autonomy), but I think Galbraith was referring to the dissonance between our better and worse selves (as we define them).

Stated and revealed preferences may be understood as two distinct framings for understanding market decisions, in line with Erving Goffman's (1974) seminal work and Amos Tversky and Daniel Kahneman's (1981) application to rational choice. Yet these are more than rhetorical frames; they are modalities of thought, what I have elsewhere referred to as cultural logics (Fischer 2001).

Revealed preferences tend to be framed by what Gudeman (2008) calls calculative reason—the cost/benefit analysis of perceived utility as represented by a dollar-and-cents value. The symbolic (and the sacred, McCloskey's "S" variables, including the solidarity of social obligations and the convictions of moral values) is often undervalued in such monetary conversions. Revealed preferences are highly sensitive to contextual and structural constraints, a necessary and pragmatic concern with what is possible. They are also influenced by what behavioral economists call "hyperbolic discounting," a bias for immediate and short-term rewards expressed by discounting future values (see Thaler 1992).

Stated preferences, on the other hand, are less bounded by the practicalities of time horizons and collective action problems. They are able to consider "what if" possibilities: what kind of person one would like to be, what sort of world one would like to live in. Even with stated preferences, disciplined aspirations are developed in a cultural and social context of what is possible (see Li 2007; Bourdieu 1977; Carrier 2010).

In the German case, consumers expressed both a strong stated preference for "quality" and "solidarity" and revealed preferences that valued material maximization (price frugality) over the qualities they said they preferred. We might expect supermarket decisions to be especially susceptible to hyperbolic discounting: money will shortly change hands in the checkout line (and in Hannover it is most often a cash transaction, underlining the fiduciary impact); one must decide the value of an immediate savings versus other, perhaps more distant, preferences for quality and solidarity.

There are also potential free-rider and collective action problems at play. If everyone else is supporting a commons (such as environmental consciousness or social solidarity), and that would be a reasonable supposition given what most respondents said, then a bit of individual backsliding would not seem particularly significant. Regulatory structures that reduce choice, such as those being implemented in Germany, would improve individual and collective wellbeing by coordinating and aligning revealed and stated preferences. In this context, remember that, despite the obvious free-rider problem, many people do in fact buy the costlier organic eggs. Their willingness to pay a higher price even when individual action has only a negligible effect on the broad areas of concern (helping the environment, promoting social solidarity) is powerful evidence of the importance of these broader moral projects.

In any case, we should not ignore the importance of stated preferences as we seek to understand what motivates economic behavior. These tend to value broad, long-range ideals and unveil a concern for common goods that often remains hidden in the immediacy of revealed preferences. As the case of the moral provenance of German eggs suggests, we might do well to promote economic structures that help us realize our stated preferences and not just cater to the quick buck made by inducing hedonistic revealed preferences.

Through such ethnographic understandings of what people say they want in their lives (their stated preferences in pursuit of the good life), anthropology brings a crucial perspective to public debates on state regulation and the economy. Indeed, it opens the door to the sort of positive anthropology I outline in the Conclusion—an anthropology that dares offer conceptual alternatives, practical suggestions, perhaps even regulatory nudges, based not on rigid models but on inductive ethnographic understandings of what people (in particular times and places) say they want from their lives.

CHAPTER 3

Moral Provenance and Larger Purposes

Things are not just things; eggs are not just eggs. There is, of course, a physical quality to eggs and other things, a material egg-ness, if you will. Yet things also have meaning, meaning that we endow them with, meaning that is often tied up with the moral projects of our lives. This is to say that the meaning of something is never merely given by its physical properties. The simple act of recognition, of naming an object, any object, even an egg, bestows cultural meaning. We ascribe meaning to the things that fill our lives: they mean something because we decide they do, even if that decision is more or less conscious and the meaning more or less laden.

It follows that when we consume things our satisfaction comes not just from the physical properties of the object of our desire. There is certainly use-value, as Marx called material utility, that instrumental value of what something actually does. But, as Jonathan Friedman (1994) and Jens Beckert (2011) remind us, even with use-value the subjective and objective properties are inextricably intertwined. Beckert goes on to lay out two other key sources of value. The first is positional, when the value of an object depends on its valuation by third parties. Objects of conspicuous consumption are the prototypical case: the value of that handbag or sports car or trophy house depends largely on the valuations other people place on them, on their exclusivity, and on what they mean culturally and say about one's social position (see Frank 2000; Bourdieu 1984). In economic terms, positional value appears exogenous to a particular market transaction.

The ideas presented here about provenance and value were developed through conversations and collaboration with James Foster. Foster and I are developing this model in more detail elsewhere.

Beckert's other value comes from what he terms "imaginative performance," the private act (albeit culturally contextualized) of imagining the future; imaginative value is endogenous, in contrast to positional value. Beckert writes about the imagined subjective utility of particular objects, but I think we can fruitfully extend his idea to broader considerations of the good life. We often look to the past to explain different cultural formations, but it is important to remember that the subjects of our inquiries are living their lives with an eye to the future. There is certainly a weight to history, as Marx reminds us.[1] But aspirations for the future, the dreams, hopes, and desires of those we study are fundamental in understanding why they make the choices they do (see Fischer and Benson 2006).

What we miss sometimes in economic abstractions is that people are more than just abstract producers and consumers pursuing their interests. They produce and consume for specific reasons, have specific expectations, express particular desires, and pursue particular moral projects. What people want—why they produce and consume—takes shape at interfaces between global political economic structures, collective processes, and cultural representations, all of which coalesce around ideas about the good life. Buying things may give us hedonic pleasure, a treat, or it may be an expression of love and caring for others. It may express greed or prosocial behavior—markets facilitate both, a point I return to later. For now, I would simply note that one key way individuals exercise agency and express moral projects is through consumption. (Another is production, which I turn to in Chapter 4.

Moral provenance has become an important consumer concern in the complicated world of global commodity chains. Moral provenance refers to the social conditions embedded in the commodity chain and the social, economic, and environmental externalities implicated in transactions; that is to say, moral provenance represents the non-supply-and-demand values encoded in the value chain. Moral provenance manifests in consumer behavior in a willingness to pay a premium for positive externalities and to punish companies for (perceived and actual) negative externalities. The concept of moral provenance highlights the fact that commodity chains are not simply a material infrastructure of points of production, exchange, and consumption, but also a corresponding flow of desire, with personal and collective preferences manufactured along the way (Fischer and Benson 2006).

Among Hannover's supermarket shoppers, we found a broad range of respondents willing to pay a significant premium for certain eggs as well as other bio and Fair-Trade products. The Südstadt supermarket shoppers who preferred organic or free-range eggs tended to talk about their preference by calling on broad notions of fairness and social solidarity, environmental concerns, and civic obligations.[2] They used a language of social obligation and moral values. For many, this was not much more than a vague and abstract idea of a common good, sometimes referred to as "solidarity." When pressed to clarify, they mentioned environmental concerns, animal rights, eradicating unfair work practices, and generally safeguarding common resources. All of the respondents said that these values were an important motivating force: an ideal, even if only broadly defined, that requires action in the real world. Such moral projects give meaning to life—and, along the way, bestow meaning on markets and on things.

Ethical Consumption

Consumer moralities offer fruitful ground for investigation in this regard. Newspapers are filled with stories of corporate social responsibility (CSR), ways that companies are doing well by doing good. It is easier than ever for consumers to act on their moral preferences by, for example, buying Fair Trade coffee, chocolate, and, increasingly, clothing. Even retailing behemoths such as Walmart and Home Depot champion their environmental friendliness and corporate good citizenship. This is partially a case of access to information—consumers have become more informed about many of the products they buy. But it also points to a set of preferences that are often excluded from economic utility functions.

People often buy things not because they have worked out a simple monetary cost/benefit analysis, but because of the allure of a brand, the politics associated with a product, or peer pressure. People also often buy things to express what matters deeply to them.

For example, in recent years we have witnessed a growing concern with the moral provenance of goods. A growing segment of consumers have shown a willingness to pay a premium for goods produced in what they consider to be just working conditions. The value of moral provenance stems from a number of areas, including fair trade practices and ecological concerns. The growing market segment concerned with moral provenance is often assumed to tilt toward an affluent demographic, but it is rapidly expanding into lower socioeconomic brackets.

Moralities and Self-Interests

From an anthropological perspective, the problem with the economic notion of self-interest is that both the "self" and one's "interests" are variable, culturally and contextually defined. In many places, the "self" is not seen as an autonomous being but as integrated into a larger collectivity. Such a perspective allows us to see multiple, contextually defined selves, with varied conceptions of long- and short-term self-interest. It also gets at a broadly conceived notion of stakeholding, in which one's self-interest is inextricably tied to the long-term wellbeing of a larger collectivity (be it family, community, corporation, or nation). This is different from so-called enlightened self-interest.

The regard for self-interest as the ethical foundation of neoclassical economics goes back to the often quoted passage from Adam Smith's *The Wealth of Nations*: "It is not from the benevolence of the butcher, the brewer, or the baker that we expect our dinner but from their regard to their own self-interest. We address ourselves, not to their humanity but to their self-love, and never talk to them of our own necessities but of their advantages. Nobody but a beggar chooses to depend chiefly upon the benevolence of his fellow citizens." Through such compelling sketches, Smith uncovers how competition between actors free to pursue their own self-interest can create efficiencies that benefit everyone. This is the core of enlightened self-interest: "Every individual generally neither intends to promote the public interest, nor knows how much he is promoting it . . . he intends only his own gain, and he is in this led by an invisible hand to promote an end which was no part of his intention."[3]

Self-interest propels human beings in many ways, and the genius of capitalism has been in harnessing self-interest toward a common good. Yet belief in the powers of the invisible hand has led self-interest to become an ethic in its own right. Today, the morality of self-interest serving the public good is called upon unflinchingly in the United States by corporate executives and the editors of the *Wall Street Journal* not as a justification of last resort but as an unassailable virtue. It is an incredibly liberating and optimistic ethic: self-interest is not to be suppressed but celebrated, for in looking out for Number One I am helping everybody. Through the mystical transubstantiation of the invisible hand, personal greed is converted into collective good. As a hegemonic ideology, it is brilliant.

Yet we should remember that Smith was writing in a particular time and place, in opposition to a monarchical system, and we must take care in transposing his pronouncements onto the current state of global capitalism. He was equally skeptical of merchants and businessmen and what he saw as their conniving, monopolistic, and greedy ways. The sort of government regulation Smith saw in 1776 is not quite the same as what we have today, even if some of the more arcane EU rules come close.

Nor should we forget that Smith considered himself a moral philosopher in the days before we broke up the human experience into the discrete areas of study that interdisciplinary efforts now try to reunite. In this light, his *Theory of Moral Sentiments* (1759) is key to understanding the complex moral stance of *The Wealth of Nations* (1776). Many see a fundamental contradiction between these works. Yet if we read the former as foundational to the latter, and understand Smith's characterization of self-interests to be intertwined with his ideas of sympathy, the contradiction melts. Smith's notion of sympathy, later expanded upon by Amartya Sen, converges with lines of thinking in the neo-virtue theory of Alasdair MacIntyre.

Sen (1979) defines sympathy as a concern for others that affects one's own welfare. The utility here comes from an increase in the welfare of another that makes one better off. This is what Sen calls "definitional egoism": helping others in order to maximize our own utility. Benefits of sympathy may be seen as positive externalities.

Commitment, on the other hand, involves a counter-preferential choice: a concern for others that does not improve one's own welfare, usually driven by a strong belief about what is the right thing to do. Because it involves counter-preferential choice, Sen's notion of commitment is more consequential than sympathy: in choosing to help others, it is possible to make oneself worse off. It is significant that the motivations here are often religious belief, moral values, or more broadly, a sense of identity.

The distinction between sympathy and commitment is not clear-cut. Very often the preferences are so complex, and even internally contradictory, that it is not always obvious that one is using "counter-preferential choice" (the defining feature of Sen's commitment). Sometimes we do things because we get something out of it (however intangible, such as a sense of identity or pride) and sometimes because it is "the right thing to do." Sympathy leads to commitment (the one bleeding into the other so that it is impossible to draw a clear boundary).

Sen's larger point is that we are motivated by factors other than blind self-interest and rationality. He points out that no economic system has ever existed that relied on blind, rational, self-interested calculation. Morals always play a role, and we need to acknowledge that and work it into our models. (If everyone were self-interested, companies would not function: they require some trust and cooperation, and workers must be committed enough to go beyond their specific job descriptions.)

The concept of sympathy can help explain the pull of collective identity encoded in stakeholding systems (see Akerlof and Kranton 2000, 2005) and the limits of narrowly defined notions of self-interest. In stakeholding systems such as Germany's, the presumed tension between self-interest and collective good becomes muted, or at least recast in a different light, because individual self-interest is not just convergent with but partially defined through the collectivity.

Consumption is one way that people express their values and pursue moral projects. It is not the only way, and marketing driven consumption orients as well as reflects consumers' values. In our Hannover sample, solidarity was frequently invoked as an explanation for choosing organic and free-range eggs (as well as other sorts of ethical products). Cindy Isenhour (2010: 521) describes a similar situation among "sustainable consumers" in Sweden who use their buying power to "attempt to rein in what many middle-class Swedes see as immoral, irresponsible, and rampant materialism among the world's wealthiest citizens."

Moral Projects and Larger Purposes

Among those who preferred *bio* and *öko* eggs in Hannover, many invoked the language of "solidarity." Solidarity is a key word in German political and public discourse. The Christian Democratic right as well as the Social Democratic left embrace the concept; it undergirds German approaches to social assistance, labor relations, and economic relations more broadly. It is about justness and fairness. *Solidarität* is one of those key words that acts as an anchor for moral meaning; more than just semantics, these concepts reflect ideas and ideals, defining and motivating certain sorts of views and behavior, in a process Dominic Boyer (2005: 39) calls "tropic condensation." The German discourse on "solidarity" reflects moral values about shared social obligations while also meaning different things to different people. The term is partly idiosyncratic in its shades of meaning while referencing salient political discourses (racist or multicultural, leftist or nationalist, corporate or labor). Its power lies in the strategic ambiguity that nonetheless carries enough common meaning to give it traction.

Now, let us assume that individuals like the Hannoverian shoppers described in Chapter 1 are active agents in the construction of their lives, that much of the work of being human is in giving meaning to the world we inhabit, and that such meanings tend to indicate culturally salient values and social obligations. It is useful to view consumer orientations, strategies, and behaviors as expressions of particular cultural logics and moral projects, linking one's life to larger purposes (Fischer 2001). Such moral projects are driven by the process of desiring, ever with a view to the future and the good life.

While ascribing cultural and transcendental meaning to life's activities, moral projects are also fundamentally contingent. Works in progress, often improvised on the fly, they respond to immediate circumstances as well as to institutional structures and long-range goals. They are highly idiosyncratic and intimately meaningful while articulating culturally salient themes and social currents in a way that gives them broader meaning. To the extent that they overlap, moral projects undergird social organization. As such we must see them as developing from particular historical trajectories and as deeply implicated in genealogies of power relations: moral projects play into the construction of particular sorts of political subjectivities.

Following Arthur Kleinman (2006), we may understand the term "moral" to denote "what really matters" to individuals and communities. This is not simple (and absolute) "morality" but rather a mode of human experience in which things come to matter deeply, in which certain goals become compelling, and in which projected, anticipated, or desired futures are thought to be up in the air. It is in relation to the things that matter most—to what people desire in their lives and in connection to those around them—that people become contentious and committed stakeholders in their activities (Fischer and Benson 2006).

In such an expansive usage, "the moral" bleeds over into what we often refer to as "the social" or "the cultural." But a few key differences make the term especially useful for our purposes. First, it implies judgments of value: what is considered good or bad, what sort of life one wants to lead, and what sort of world one wants to live in. Second, a concern with "the moral" gets at key foundational aspects of "the social": a concern for others and the practical accommodations of living together, the social contract, and the delicate balance between private gain and public good. Finally, a concern with the moral speaks to problems of governmentality and the relationship between what people believe they ought to be doing and how things actually are (Foucault 1979).

Morality in this sense does not comprise absolute categories, but rather emerges from the many moral projects that are constructed around livelihoods and economic behavior; moral projects involve making value judgments in a world inhabited by others. Any one person, and much more any group, holds many different, shifting, and sometimes competing moral values that are impossible to fully disentangle. These come together in the ongoing, active creation of life projects, given coherence at any particular moment in a biographical narrative while also converging at times around salient themes and shared value judgments.

This is to say, moral projects are actively constructed by individuals and fit into the ongoing particulars of their lives, while at the same time they tap into larger cultural currents. Social structures and institutions condition these projects, shaping their flow without absolutely determining their path, in ways that can give the impression of more homogeneity than is actually the case. In constructing moral projects, individuals tap into cultural flows. These flows tend to consolidate around particular ideas and key words whose power lies with their strategic ambiguity—meaning many slightly different things to different people—while converging sufficiently to give the impression of consensus, about what is "fair," for example.

In popular usage, the term "moral" often serves as a synonym for "good," "proper," or "correct." Yet we should take care to clearly bracket such emic normativity and separate it from our analytic project. There is a dark side to collective moralities that such language belies; values that are social, shared, and communal can promote tyrannies as well. Moral projects, in defining moral communities, exclude as well as include—the silenced voices and thwarted lives that fall on the other side of a given morality are also part of the story. Such collective moralities may lead to totalitarian and fascist extremes, as happened with National Socialism in Germany. For Emmanuel Levinas (1969), the expansion of self-interest and its expression in societal mores is a form of aggression and war. And the Levinasian critique would entail what Peter Benson calls "narrowly defined other-interest," putting a face to compassion and sympathy and other-regard.

Ample cautionary tales punctuate the German example. The institutions and moral projects that produce positive outcomes around solidarity can also uphold xenophobic attitudes toward immigrants, as well as incentive structures that are unfriendly to woman and primary childcare providers and that promote other forms of social exclusion and marginalization. In Chapter 4 we examine the exclusion that goes with solidarity. For now, let us look at how, through a concern with moral provenance, the shoppers in Hannover explicitly expressed a set of preferences based on a sense of social obligation, environmental solidarity, and moral projects.

The Meaning of Things

As mentioned, things are not just things; but rather than speak in abstractions, let us think of real objects. A spoon, for example. Clearly a utilitarian device, the spoon allows us to eat soup and cereal and many other things. Made of wood, metal, or mother-of-pearl, a spoon is an instantly recognizable thing that we can see and touch and possess. And yet each and every spoon has its own life history, full of cultural meanings. Some may be ostentatiously endowed with sentiment—that old silver spoon passed down in the family for generations; others find meaning in their ordinariness, such as a spoon bought at Target. Arjun Appadurai (1986) and Igor Kopytoff (1986) have explored the fruitful nexus of values revealed through the biographies of things.

Often, the precise biographies of objects remain hidden; comforting (or just overwhelming) marketing images conceal the life stories of the mundane products we buy day in and day out, often assembled in faraway places by individuals with distant hopes and dreams and fears for their lives. Every pen, every toy, every egg holds a multitude of such life histories, giving these objects far more meaning than we can readily comprehend.

While every spoon has a unique biography, taken as a category ("spoons"), they also have a fundamental shared cultural meaning. Spoons are easily recognizable in societies around the world; to a large extent they are inter-changeable (from a utilitarian perspective, a spoon is a spoon is a spoon); and yet what they mean is not inherent in the physical properties of a spoon. Material form does not give rise to semantic function. Culture teaches us the very utility of the spoon, and how to take metal or wood from its natural setting and transform it into what we recognize it could be.

My point is simply that objects—despite the way we may talk about them—have no intrinsic meaning. We give meaning, and thus life, to the things in our lives. Thoughts and beliefs turn water to wine—a cultural al-chemy that is no less powerful for its scientific impossibility. The meanings we bestow can take on power to motivate our actions. Paradoxically, we may even come to feel as if objects control us (think of the way we talk about certain things: the pull of something, the hold it has on us, the seductions it carries).

Karl Marx was fascinated by the 18th- and 19th-century shift from indi-vidually produced artisanal goods to mass-produced commodities. Before the rise of factories, most goods in English towns were produced locally by known craftsmen, and consumers had some sort of social relationship with the producer. Such goods were embedded not just in economic trade but in a whole web of social relations and cultural meanings. Commodities, in contrast, were mass-produced, not associated with an individual producer and divorced from local mores; following Marx, we may define a commod-ity as something produced for the purpose of exchange. And of course, the commodities capitalist enterprises were able to produce were significantly cheaper than artisanal goods. Factory-produced textiles sold at a fraction of what individual weavers could sell them for, putting the artisans out of busi-ness. In factory production, the division of labor and control over the means of production required the forfeiture of artisanal personal ties for greater efficiency.

Commodities are defined by their uniformity and, for Marx, by their alienation. (Although artists from Andy Warhol to Thomas Kinkade have played with the relationships between art's uniqueness and commodities' mass production.) Original art, in its singularity, is the anti-commodity. Each object is unique, embedded in a particular social relationship; it is not alienated. Gifts derive value from the sentiments and social relations at-tached to them, and art is valued partly through its singular relationship to the producer.

The switch to commodities was a fateful move, one that alienated workers from the social relations that gave meaning to their work. As a result, commodities come to stand in for those social relations, giving them weird animistic qualities. In *Capital*, Marx writes of the peculiar qualities that commodities take on:

> A commodity appears at first sight an extremely obvious, trivial thing. But its analysis brings out that it is a very strange thing, abounding in metaphysical subtleties and theological niceties. So far as it is a use-value, there is nothing mysterious about it, whether we consider it from the point of view that by its properties it satisfies human needs, or that it first takes on these properties as the product of human labour. It is absolutely clear that, by his activity, man changes the forms of the materials of nature in such a way as to make them useful to him. The form of wood, for instance, is altered and a table is made out of it. Nevertheless the table continues to be wood, an ordinary, sensuous thing. But as soon as it emerges as a commodity, it changes into a thing which transcends sensuousness. It not only stands with its feet on the ground, but, in relation to all other commodities, it stands on its head, and evolves out of its wooden brain grotesque ideas, far more wonderful than if it were to begin dancing of its own free will.[4]

Tables are just tables. They serve a function—they have use-value. But tables, like all objects, are given meaning by us (humans); they take on cultural values (a Japanese tea table, for instance) and idiosyncratic meanings as well (Aunt Shirley's picnic table that was the setting for so many family reunions). In this sense, tables are not just tables but containers of meaning and social relationships. Their provenance gives them a symbolic value tied to the material object but not limited to its material utility.

Marx was concerned with the different sorts of meanings and values that commodities can embody. On the one hand, there is use-value: the simple utility of an object (one serves food on or works at a table). But in taking on value through anonymous exchange (as when the medium of money removes the need for more personal relations), commodities are endowed with a special sort of meaning. In the first instance, there is a loss—the loss of the personal relationship between producer and consumer and between producers and the fruits of their labors.

Every time a product is used, it invokes a social relationship with the producer that can be hidden or can be apparent. With commodities, Marx argued, this relationship is hidden. Objects still take on individual meanings. Mass-produced cars take on highly personal meanings for individuals (recall Henry Ford's famous quip that you could have a Model T in any color you wanted as long as it was black). And even utilitarian items take on subtle meanings—the wooden bowl made by a friend, the saw that was borrowed and never returned. Yet commodities are given meaning through consumption and not from the social relationship with the producer. By being exchanged—reduced to an anonymous monetary abstraction of their labor—they become alienated from the hopes and dreams of the individuals that produce them.

Objects—commodities, gifts, natural things—also serve as vehicles through which we present our identity to the world. Jean Baudrillard (1972) remarks that where we once defined ourselves through what we produced, we now define ourselves by what we consume. Indeed, we must often appear to the world (or at least to marketers) as merely the sum total of our consumption, a unique confluence of product preferences, lifestyle choices, and identities.

Thus things, both common and uncommon, serve as powerful repositories of identity. The clothes we wear, the cars we drive, the brand of coffee or beer or whiskey we drink—all convey messages about who we are and how we see ourselves. And these messages are for us as well as others. But like all such cultural-yet-idiosyncratic messages, the reading may be different from that intended. There may be a disconnect between what we mean to say and what we are understood to say. Indeed, there is always a dialectic dance between meaning intended and meaning perceived. We all give idiosyncratic meanings to objects, events, relationships, and so on. But it is very hard to interpret idiosyncratic messages. And the image we present to the world might be based on some momentary impulse and not some essential quality of our being.

Consumers increasingly yearn for more personalized interactions in their transactions. These may be pursued by patronizing local businesses, interacting with workers or owners, or participating in formal or informal consumer groups. They may also be revealed in virtual relationships—knowing where products came from and broadly who made them. These acts and associations de-commodify products and make them more personal and unique, and thus also de-alienate products and production processes from consumers. Thus we see the increasing popularity of personalized goods and "markets of one" (see Gilmore and Pine 2000). We see new relationships emerging between producers and consumers, and a growing number of "consumer-activists" (Wilkinson 2007: 219), who buy with political motives in mind.

Anthropologists have long noted the role of provenance in the value of goods, focusing particularly on the distinction between commodities and gifts and the different social valences of each (see Mauss 1924; Malinowski 1922). Igor Kopytoff (1986) observes that all goods have life histories, for which the commodity phase may be only one aspect. Objects move in and out of commodity status over time and across contexts—consider items bought at a garage sale, for example. He describes competing processes of "singularization" (making an object more unique) and "commoditization" (the homogenization of economized mass production and the obfuscation of provenance). The mid-century modernist project moved toward replacing traditional provenance with corporate brands—a Big Mac or a Hilton hotel room anywhere in the world being more or less the same. By the end of the millennium, however, provenance had resurfaced as an important vector of consumer choice.

Provenance

Speaking of provenance calls to mind Bordeaux wine and Parma ham and fine art. Yet there are many sorts of provenance, signaling moral values, ecological externalities, identity, and other elements, as well as quality, taste, and authenticity. The notions of "fair trade" and "union made" are based on provenance. eBay's seller rating system is so successful because it can provide some assurance of provenance in the context of anonymous, distant, and likely one-time transactions. Even the mortgage-backed-derivative crisis of 2008 and beyond comes back to an issue of provenance (the misleading origins of underlying securities).

Provenance is an increasingly important component of value in consumer decision making. This is most evident among retail consumers in the exploding market for Fair Trade, organic, and other socially and ecologically conscientious products. Provenance can also send signals about product safety, as seen in news reports about lead-tainted paint on toys and antifreeze-laced toothpaste (both of which had Chinese provenance). Such cases point us toward the dramatic impact provenance can have on market value. As James Foster and I argue, "provenance" may serve as an important frame, or analytic tool, for examining sources of and perceptions of value.

Price, quality, and convenience are three key features consumers consider when making a routine purchase (along with the subsidiary qualities of service, variety, packaging, and so on). In economic terms, consumers must weigh utility in each of these domains to calculate an overall utility bundle; how people do this varies from person to person, item to item, and context to context, but often they express a preference for low price over convenience. In recent years, as convenience and price have become ever more important in the United States, quality premiums have lost value (though at the same time a wealthy demographic has come to value quality and durability—think of industrial kitchens in upscale housing). Consider MP3 music files: the low cost (approaching zero with some file-sharing networks) and convenience (instantly download the tracks you want onto your computer) seem to far outweigh the quality degradation and original packaging for many young consumers. Bootlegged DVDs are an even better example—DVDs bought off the street often are of poor quality, but it is good enough for many given the low price and convenience. In a 2004 interview with BBC News, Iggy Fanlo, chief revenue officer at Shopping.com, said, "The single biggest reason people went online before this year was price. The number one reason now is convenience" (BBC News 2004). Looking at the growth of retail health clinics inside pharmacies and big retailers, Forrester Research consultants found that "convenience trumps service and quality" (Holmes and Snyder 2007).

Along with price, quality, and convenience, consumers have long factored provenance into consideration of value. In particular, geographic provenance can signal fine quality, especially with high-end foods and wine. Yet today consumers are increasingly concerned about other sorts of provenance as well—exclusivity, authenticity, security, and morality are all linked to different forms of provenance. Protecting intellectual property rights from piracy and brands and trademarks from counterfeiting are ways of safeguarding the authenticity of the production and distribution chain (see Brown 2004). Real designer goods command a premium over counterfeit versions because their provenance can be verified. In the opaque markets of the intelligence world, the provenance of information is crucial in considering its value, and Colin Powell's 2003 testimony before the UN Security Council (in which he asserted that Saddam Hussein possessed weapons of mass destruction) shows the risks of not properly assessing provenance. In a similar fashion, virtual provenance has taken on new importance in Internet commerce and computer security (anti-spam programs work provenance prominently into their algorithms). And environmentally friendly production practices similarly play to a concern with externalities encoded in provenance (as does the reverse provenance of waste management). While price and quality remain the top two criteria affecting consumer choice, environmental and social considerations now compete with convenience as the third.

Provenance captures a wide range of preferences united by common concerns; as such, provenance provides an analytic lens through which we can examine the increasingly complex ways that goods are valued and the intangible considerations consumers reveal in their preferences. Such provenance may be geographic; it may signal elements of quality; it may have moral valences; and/or it may be concerned with security and authenticity. But in each of these realms, tracing provenance provides a new angle for understanding value, as well as how economic value and moral values intersect in consumer behavior.

Attributions of provenance work along three key axes:

- **Quality**, as a signal for properties associated with a particular provenance;
- **Authenticity and exclusivity**, as with brand names as well as individualized items (e.g., souvenirs, gifts, original art); and
- **Moral preferences**, including social obligations, environmental concerns, and virtue ideals.

This is not an exhaustive list; nor are the categories mutually exclusive. Indeed, the value of provenance as an analytic concept is that it encompasses a wide range of valuation criteria, both tangible and intangible. Moral provenance captures the ways externalities (positive and negative) are internalized into product costs. A standard model of consumer sovereignty and utility maximization focuses on immediate monetary returns from a particular transaction, leaving little room for moral considerations. This same framework, however, may be more expansively conceived in terms of Weber's (1978 [1914]) "substantive rationality," the idea that decisions are not reducible to only material considerations or narrow self-interest. The ways in which substantive rationality is enacted bring to bear cultural norms and moral considerations on economic behavior and identity formation.

Provenance and Quality

Provenance often serves as a signal for quality, especially for food and drink but also for cars (e.g., German engineering), clothing (e.g., Italian design), thread (e.g., Egyptian cotton), and other commodities. Brands serve as a labeling device to ensure quality by assuring provenance. Conversely, provenance can be seen as a form of branding. Vidalia onions, Champagne, and Parma ham, among many examples, are almost indistinguishable from traditional brands, and their official designations command a hefty authenticity premium. Amid much uproar, a French regulatory body has been considering expanding the Champagne region beyond the traditional 1927 boundaries, and the battle for inclusion in the early 2000s demonstrated just how valuable the designation is. The European Union's "Protected Designation of Origin" and the French "Appellation d'Origine Contrôlée" promote quality claims based on geographic and historical provenance. The quality/provenance link is also concerned with honesty in describing products; CARFAX, for example, has successfully provided provenance reports to automobile buyers worried about hidden histories of trouble or damage.

Food is a particularly rich domain in which to examine the influence of provenance. The commodity chains of wine, chocolate, , coffee, sugar, salami, and even broccoli have been well examined (see, e.g., Urry 1995; Terrio 2000; Roseberry 1996; Mintz 1985; Cavanaugh 2007; Fischer and Benson 2006). Only more recently have the public health implications become clear. Being able to trace provenance turns out to be crucial in stymieing outbreaks of e. coli, salmonella, and other food-borne illnesses. In a twist on this, cigarette manufacturer Philip Morris has become a vocal proponent of FDA regulation of tobacco; the company sees it as a way of documenting provenance to control the introduction of contaminants, which in turn may bolster consumers' sense of cigarettes' safety and purity (Benson 2012).

For certain goods, particularly those associated with recognized notions of geographic provenance, the designation of a specific *terroir* (from the French *terre*, "*land*") can command a substantial premium. This first developed around French wine in the 19th century; in 1855 the French "*cru*" designation was formalized, building on the idea of terroir (Pratt 2007). Today, concern with provenance and geographic designations has spread to olive oil, caviar, and diamonds. Chocolate and coffee, in particular, have become, at the upper end of the market, valued through notions of terroir. Terroir is used to signal overall quality as well as particular gustatory qualities, and documenting terroir allows certain firms to collect monopoly rents.

The French Champagne industry spends heavily on advertising to reinforce the value of its authenticity and its difference from other sparkling wines. Parmigiano-Reggiano, Lübecker Marzipan, and Café de Colombia all call on notions of qualities inherent in terroir, as well as the historical and social conditions of production, to command a premium.

There are material, intrinsic properties of certain foods and drinks endowed by geographic provenance—the soil quality, climate, water qualities, and so on. These intrinsic qualities are also linked to prestige hierarchies (Bourdieu 1984). (While Veblen [1899] was dismissive of the intrinsic qualities of luxury goods, it is the combination of material quality of intangible prestige associations that make up their value. Why buy a BMW? There are objective qualities as well as elements of prestige involved; it is not an either/or proposition.)

Colombian coffee has long tried to promote a sense of social relationships expressed through its products. Early attempts used the character "Juan Valdez" to personalize and humanize the production process; significantly, the actor who played Valdez was replaced in recent years with an actual (and still photogenic) coffee farmer. Coffee producers have recently expanded the notion of terroir to the upper end of the market (Blue Mountain, Kenyan AA, Guatemalan Antigua, etc.), and in 2007, Colombian coffee became the first foreign product given EU geographic origin protection. My own favorite coffee, from the El Injerto finca in Huehuetenango, Guatemala, has earned a Gran Cru designation from the French authorities, and it has been able to command a significant premium for its quality, as denoted by the provenance (see Chapter 5).

Even more than coffee, gourmet artisanal chocolate has adopted French wine's language of provenance. With labels touting "Premier Cru" and using terminology such as "terroir," producers of high-end chocolate bars promote the uniqueness of their origin (from a single-plantation) and high cacao content. Long treated and traded as a more-or-less homogeneous commodity, cacao producers now seek to distinguish their beans' unique qualities ("earthy with a dry finish" or "a complex marriage of berries, tobacco, and licorice") with ties to their particular provenance (Venezuela or Madagascar).

The organic and local food movements likewise stress provenance. Buying produce grown within a 100-mile radius of one's home, activists argue, puts consumers and producers in closer contact, imparting a sense of environmental as well as social security. It also makes consumers feel more confident that the products will be free of unknown contaminants. Organic foodstuffs are now a $30 billion a year industry, and growing rapidly. Jeff Pratt (2007) shows how products labeled "natural," "organic," and "local" are symbolically positioned in opposition to "modernity." In this context, "local" is equated with "authentic" in a discursive framing that seeks to connect producers and consumers.

Provenance and Authenticity

We perhaps associate the term "provenance" most readily with art. Indeed, the value of original pieces of art is closely bound to provenance. In the fine art market, unequivocal documented provenance from the artist's easel to the present ensures the highest value for sellers (and minimizes the buyer's risk that a work is inauthentic or a forgery). In this sense art is the quintessential anti-commodity: each piece of original art is unique and derives its value in part from that fact. Each object is produced by a known person with whom the "consumer" has some sort of real or imagined personal connection. Pieces of art are thus embedded in a known social relationship; they are not alienated, in Marx's sense. Just as gifts are worth more because of the sentiments they reflect, so too is art valued partly through its singular relationship to the producer. Reproductions are worth less than originals, even when the aesthetic value might be the same, and in good galleries clerks are quick to tell the story of the artists, creating a sort of proxy relationship with them. To ensure this singularity, provenance is paramount.

The same is true in the vast market for collectible items once owned by famous people. A string of fake pearls worn by Jacqueline Kennedy fetched $112,500 at Sotheby's in 1996; a guitar once owned by Jimi Hendrix sold for $168,000 in 2005; and provenance even extends to chewing gum spit out by Brad Pitt and hair cut from Britney Spears's head.

To the extent that brands serve as signals of quality, consumers must have trust in those brands and trust that items are not pirated or counterfeited. This is especially true for luxury goods, medicines, and other high-value products whose underlying utility can be replicated. Authenticity is linked to honesty in labeling and represents a good's quality with security of provenance. Interestingly, for younger consumers of digital materials (CDs, DVDs), provenance and the quality associated with it seem to be much less important.

Trademarks are signals of a brand's authentic provenance and build on past good will and brand equity. The intangible assets of the brands of companies such as Procter and Gamble, Nike, and others make up a significant part of their products' market value. As Giovanni Ramello (2006: 1) notes, a "trademark is a sign introduced to remedy market failure. It facilitates the purchase decision by indicating the provenance of the goods, so that consumers can identify specific quality attributes deriving from their own, or others', past experience." It can also promote rent-seeking behaviors.

Given the links between provenance, quality, and authenticity (and the associated prestige premium), it is not surprising to find examples of fake or misleading provenance. In the beer industry, for example, there are a number of pseudo-microbrews. Blue Moon ales look as if they come from a small microbrewery, even if its location in Golden, Colorado is suspicious. Blue Moon Brewing's quirky and colorful bottle labels give the impression that its ales are produced by a microbrewery, although the brand is owned by brewing behemoth MillerCoors. Such stealth branding allows companies to tap the authenticity premium. In the early 2000s, a controversy erupted over the implied provenance of Dasani water (bottled by Coca-Cola), which, as it turned out, is filtered tap water.

Kevin Roberts's (2004) book *Lovemarks* made a splash in the advertising world for declaring this a new age of brands. No longer are brands now mere emblems of a certain quality; they are built on the imagined relationship a consumer has with a brand (see also Thomas Frank 1997; and Carrier and Miller 1998).

Provenance and Moral Preference

Moral provenance often signals quality based on geographic provenance, but it is different from terroir in that it can be applied to complex commodity chains. Looking at moral provenance is a way of seeing how consumers connect moral preference with economic value. Those who do so pay for externalities: customers pay a premium for perceived positive externalities or are willing to punish companies for (perceived and actual) negative externalities. Increasingly, consumers are supporting moral projects through their purchases. This includes choosing products that are "made in the U.S.A.," environmentally friendly products, and Fair Trade products. Knowing a product's moral provenance allows consumers to support what they consider to be ethical social relationships through product choice.

Although the importance of moral provenance has taken off in recent years, the idea is nothing new. Sugar boycotts of the late 18th and early 19th centuries were based on the anti-slavery moral stance of the Anti-Saccharine Society.

For self-interested reasons, consumers are increasingly concerned about the dangers posed by products, such as lead in toys and pesticides on produce. Documenting provenance, such as with organic certifications, addresses such concerns (and allows for rapid responses to lapses of quality control). Such personal concerns are also linked to broader desires to safeguard a perceived common good, environmental and social, which often involves a trade-off with price and/or quality. The trend is expanding beyond upscale markets as well. Walmart has moved to make its stores more green by using compact fluorescent lightbulbs and other "green" products and techniques; the company is also working with its suppliers to reduce the carbon footprint of the products its stores sell. The EPA and Commerce Department have started the Green Suppliers Network to help identify environmentally friendly producers, and many are calling for unified standards to help monitor and control the supply chains.

Outsourcing is most often discussed today as producing negative value derived from provenance. Nike and other apparel companies in particular have been hit with consumer backlash against child labor and sweatshop conditions in overseas assembly plants. American Apparel uses its U.S.-based workforce and the employee benefits the firm provides as explicitly politicized selling points. The increasing length and complexity of commodity chains makes it easier to whitewash (or greenwash or sweatwash) the specific links that consumers might find troublesome (see Micheletti and Follesdal 2007). Such "provenance laundering" can be a conscious strategy or simply expedient for companies pushed to find the lowest production costs. The anonymous nature of commodities allows this loosening of provenance. Likewise, there has been a proliferation of "astroturf" social movements (the opposite of "grassroots" movements) funded by outside special interests.

In this light, new labeling regimes that mimic brand signaling have emerged. Fair Trade–labeled products represent a multibillion-dollar market that has been growing rapidly. The idea of Fair Trade goes back to the 1950s in Germany, and the international umbrella organization for socially conscious labeling that emerged in 1997 is the German-based Fairtrade Labelling Organizations (FLO) (Wilkinson 2007). As Torsten Steinrücken and Sebastian Jaenichen (2007: 205) argue, "Fair Trade products are a product bundle" that allow consumers to exercise preferences about the production process "even if it does not affect product quality." Concern with the production process contributes its own utility to the product bundle (a concern with externalities), and the success of Fair Trade products show that consumers are sometimes willing to pay a premium over that merited by functional utility. "Shopping for human rights is a wallet-based and knowledge-intensive activity," observe Michele Micheletti and Andreas Follesdal (2007: 170). It is also one that seems to kick in only above a certain income threshold, and it is based on access to information. Social labels, such as that of the Fairtrade Labelling Organizations, help streamline the information gathering process for concerned consumers. "Social labels," according to Simon Zadek et al. (1998), are "the words and symbols on products which seek to influence the economic decisions of one set of stakeholders by providing an assurance about the social and ethical impact of a business process on another group of stakeholders." For socially conscious consumers, labels reduce the cost of seeking out information on their own.

The fair trade market is currently centered on high-end coffee, cacao, and cotton products, but is expanding outward. The FLO seeks to combat the "injustice of low prices" by ensuring that producers and workers are paid a living (fair) wage. For coffee, this translates to a premium paid to producers of $1.29 a pound or $0.05 above the market rate, whichever is higher. In late 2007 this was a $0.24 premium per pound over market rates paid to Fair Trade producers; still, by some calculations, less than 10 percent of the retail Fair Trade premium makes it back to producers. Fair Trade products are especially strong in select markets: 47 percent of bananas in Switzerland are Fair Trade, 20 percent of coffee in the UK (Wilkinson 2007: 224). And Fair Trade is going mainstream: Dunkin' Donuts, McDonalds, and Starbucks are all major buyers of Fair Trade coffee.

Moral Projects and the Good Life

Moral provenance appeals to certain consumers' sense of the good life and desire for a better world. As a distinguishing attribute and a competitive advantage, morally provenanced goods allow consumers to (voluntarily) place a monetary value on intangibles such as justice, solidarity, thrift, and environmental stewardship. Their purchases are a visible expression of a commitment to a larger purpose.

Looking at moral provenance is a way of seeing how consumers are driven to pursue their moral preferences, and at what economic cost. If moral projects give meaning to people's lives, reflecting what matters deeply to them, it follows that such projects are also an important source of identity (Taylor 1985). Alasdair MacIntyre (1984, 1988) calls attention to the ways moral projects saturate our everyday lives and how moral communities define virtuous practice. In his neo-Aristotelian view, identity and locally contextualized moralities are essential components of the good life. Economists such as George Akerlof and Amartya Sen write about the powerful role of identity and culture in conditioning the social networks that embed economic activity (Akerlof and Kranton 2005; see also Sen 2006).

From an economic perspective, if preference structures are not oriented only toward immediate material rewards, we may consider a broader range of socio-cultural resources and constraints that touch on the realm of identity formation. Some of these concerns can be worked into self-interested utility functions—the long-term payback from maintaining a reputation (e.g., for honesty) or the negative utility produced by sympathetic suffering. Others require a fuller understanding of the socio-cultural context.

There is ample empirical evidence of unmet moral demands on our market system. These range from the dramatic to the mundane and encompass a range of moral positions. Michael Hiscox and Nicholas Smyth (n.d.) present convincing evidence that consumers are often eager and willing to pay a premium for moral provenance. Using a clever experimental design, they found that a significant number of shoppers at ABC Carpet & Home in New York City prefer articles labeled as having been made under fair labor conditions and were willing to pay a premium for these. Not only were sales for such items higher, but demand for them rose when their price was increased by 10–20 percent. Such strong latent consumer demand for fair labor standards suggests that other sorts of moral provenance are equally valued. The research by Hiscox and Smyth raises the possibility that morally provenanced goods might be that rarest of economic beast, a Giffin good, for which demand rises with increased supply (holding quality and price constant).

Ethical consumption and a concern with moral provenance are revealed preferences for certain moral values that feed into our sense of self, self-worth, and wellbeing. In fact, James Carrier (2012) and others argue that ethical consumption is often more about the identity of the consumer than about effecting real-world change; in our virtualized economy, the subjective feeling of agency substitutes for real power to effect change. There is certainly truth to this: working within the framework of an open market to promote just social relations may mean that one fails to act in ways that would further one's aims more effectively. And yet, I argue, we need to have a double consciousness about these things (DuBois 1903): imagining a better future unconstrained by the solidity of the existing structure while also finding ways to make the system work more fairly in the short run.

Such potential shows how markets may respond to moral demands and effect change along supply chains. But it is not enough to say we should just let the market do its work. Markets operate within a given institutional structure, overlaid with formal and informal power relations. Pursuing the good life is not something we do alone; it requires the coordination of social structures and political-economic orders.

CHAPTER 4

Solidarity, Dignity, and Opportunity

In 2009, Munich-based automaker BMW reached a historic wage agreement, not with its blue-collar employees but with upper management. BMW announced that it would henceforth peg all management salaries to worker wages to ensure that the two would grow at the same rate and that wage inequalities would not increase. The highest-paid employees were to be limited to salaries no more than twenty-five times the company's average salary (*Deutsche Welle* 2009).

BMW's move bucked trends in the United States and England of ever higher executive compensation, even in the aftermath of the 2008 financial crisis. In the United States, CEOs earn, on average, more than 300 times the average wage of workers. The comparable figure for Germany is less than twenty times average wages (so BMW is still on the upper end of the German inequality spectrum), and for Japan less than twelve times average wages.

Volkswagen's global headquarters are in Wolfsburg, not far from Hannover. In 2011, VW announced that its corporate BlackBerry server would stop sending message to employees' devices thirty minutes after their work-day ended and would not begin again until thirty minutes before the next shift. This change resulted from an agreement reached with VW's powerful works council (*Financial Times* 2011). As in all large German companies, VW's works council, elected by workers, holds just under half of the cor-porate board seats. From an American perspective, this ratio is incredible, almost unthinkable. But under the German model of "co-determination," which treats employees as stakeholders alongside stockholders, it works pretty well. As the VW action shows, workers are wary of gains through increased productivity that are made possible by 24/7 accessibility. They are willing to fight not only for wages, but also for quality of life, and indeed, independence and dignity, to avoid being at their employers' beck and call.

"Institutions matter," as Douglass North (1990) observed. But institutions do not operate in a vacuum—they emerge from, are folded into, and shape cultural perspective and individual behaviors (Portes 2008; Giddens 1984).

BMW, VW, and much of German business have a system of co-determination between capital and labor that places a high value on solidar-ity, a theme that permeates the German stakeholding variety of capitalism. The structure of capital markets and the system of co-determination by labor and management create institutional incentives that value stability over rapid growth and operate with long-term horizons. As such, Germany presents an example of a balance between regulation and liberty, between public goods and private interests, that seeks to maximize overall wellbeing.

Moral values condition the economic systems found in different societ-ies. At the same time, political-economic relations and structures condition moral values. The German balance between individual self-interest and the common good differs in significant ways from that in Anglo-Saxon econo-mies. A set of institutional structures—a "variety of capitalism" or "social market economy"—creates incentives to pursue long-term goals through the system of co-determination between labor and capital. BMW's wage structure and VW's leisure-time policies reflect their corporate cultures, but they also arise from larger institutional contexts.

This chapter focuses on how institutional constraints and cultural val-ues play into the formation of particularly German forms of capitalism and market relations. I examine the broad structural framework of German cap-italism—finance, labor relations, and consumer regulations. Opportunity structures channel the paths that are open, and the choices presented, to individuals; recognizing this does not negate individual agency but places it within a structural framework of possibilities. The consumer desires and agency I discussed in the previous chapters are crucially important, but they must be understood within institutional contexts and opportunity structures.

The German Variety of Capitalism

Reading the major German newspapers (*Die Zeit* and *Frankfurter Allgemeine Zeitung*, although perhaps not the more mass-market *Bild* tabloid), one is struck by how often the word "*Kapitalismus*" (capitalism) appears—much more often than in the *New York Times* or the *Nashville Tennessean*. The U.S. press talks a lot about "the economy," but that takes a particular free-market variety of capitalism for granted, assuming that it is simply the way things are. Explicitly naming the system ("capitalism") highlights the more overtly negotiated nature of the German variety of capitalism—not so taken-for-granted that it can be left unnamed, not yet a part of a hegemonic common sense. (I should also note that *Kapitalismus* is sometimes used by German journalists as pejorative shorthand for market excesses.)

Germany's *soziale Marktwirtschaft* (social market economy) tends to be more regulated than the Anglo-American capitalism. An overarching mandate for German economic and labor policy is the *Grundgesetz* (the postwar stand-in for a constitution that still governs), which states that all have a right to "*ein menschenwürdiges Leben*" (a life of dignity—literally, a human-worthy life). This principle is generally interpreted to guarantee a minimum standard of living, and it is operationalized through a number of government programs. For example, lower limits for wages are set by the "immoral wage" (30 percent or more below customary wages), and welfare (*Sozialhilfe*) payments must be sufficient to ensure a *menschenwürdiges Leben*.

This speaks to "is" and "ought" questions: What is the right balance between labor and capital interests? What should be the trade-off between leisure time and income? Rather than defer to mathematically modeled market forces, how can we ensure that our economy is producing the greatest utility (as broadly conceived) for the greatest number? A "varieties of capitalism" approach "distinguishes different types of political-economic systems and explores the different institutional arrangements and behavioral 'logics' that sustain them" (Thelen 2001: 72; Hall and Soskice 2001).

Plate 7: Smash Capitalism

On editorial pages, in subway graffiti, and in daily conversation one finds in Germany a widespread critical perspective on capitalism. Even Hannover's neighborhood *Südstadt Magazin* (which is filled mostly with ads from local businesses and announcements of neighborhood events) takes this tone: in 2009 a letter from the editor warned readers that "capitalism demands its tribute, and it demands it first and foremost from the place that appears weakest" ["Der Kapitalismus fordert seinen Tribut, und er fordert ihn genau an der Stelle, die ihm zunächst am schwächsten erscheint." (Haas 2009)]

A 2008 survey by the Bertelsman Foundation found that 75 percent of Germans felt that economic conditions in their country were "unfair." Overwhelming majorities agreed or strongly agreed that workers deserve a bigger share of company profits and that managers should worry less about profits and more about the social impact of their decisions (96 percent and 93 percent, respectively). More Germans than ever had lost confidence in the German "social market" economy (*Der Spiegel* 2008). What Germans see as so unfair would seem downright socialist to many Americans.

Stakeholding, Co-Determination, and Works Councils

The German variety of capitalism emerged relatively late and was concentrated in coal, steel, and other capital-intensive industries; this led to a close association between firms and banks and was a key foundation of Bismarckian forms of 19th-century corporatism (Busch 2005).

The current institutions of German capitalism took shape in the postwar reconstruction period and were associated with the "ordoliberalism" of the Freiburg school of economic thought, in particular the work of Walter Eucken (Witt 2002). In this blending of economic liberalism and social welfare corporatism, organized labor took on an especially strong role (Turner 1998). Today, the key employee and employer associations are IG Metal and Gesamtmetall, respectively, and they set the tone for sector-wide bargains between labor and capital. While this sort of cooperation results in high labor costs, Kathleen Thelen (2001) argues that employers appreciate the stability of industry-wide bargaining: with everyone in the same boat, there is more stability. And the high labor costs were long financed by the post–World War II *Wirtschaftswunder* (economic miracle) that Germany enjoyed until the mid-1970s (and then in the 2000s by focusing on high-value exports).

Definitions of contemporary German capitalism vary in emphasis but tend to cluster around several key traits.[1] Wolfgang Streeck identifies German capitalism with strong national unions; an education system that channels students into trades and apprenticeships; regulation that limits retail competition; a strong welfare system; a high savings rate; works councils and other stakeholding mechanisms; and tightly held equity with companies tending to finance expansion through bank credit. He argues that the structure of capital holdings allows German companies to take a longer-term perspective on returns on investment (see Streeck 1997; Kitschelt and Streeck 2004; Streeck and Thelen 2005).

Germany's corporate capital structure is markedly different from that of the United States. For example, of the country's 1,000 largest companies, only 170 are listed on the stock market. German companies, and especially the *Mittelstand* (mid-sized) engines of the export economy, raise most of their external capital through borrowing rather than through the stock market. They are more concerned with steady and safe returns, while the market rewards riskier, short-term gains. Thus the incentives and time horizons for

German corporate leaders are more aligned with those of stakeholders, not just stockholders.

Sigurt Vitols (2004) distinguishes German stakeholding from Anglo-American shareholder systems in that it involves "negotiated shareholder value," meaning that shareholder interest cannot simply be implemented by management and that shareholder value is worked out in negotiations with other stakeholders. Stakeholders include large investors (banks, families, state governments, insurance companies), employees (works councils, unions), the community, and suppliers and customers.[2] Vitols (2004: 371) compares the distribution of net value added in Anglo-American and German firms (see Table 4.1). The figures in the table reflect dramatic differences in the priorities and incentive structures in German and Anglo-American businesses.

While German labor's percentage share of value added declined over the 1990s (and through the early 2000s), it is still substantially higher than that of the Anglo-American world. This reflects both the power of German organized labor and a cultural norm regarding equity that flows from *Mittelstand* labor relations. (Mittelstand firms are small- and medium-sized companies with fewer than 500 employees and less than €50 million in revenue.) Labor still takes a sizable portion of Anglo-American value added, but returns to capital in these countries are much greater than in Germany. As these figures show, Anglo-American companies place a much higher value on shareholder returns, while German companies allocate more to labor at the expense of capital.

Germany experienced a period of substantial market liberalization in the early 2000s. As Wolfgang Streeck (2009: 33) shows, this resulted in "market forces slowly taking the place of political decisions" in various sectors,

Table 4.1: Distribution of Value Added in Anglo-American and German Firms

Stakeholder	Anglo-American, early 1990s (percent)	Germany, early 1990s (percent)	Germany, late 1990s (percent)
Labor	62.2	85.3	78.4
Credit	23.5	5.4	4.3
Government	14.3	5.2	6.8
Retained earnings	3.2	5.2	7.8
Dividends	15.0	2.0	2.8

SOURCE: Vitols 2004: 371.

including labor relations and public finance. Although in line with global trends toward neoliberal political economic orders, the German case was also driven by domestic concerns and Chancellor Gerhard Schröder's (1998–2005) "third way" politics. An additional, and surprising, motor for liberalization has been the European Union. Legally enforceable EU regulations can overrule what are deemed to be anti-competitive national laws; the EU goal of fully integrating capital markets and harmonizing corporate regulations poses a serious threat to the German model.

The result of high taxes, strong labor, and an extensive social safety net is much greater income equality in Germany than in the United States (as well as a significantly lower GNP per head). For example, the income of professionals such as physicians is much lower than in the United States: in 2006, the average salary of hospital doctors in the United States was $267, 993, while in Germany the equivalent figure was $56,455 (spiegel.de 2006). For working-class jobs, the hourly wage in western Germany averaged €27.60 in 2005 (€18.80 in the United States, €17.20 in eastern Germany). Although these are some of the highest labor costs in the world, worker efficiency makes up much of the difference.

While Germany has much lower levels of inequality, the country's GDP per head ($29,461) is also significantly lower than that in the United States ($41,890). In 2005, average German household income was €33,700 (about $43,136) (Statistisches Bundesamt Deutschland 2006); in the United States it was $55,238 (with a lower median). The poverty level in Germany is set at 60 percent of average income. In 2000, the poverty rate among the working-age population was 8 percent in Germany (as compared with 13.7 percent in the United States); at the same time social spending was 7.3 percent of GDP in Germany (as compared with 2.3 percent of GDP in the United States (*International Herald Tribune* 2005a: 16). In Germany, unemployment benefits replace about 29 percent of lost wages, and only about 14 percent in the United States.

A key component of the liberalization of the German economy in the early 2000s was labor market reforms. In 2002, Peter Hartz (chief of personnel at Volkswagen and close adviser to Chancellor Gerhard Schröder) headed the Kommission für moderne Dienstleistungen am Arbeitsmarkt (known as the Hartz Commission). Focusing on ways to make the labor market in Germany more flexible, the Hartz Commission developed key provisions in Schröder's Agenda 2010 that came to be known as Hartz I,

Hartz II, Hartz III, and Hartz IV, and these were enacted from 2003 to 2005. The Hartz provisions sought to make welfare less attractive and to provide incentives for the unemployed to reenter the market. The Hartz laws reduced unemployment payments from thirty-two months to sixteen months (in 2003). It also enabled workers to earn up to €180 a month without losing benefits (through what are pejoratively called "one euro jobs"). In 2005, 30 percent of German workers were in part-time or temporary jobs, such as the one euro jobs (*Economist* 2005b: 55).

Germany has a much more regulated economy than the United States or Great Britain and usually does not score high on indices of business-friendliness. Germany boasts the highest corporate tax rates in Europe, and according to the World Bank's ranking of rigidity in labor markets, Germany ranks 95th of 144 countries.[3] Germany's rules governing hours worked and firing costs are particularly rigid. The inflexibility in German capital, labor, and production has made it difficult for German firms to compete (especially in lower-end products) in the turn-of-the-millennium fast-paced global markets. During the fat years, labor made huge gains in reducing work hours and increasing pay and benefits, but these are hard to sustain in leaner times.

Since the Hartz reforms, "flexibility" has entered German political discourse as a new key word. It covers a whole range of labor regulations that make it easier to hire and fire workers. But there are also deeper cultural overtones associated with "flexibility": that the German economy needs more entrepreneurship and German society is too immobile. This flexibility stands in contrast to another, longer-standing, key concept in German public discourse: "solidarity," a strategically nebulous value of cohesion that even the pro-business Christian Democrats find hard to oppose. And while there is widespread discontent with the tax burden, it is also politically costly to cut programs perceived as buttressing solidarity. Solidarity is at the cultural heart of the German stakeholding system.[4]

Financial Structure and Cross-holdings

The German social market economy since World War II has relied on an interwoven network of financial arrangements whereby banks and large insurance companies maintain large cross-holding stakes in various industries. Based on financing by banks, insurance companies, and quasi-governmental investment vehicles (with what Andreas Busch [2005] terms "patient capital"), stable cross-holdings extend the horizon for expected returns. Streeck (1997) argues that cross-holdings allow a firm to look beyond quarterly or annual returns. With longer timelines, the incentives of investors and managers differ from those of shorter-term speculative stock traders. (The German structure also insulates against hostile takeovers and shareholder actions.) In fact, in popular discourse, speculation is often demonized. "Hedge fund" has become a code word for short-term speculative capital that often destroys social goods. In contrast, the German variety of cross-holdings supports an expansive concept of who should benefit, from individual stockholders to a wider group of stakeholders.

Martin Höpner and Lothar Krempel (2003) diagram the dense web of German corporate cross-holdings, which looks like a spider web with banks and insurance companies anchoring individual nodes (see Figure 4.1). The web is changing rapidly as Germany, on its own and in some cases under EU coercion, continues to liberalize capital regulations. Krempel maps cross-holdings every two years, and his depictions of more recent networks are much less dense. Vitols (2004: 361) shows that in the mid-1990s the median size of the largest shareholding bloc in German companies was 57 percent. In the United States the equivalent figure was just 5.4 percent. This significant difference means that, on average, large stockholders in German companies have much more power than their U.S. counterparts.

A key component of this system are the Mittelstand companies, which account for 70 percent of employment in Germany. These are mostly privately held (GmbH, Limited Liability Corporations), and are typically largely owned and managed by a family. In fact, the Institut für Mittelstandsforschung (2004), defines Mittelstand in part by the identification of an owner with the enterprise and vice versa, as well as a close relationship between owners and employees. Vitols (2004) notes that the Mittelstand companies tend to focus on high-quality, small-batch, high-margin production. Many make specialized machinery—condom machines, robotic welders, and so on—and have a dominant share of their niche markets. The Mittelstand account for 40 percent of German exports, and exports produce about 30 percent of GDP. Thus the Mittelstand are often considered the pillars of the German economy. Nonetheless, equity financing provides less than 15 percent of Mittelstand funding (in other OECD countries the figure is about twice that) (*Economist* 2009).

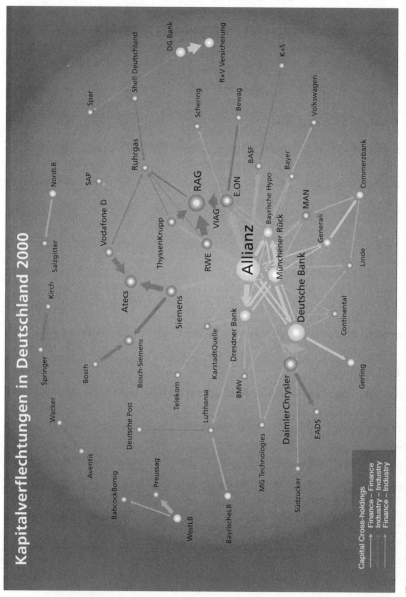

Figure 4.1: German Capital Cross-holdings in 2000

(courtesy of Lothar Krempel, Max Planck Institut für Gesellschaftsforschung)

The Mittelstand and other German companies rely much less on the stock market for capital than do their counterparts in the United States; most financing is provided by bank loans. There are only about 750 German companies listed on the stock exchange, less than 10 percent of the U.S. total, and there are high barriers to entry and cultural resistance to the stock market. Vitols (2004: 361) reports that in the mid1990s the median size of the largest shareholding bloc in Germany companies was a whopping 57 percent, while for U.S. corporations it was only 5.4 percent. In 1999, German market capitalization was only about 52 percent of GDP ($1.1. trillion), while U.S. market capitalization was 161 percent of GDP. Many fewer Germans own stock—around 10 percent—as compared with over 40 percent in the United States (including mutual funds). A survey of Mittelstand companies found that 75 percent planned to raise funds for growth from their own resources (retained profits and bank credit lines) rather than sell equity (von Rosen 1999).The result is that most equity capital is not traded on the stock market but held in elaborate webs of cross-holdings.

Market liberalization reforms in Germany in the early 2000s brought about a crucial shift in financial regulation. A 2003 law allowed German companies to sell cross-holdings in other German companies without paying capital gains taxes, making it possible to break up the web of cross-holdings that had long constituted "Deutschland AG." Companies such as Deutsche Bank, Allianz, and Munich Re began to sell significant stakes in Bayer, Karstadt, Continental, DaimlerChrysler, and others. This allows them to raise earnings per share and increase shareholder value. The benefits include more liquidity in the market, with companies better able to raise capital through equity stakes rather than traditional bank loans. It is also hoped that a more diverse group of stockholders will take an active interest in performance and push the companies to pursue growth and realize efficiencies. At the same time, there has been a move away from "stakeholding" interests (including those of workers) and a greater emphasis on stockholder interests, maximizing stockholder value, often in the short-term and potentially at the cost of long-term health and growth.

No company better exemplifies cross-holdings than insurance giant Allianz, which has been at the center of the web of post–World War II corporate links. After a 2003 shift in tax rules, Allianz began selling off cross-holdings (e.g., stakes in Beiersdorf, Bayer, Dresdner), reducing its holdings in them from 35 percent of assets in 2002 to less than 15 percent by 2007.

In 2006, when Allianz AG (*Aktiengesellschaft*) became Allianz SE (*Societas Europaea*), it was no longer governed by German rules for public companies but a new set of more liberal rules enacted through the European Union. Under the new rules, Allianz's twenty-member board was reduced to twelve. Of these twelve, only six (yet still half) are employee representatives; and further, only four of these come from German operations, reducing German employee representation from ten members to four, and from 50 percent to 33 percent of the board. Brokers at the hundreds of neighborhood Allianz offices throughout Germany have protested their diluted influence (Dougherty 2006), yet Allianz closed many of these small branches and moved more business online (*Economist* 2005a). Such moves do make German companies more flexible by giving boards more freedom to make tough decisions.

Banking: Landesbanken, Sparkassen

Another key element of Germany's institutional framework, public savings banks (*Sparkassen*), are undergoing major restructuring as well. Over half of all private savings in German are held in Sparkassen, which are majority owned by the local government but with semi-independent management. The Sparkasse brand (and its ubiquitous red "S"-and-dot logo) has high recognition and loyalty in Germany, and Sparkassen make more than 20 percent of the country's loans. They are closely linked to the regional wholesale *Landesbanken*.

First established in the early 1800s, Sparkassen by law must serve the "common good." This normally means supporting local development and providing banking services to those who might not otherwise qualify in the private market. They have been able to do so and still make a profit because their debt is guaranteed by their respective local regional governments. That arrangement has now been successfully challenged by EU competition authorities.

Germany's 500 Sparkassen are closely associated with their home cities and are prohibited from operating outside of their home region. They do not pay taxes and have an obligation to invest locally. Their connection to the state allows them to borrow at AAA rates, as they are implicitly and explicitly backed by local governments.

The Sparkassen and the regional Landesbanken, which serve as clearinghouses for the Sparkassen, represent—and fund—the German model of a "social market economy." Sparkassen are obligated to support local development and provide banking services to those who might not otherwise qualify on the private market. They are able to do so and still make a handsome profit because their debt is guaranteed by their respective local and regional governments, giving them superior credit ratings and access to capital at below-market rates. But that changed in 2005, when, owing to EU ruling, their debt stopped being backed by the government guarantees.

From a free-market perspective, this was a much-needed reform—the Sparkassen distort the market through their unfair advantage. Now they have to pay market prices for their capital, and pass those costs along to their consumers. However, the Sparkassen serve an important function that will not be replaced by the private sector—there are greater public benefits that accrue from their existence than their opportunity costs to the private sector. Their function is not just private market lending but also local and regional development.

Stakeholding and Co-determination: Mitbestimmung

The signature feature of German stakeholding capitalism is the idea of co-determination embodied in works councils. By law, all German companies must make special provisions for workers and reserve half of supervisory board positions for workers and union representations. At Volkswagen, the works councils are especially strong. Indeed, VW went beyond what is legally mandated and in 1999 created a World Works Council to enfranchise all their employees, not just the German ones; this global council has twenty-seven members, eleven from Germany and sixteen from the foreign operations). VW has an exceptionally strong works council and union representation on the board of supervisors, with labor, capital, and the state having roughly equal roles in the VW corporate structure.[5]

It is also significant that the state of Niedersachsen controls a 20.1 percent share of VW voting stock.* The 1960 "Volkswagen Law" prohibits any

---

* In 2008, privately held Porsche (which has long family ties to VW) attempted a semi-hostile take-over of the much larger VW. Porsche's bumbling moves and frenzied short sellers pushed VW stock to new heights, making it briefly the most valued company in the world. In the end, in a series of complicated cross-holding moves, as of this writing in 2013, VW has effectively taken control of the Porsche car business.

stockholder from taking more than a 20 percent share of voting rights in VW, giving Niedersachsen unparalleled power in VW corporate affairs (including decision making on layoffs, future plant locations, and so on). In 2007, the European Court of Justice ruled against the German government, declaring the law illegal on the grounds that it is anti-competitive by hindering the free movement of capital across national borders. In response, in 2008 the Bundestag passed a modified version of the Volkswagen law to protect the share of voting shares held by the Niedersachsen state. Further challenges are expected from the EU competitiveness office.

The co-determination (or *Mitbestimmung*) system and works councils (*Betriebsräte*) are part of what Vitols (2004) calls "conflictual partnership." Mitbestimmung laws require companies with over fifty employees to allocate half of the seats on the corporate supervisory board to labor (see Streeck 1997; Schumann 2005, Frege 2002; Turner 1998). (The supervisory boards appoint the managing board and fill top executive positions.) Works councils (along with unions) organize workers within companies and feed into the labor slots on the board. (A 2001 law, the *Betriebsverfassungsgesetz*, substantially strengthened the rights of works councils and made them easier to form with smaller numbers.) Works councils are key elements of a system that enfranchises workers and helps companies maintain a long-term perspective on their finances and growth.

Michael Schumann (2005) identifies the key aspects of Betriebsräte and Mitbestimmung as teamwork and worker self-organization along with a loose hierarchy to help problem solving and the development of innovative ideas. Works councils do certainly increase information flow (Frege 2002). In a survey of recent literature on German works councils, Carola Frege found that most studies show that the impact of works councils on the firm's finances is not seen as a problem by most managers; if anything, works councilors tend to overestimate the influence. Thelen and Turner (1997) argue that the increasing mobility of capital, which encourages transnationals to shop between countries for the best deal, can weaken works councils.

In 2005, news from the Volkswagen headquarters in Wolfsburg could have provided the plot for a mini-series involving bribes and secret front companies, prostitutes and Viagra, and leading business figures with close ties to the ruling government. The misdeeds were actually part of several different, although interrelated, scandals. At the heart of the issue was the way VW management seemed to be buying off its powerful works council.

In 1993, VW's Peter Hartz, the architect of Germany's wide-reaching labor reforms, instituted a new Volkswagen 5000 plan: hiring 5,000 additional workers under a new contract to be paid DM5,000 per month, below union wages, but promising not to move assembly abroad.

Labor went along with Volkswagen 5000 and a series of later plans in exchange for continued job security. As it turns out, the worker/management harmony at VW was greased by payments to works council leaders (through investments in dummy subcontracting firms) as well as junkets to Brazil and other exotic locations. In 2005, Hartz resigned from Volkswagen. And for many, the VW scandal called into doubt the value of works councils in the global marketplace. The *International Herald Tribune*, the *Economist*, and the more conservative Germany dailies called for scrapping the laws of co-determination.

Yet, works councils provide a crucial function in worker engagement and dedication to the job—those qualities that make German workers, by some measure, the most productive in the world on a per hour basis. If workers are part of the decision-making process—if they feel as if their occupation is more than just a job—they are more dedicated, more productive, and more reliable workers. Also, crucially, they are more willing to make concessions for the company when called upon to do so; they are willing to share in both the gains and the pain. Hermann Kotthoff (1994) shows workers most interested in creating a moral structure within their firm. Such a moral community is the prerequisite for a functioning partnership and underlies the German stakeholding system.

Regulating Work and Leisure

Many Americans find German stores' business hours frustrating and oppressive.* The *Ladenschlussgesetz* (the federal store-closing law) governed retail hours until 2006, when that power was devolved to individual states (*Länder*). Under the federal law, stores were closed on Sundays and holidays, open until 2:00 P.M. on Saturdays and until 6:00 P.M. Monday through Friday.

---

* Other regulations can be similarly frustrating, including restrictions on hanging laundry out on Sundays, enforced quiet times, and the complex rules governing recycling and trash.

Plate 8: Öko-Druck Laden

By law, German workers get four weeks of paid vacation, although the national average is a much higher 7.8 weeks of vacation (paid and unpaid). Long vacations may be nice for employees and shop owners, but they are also an inconvenience for customers. Running errands in August, one is often thwarted, with stores closed and little signs in the window saying that they will reopen after the summer break (Sommerpause).

Average number of hours worked per year		Vacation and holidays (weeks per year)	
South Korea	2,380	Germany	7.8
United States	1,824	France	7.0
Japan	1,789	Britain	6.6
Britain	1,669	United States	3.9
France	1,441		
Germany	1,440		

SOURCE: International Labor Organization (www.ilo.org).

Most cities also designated one Saturday per month as a *langes Samstag* (long Saturday), allowing shopping until 6:00 P.M. These restrictions have been loosened in Niedersachsen, but most stores must still close on Sunday, and in fact most maintain their former 9:00 A.M.–6:00 P.M. schedule; larger retailers stay open until 8:00 P.M. and a few grocery stores are open until 10:00 P.M.* Germany has for several years been trying to increase domestic consumption, recognizing the weakness as well as the strength of export dependency (as the world's largest exporter in dollar terms, exports account for about a third of Germany's GDP). The financial crisis of 2008–09 brought greater urgency to stimulating domestic consumption by lengthening store hours.

While infringing on consumer sovereignty, having official store hours produces a number of social externalities. When everyone has to shop at the same time, deep social ties between classes may not be the result; but even coming into casual contact with many others who are doing the same thing can produce a sense of solidarity, a realization that one's own life is inextricably linked to those of one's neighbors. Store hours also provide common time off for everyone, facilitating social interaction with friends and family. To be sure, store-closing hours are often inconvenient. If one forgets to pick something up from the store, or runs out of time, then one just makes do. (And perhaps it is a good thing, both psychologically and socially, to sometimes have to figure out alternatives to easy consumption.)

Laws governing business hours, price controls, and other such restrictions act to protect small and medium-sized firms from competition. In many other ways, German regulations act to limit competition. Until recently, strict laws governed when retail sales could be offered and the extent of discounts. Even today, bookstores are prohibited from discounting titles, a policy that undoubtedly helps many small bookstores stay in business. In Hannover, one can order almost any book from a small neighborhood store and pick it up there within a day or two.

Germany is also famous for its short work week and long vacations. Unions have had great success in reducing work hours. In the early 1970s, they began to push a "work less, work all" platform, and by the 1980s conflict between labor and companies had resulted in significantly reducing the

---

* There have long been formal exemptions from the business hours law for shops in train stations (which may stay open Sunday and nights) and gas stations (*Tankstelle*), which have also expanded their food offerings to look like the convenience stores at gas stations in the United States.

number of hours worked annually and allowing more scheduling flexibility while holding wages steady (Thelen 2001). There is even a German word for working less for the same pay: *Lohnausgleich*. Per hour, German productivity is higher than that in the United States, although U.S. companies produced 45 percent more income per employee.

As another way of valuing leisure time, Germans also tend to make a clear distinction between work and private life, being careful not to let the one bleed over into the other. *Feierabend*—that time after the workday is officially over—is taken seriously even by many professionals in a way Americans would find odd.

Exclusion and Community

Structures that promote solidarity also promote exclusion. This is a delicate subject in Germany, given the legacy of the Holocaust, and one that has seen much debate over the role of immigrants in German society. Ample cautionary tales punctuate the German example. The institutions and moral projects that produce positive outcomes around solidarity can also uphold xenophobic attitudes toward immigrants, incentive structures that are unfriendly to women and primary childcare providers, and other forms of social exclusion and marginalization.

One element of Germany's legal contrition following World War II was the institution of generous asylum laws. But while it is relatively easy to enter the country and gain refugee status, it is difficult to enter the legal labor market. These restrictive labor rules heighten barriers of language and culture, isolating immigrant populations and inflaming the passions of both pro- and anti-immigrant groups.

Germany has long depended on immigrant labor. In the 1950s, 1960s, and 1970s, many Turkish "guest workers" stayed in Germany and raised families despite restrictions on gaining citizenship. The Turkish *döner kebab* competes with bratwurst as the country's "traditional" fast food. Berlin is the second largest Turkish city in the world by population citizenship. Today, Russians and Poles compete with Turks for jobs in Germany's export economy.

Despite record low unemployment rates in recent years, violence against immigrants is on the rise. Extreme right-wing groups, while still a small minority, have been attracting ever more young men, especially from the former East. These developments point to the dangerous aspect of moral communities that Habermas pointed out, that the consensus such communities require can as easily be oppressive as it is nurturing.

Conclusions

It is clear that certain German institutions and cultural processes condense around themes of stakeholding and collective goods. The balance between moral and economic concerns that many Germans seek speaks to the philosophical foundations of economics. As Doug Meeks (2000) points out, the word "economy" comes to us from *oikonomia*, based on the Greek *oikos* (household) and *nomos* (law, word), and this "law of the household" was a morality of provisioning (a sort of "from each according to his abilities, to each according to his needs"). In this vein, John Ruskin (1862) wrote that the merchant's value to society and very duty is "to provide for the nation. It is no more his function to get profit for himself out of that provision than it is a clergyman's function to get his stipend. The stipend is a due and necessary adjunct, but not the object of his life, if he be a true clergyman, any more than his fee (or honorarium) is the object of a true physician. Neither is his fee the object of life to a true merchant."

Ruskin's call for the merchant to "provide and provision" concerns the dignity of a calling and a trade as well as the importance of commitment to larger projects. Stakeholding—seeing one's future and self-interests as intimately tied to those of a larger collectivity—complicates easy, neat notions of self-interest: if I define myself as part of something larger, my self-interests are based not just on my narrowly defined material wellbeing, but also on a willingness to sacrifice for the greater good.

Although rapidly changing, German political economic institutions of co-determination support a particular balance of individual self-interests and collective goods. Such stakeholding can be seen both in national policy and in consumer behavior. German consumers put a high value on the moral provenance of goods and how these contribute to the common good. Such stakeholding constitutes a form of imagined (and usually unarticulated) moral community that informs the ways that (ever contingent) identities emerge. Widely held German notions of stakeholding create imagined moral communities in which solidarity and fairness balances narrow self-interest.

The German system of co-determination and market regulation creates a particular set of opportunity structures for workers and consumers, limiting choices in many areas to promote a balance of dimensions of wellbeing. It is an expensive system, and despite Germany's higher per worker productivity, take-home wages are much lower than in the United States. In addition, retail prices are high by American standards, and part of that premium goes into vocational and professional training for workers, reinforcing the dignity of their jobs. Wages are spread more evenly than in the United States, and the German system distributes dignity of work more broadly. The system itself has the legitimacy to function to the extent that it constitutes a meaningful, moral project (often expressed as "solidarity") for most people most of the time.

PART TWO

Guatemalan Coffee, Cocaine, and Capabilities

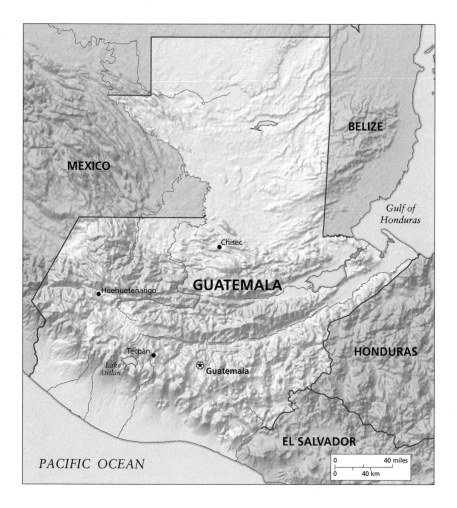

MEXICO

BELIZE

Gulf of
Honduras

Chisec

GUATEMALA

Huehuetenango

HONDURAS

Tecpán

Lake
Atitlán

⊛ Guatemala

EL SALVADOR

PACIFIC OCEAN

0   40 miles
0   40 km

CHAPTER 5

Provenance and Values

The Case of Guatemalan Coffee

Although you may not have spent much time thinking about where your eggs come from, there is a good chance that you have considered the origin of your coffee, if only to order the Antigua mild or the Colombian blend at your local coffee shop.

As with fine wine, provenance and terroir have become key elements of value in the world of high-end coffee. Coffee's complex flavor profile (like wine's) is sensitive to climate, moisture, and soil conditions; and the highest-priced coffees are varietals whose provenance is a single estate. In 2012, Korean buyers paid $500.50 a pound for a microlot of that year's mocha varietal from the Guatemalan *finca* (plantation) El Injerto.[1] This entire lot was only eight pounds, but the benchmark New York commodity price at

---

This chapter is based on collaborative research conducted with Bart Victor. The ideas presented here developed through conversations and joint writing with Victor, and portions of this chapter were previously published in Fischer and Victor 2013.

113

the time was just over $170 per hundredweight, meaning that the El Injerto beans sold for about 300 times the going rate.

I did not try this $500 coffee, but I have sampled a number of El Injerto's more reasonable (if still pricey) alternatives. They produce one of my favorite coffees; it has a deep, almost smoky base and highlights of dark berries and citrus. Tastes vary, but by almost any standard El Injerto holds its own with the very best.[2] El Injerto's owner, Arturo Aguirres, told me that until the late 1970s he transported all of his coffee by mule because there were no passable roads for cars, and that he continued to plant the high-altitude exotic varietals (Mocha, Pacamara, Maroquipe, etc.) even when they were not selling, because they were good coffees and he took pride in his coffee production. When others were switching their land to other uses, Aguirres held out. And now his efforts are paying off with the premiums his specialty coffees command.

Are his coffees worth $6.60 a cup *wholesale* (FOB Huehuetenango, Guatemala)? If it is what the market will bear, one could argue, then it seems that they must be. Objective quality (according to established tasting standards) and market scarcity play an important role, but we cannot discount the symbolic values at play: the relative positioning of conspicuous consumption; the imagined personal relationship with a producer (and his inspiring story); and underpinning it all, the cultural and market shift among the global affluent toward artisanal and singular products.

In this chapter we turn our sights to highland Guatemala, an area of volcanoes and verdant valleys. The region is home to millions of Maya peoples, who make up the majority of the population; they speak one of the more than twenty Mayan languages of the country. Rural Guatemala is an impoverished place, but by any measure (income, land holdings, education, life expectancy, access to electricity and potable water), the Maya make up the overwhelming majority of the Guatemalan poor. Guatemala's modest per capita GDP ($4,167 in 2011 U.S. dollars) is reinforced by highly unequal land holdings and income distributions, resulting in one of the highest poverty rates in the hemisphere (between 44 percent and 80 percent, the variation in estimates reflecting the political and methodological problems with measuring poverty). While there are many poor *ladinos* (non-Maya), it is also true that the country's political and economic elite are overwhelmingly ladino (and many take pride in their non-indigenous blood lines).

This chapter focuses on smallholding Maya farmers who have entered the coffee trade in Guatemala in recent years, and what this means for their conceptions of the good life. Aguirres is not typical of the group—he is a third-generation ladino coffee farmer—but the prices his provenanced coffee commands dramatically illustrate the high end of this new market, and the potential for other farmers. El Injerto operates at the very upper end of the market, but the demand for quality and provenance has driven up prices for all of the high-altitude Guatemalan producers.

While not quite Germany's exact geographic antipode, Guatemala seems nonetheless a world away. But it was there that, well over a century ago, intrepid young German planters and merchants came to grow and export coffee. Guatemala had ideal growing conditions for coffee, and forced labor laws provided a ready supply of Maya workers. The Guatemalan ladino elite had long felt embattled by the Maya majority, and the 19th-century policies to attract Germans and other European immigrants were driven not only by a desire to stimulate economic growth but also by a politics of eugenics that sought to dilute Maya bloodlines.

(In the late 1970s and throughout the 1980s, Guatemala was a hot spot in the Cold War, with U.S. military aid funded scorched-earth assaults and terror campaigns aimed at Maya areas. The Guatemalan military response was devastatingly out of proportion to the size and threat posed by the various revolutionary groups (see Chapter 8) . The violence was felt especially hard in the coffee-producing regions, home to much of the country's indigenous population, and its legacy is still palpable.)

Up until 1900, Guatemala exported most of its coffee to Germany. In those early years, the German market had exceptionally high standards for coffee, establishing a legacy in Guatemala of quality production. While most of Guatemala's 19th-century coffee would be considered inferior in the contemporary specialty market, it was some of the best available at the time (as witnessed by various awards at world expositions).

Throughout the twentieth century, coffee production in Guatemala was a highly concentrated industry composed of a small number of very large producers. These *cafetaleros* operated privately owned fincas and depended on temporary migrant labor to deliver what had become a high-volume, low-cost commodity product. The large producers traded with equally large and concentrated exporters and roasters who then completed the global value chain; this was the coffee that found its way into cups around the

Plate 9: Milpa and Nutrition

Milpa, traditional plots of maize and beans, have provided the agricultural basis for Maya communities for thousands of years. According to the *Popol Wuj* (a book of Maya mytho-historical narratives) and contemporary oral tradition, humans were created from maize, and the plant remains at the heart of Maya culture both materially and symbolically. No meal is complete without a stack of corn tortillas, and a humble diet consists of little more than tortillas and beans.

Yet one does not live from maize and beans alone. Protein, fats, and micronutrients from vegetables and fruits are also needed. Because of land shortages, high food prices, and an influx of cheap processed foods, almost half of all Guatemalan children under age 5 suffer from chronic malnutrition, and the rate reaches 80 percent in many rural Maya communities. Chronic malnutrition leads to stunted growth, lower academic performance, and lower earnings as adults. The World Bank estimates that it costs Guatemala more than $300 million a year in lost GDP (see www.maniplus.org). Robert Fogel and other economists have used height as an indicator of overall development (Floud, Fogel, Harris, and Hong 2011).

	AVERAGE HEIGHT (METERS)	
Country	Men	Women
Guatemala (Maya)	1.59	1.47
United States	1.77	1.63
Germany	1.81	1.68

SOURCE: Bogin (1999, 2012) and www.fao.org.

world as Folgers, Maxwell House, and hundreds of other brands. In the largely Maya highland communities where labor was recruited, working on coffee fincas was, and is, seen as employment of last resort because of the low wages and harsh conditions.

Today a large number of former coffee laborers and subsistence farmers support their families by growing and selling their own coffee. The rapidly proliferating number of small producers—at least 50,000 new growers since the mid-1990s, doubling the number of producers in Guatemala—has significantly altered the face of Guatemalan coffee.

In the Western Highlands, the vast majority of these new producers are indigenous. They are cultivating increasingly differentiated varieties of high-quality coffee on their own small parcels of land using family labor as well as day workers; a majority process and sell their coffee through a co-operative. Their production is sometimes sold as domain-specific varietals directly to small and medium-sized roasters around the world rather than disappearing in vast, undifferentiated lots of commodity.

Growing coffee is back-breaking work, and most of these farmers live in very modest circumstances, with limited resources and opportunities. They are acutely aware of the perils of dependency on fickle global markets; and while coffee prices have moved steadily up in the 21st century, this trend follows a historic low in 2001. Yet, as the farmers describe it, coffee represents an opportunity in a context of few opportunities, an imperfect but valued means of realizing their desire for a better life.

In a study of smallholding coffee producers in the Guatemalan town of San Juan La Laguna, Sarah Lyon (2011: 6). reports that locals refer to the new coffee production as "'the bomb' that exploded in the community, bringing income that enabled families to end their seasonal migration to lowland plantations, build cement-block houses, and educate their children." Lyon points out the power inequities and flaws in even fair trade coffee practices, but she also finds that coffee is valued by most growers as an important tool to help them realize the futures they envision (see also Martinez-Torres 2006). Daniel Reichman (2008: 3) reports that "Honduran farmers do not see the coffee trade as fundamentally unjust or exploitative." Likewise, the small producers we interviewed view the coffee market as neither good nor bad but as a tool, a technology, a means to achieve other ends, a vehicle for their desires. This is not to say that the coffee trade is free or just; there are structural inequities and inconsistencies, even in the fair trade segment, that disadvantage small producers (see Reichman 2011; Lyon 2011; Jaffee 2007).

The emergence of this new class of small producers was unintended but far from accidental. Critical factors that have contributed to the new coffee producers' growth and success include the macro-dynamics of the global coffee market, the policies and actions of the traditional Guatemalan coffee elites, the interventions of NGOs and international agencies, and advances in communication and transportation technologies. It was the collapse in the price of the commodity-grade washed Arabica grown on the lower-altitude fincas that created the necessity for former coffee workers to find a new source of income. It was the shift in first-world taste and style that induced the Guatemalan coffee industry to move its production up into the higher altitudes where the high-quality strictly hard bean coffee would grow. It was a consequence of the history of land ownership in Guatemala that pushed the poor, indigenous population high up on the slopes of the country's vertiginous landscape, just where that high-quality coffee could be grown. But it was the preferences and desires of the farmers themselves that determined just how this coffee would be planted, cultivated, harvested, processed, and marketed, as well as their own visions of the good life.

Coffee is a business, an often brutally unsentimental one. Yet it is laden with all sorts of valuations and moralizations—much more than wheat or sugar or mahogany and much more personal than oil. Coffee stands as a symbol of the best and the worst of global trade and North/South relations—from the harsh realities of much plantation labor to the bright promise of fair trade. These values are ascribed to not only by affluent Northern consumers, but also by the mostly poor, rural coffee producers. Here we will see what the dramatic changes in the global coffee market have meant to smallholding Guatemalan producers, and how their desires for a better future orient their engagement with this new market.

Broccoli, Coffee, and Algo Más

In 2011, working with a team of Guatemalan graduate students, Bart Victor and I conducted interviews with a sample of eighty-two new small-scale producers; we also interviewed the staff and leadership of Anacafé, the Guatemalan national coffee producers' association. We asked farmers what got them involved in coffee production and how coffee affects their lives and livelihoods. We also explored why Anacafé, whose interests have historically been aligned with the landed coffee elite, came to promote high-quality regional varieties over the commodity product most large fincas produced.

This project builds on my previous fieldwork with Maya farmers in highland Guatemala. Many grow *milpa*, the traditional subsistence plots of maize and beans. As Peter Benson and I describe in *Broccoli and Desire* (2006), a significant and growing number of Maya farmers produce exotic crops such as broccoli and snow peas for export to the United States. We found that Maya farmers largely viewed the broccoli trade as a positive economic alternative, one that allowed them to retain control over their means of production and maintain the social rhythms of an agricultural lifestyle. They saw export product not as a cure for all of their problems, but as a means of working toward a vision of the good life. Smallholding farmers in the Guatemalan highlands enter into the global food system, with its risks and uneven benefits, as a way of resisting, or at least avoiding, other alternatives. The job insecurity, risk of crop failure, and price fluctuations are more than offset, most Mayan farmers reported, by the independence and flexibility such production allows. To work for someone else, more than one farmer told us, is a form of slavery. Retaining control of their means of production was seen as an important gain.

The global broccoli trade reinforces certain structural inequalities and political-economic structures, but not through simple coercion or deterministic consensus. The global broccoli trade plays into a sense of the future as open and ambivalent, capable of being practically engaged and realized. Maya broccoli farmers seek a more expansive and inclusive global marketplace, not a romanticized subsistence enclave. When asked about their vision of the future, many insist that their children will maintain the land and will themselves be farmers. But most also speak of sending their children to school, having them get an education so that they may do "more in life," such as becoming a schoolteacher or opening a store. The decision to enter export crop production reflects and reinforces these future-oriented desires and an emergent sense of modernity related to transnational connections.

Although their circumstances are humble by North American standards, most Maya farmers involved in export trade have enough land to supply their basic subsistence needs and produce a surplus. They want to get ahead, to achieve *algo más* ("something more," or "something better"), with all the multiple meanings and risks that implies. They have a stake in their heri-

Plate 10: Broccoli Truck

Broccoli consumption in the United States increased by 1,000 percent between 1985 and 2010. Broccoli, once fairly exotic, has become a staple green
vegetable for many American households, even if it is also the butt of a disproportionate number of disparaging comments and jokes.

A significant amount of that broccoli comes from Guatemala. Guatemala's
cool highlands offer perfect environmental conditions for growing broccoli,
snow peas, and other formerly exotic crops. And geographically, Guatemala is
closer to Washington, D.C., than is Santa Barbara, California, the other big
producer of broccoli. The logistics are amazing: broccoli is harvested in the
afternoon by farmers and their families and loaded onto trucks. It is taken to
a packing plant where it is washed and packed into boxes already labeled for
U.S. supermarket shelves. It is then trucked to the airport in Guatemala City,
put on a late-night freight flight to Miami, and with a little luck can clear
customs by early the next morning. It is loaded onto refrigerated trucks and
shows up on supermarket shelves along the East Coast twenty-four to forty-
eight hours after harvest.

Next time you eat broccoli, think about where it came from—and how
your desire to eat healthfully, lose weight, or be a certain kind of person in-
tersects with the desires and aspirations of Maya farmers growing these crops
for export.

tage as farmers, but they also envision a better future for themselves and their children, a modern future that is not ironic or cynical. These views are largely shared by new-entrant coffee producers (although note that our research was done during boom years in the broccoli trade, just as the work I describe here was done at the height of the coffee market).

Coffee and Labor

The history of Guatemala is deeply intertwined with coffee; there and elsewhere in Latin America coffee has historically been associated with the worst forms of colonial exploitation and marked by the dramatic boom-and-bust cycles of such primary commodities (see Roseberry, Gudmundson, and Kutschbach 1995).[3] Coffee was first introduced to Guatemala in the mid-1800s, just when the indigo and cochineal booms were ending, unable to compete with the synthetic dyes developed in Europe. In 1860, coffee represented 1 percent of Guatemalan exports; this rose to 44 percent in 1870 (Woodward 1990: 50). It has been the most important single export ever since, and national politics historically followed closely the fortunes of the coffee oligarchy (Lovell 2005; Paige 1997; Wagner 2003; Williams 1994; Carey 2001).

Dictator Justo Rufino Barrios (1873–85) made promoting coffee production a backbone of his economically liberal reforms in the 1870s. He expropriated lands from the church and confiscated communally held Maya lands and then sold these on favorable terms to those who would become the coffee barons, primarily German and English immigrants (Cambranes 1985). The Germans living in the area around Cobán especially came to be associated with Guatemalan coffee production, and Germans and coffee continue to be linked in Guatemalan popular discourse (Wagner 1991).

Throughout the 19th and 20th centuries, the Guatemalan coffee oligarchy controlled production more tightly than their peers in other countries (except perhaps Mexico (Chiapas) and El Salvador) and exerted their influence effectively over the affairs of state (Paige 1997). This classic, tightly held, large plantation structure was closely associated with exploitative legal, political, and social structures (Williams 1994; Rice 1999).

Coffee requires massive seasonal labor inputs at harvest, and labor was scarce in Guatemala in the areas around the large plantations. In response, in the 1870s the state began requiring peasants work a certain number of days per year (if they were not fully employed) on projects mandated by the government. Directed largely at indigenous campesinos, *mandamiento* labor was used for public works, but it was also official policy to assign workers to coffee plantations to support this crucial sector of the export economy. Formally, the mandamiento system lasted until the 1920s; informally, similar forms of debt servitude and coercive labor practices continued (Lovell 1988; McCreery 1994; Carey 2001). Even today, workers are recruited for the onerous labor from distant communities, often lured by loans and alcohol.

Up until 1900, Germany, with its exceptionally high standards for coffee quality and the appearance of beans, was Guatemala's primary export market. As a result, the German coffees had to be wet-processed (McCreary 1994), establishing a legacy of producing quality washed beans. The Guatemalan standard of shade-grown, wet-processed Arabicas requires more labor and more water than dry methods (Pendergrast 2010) but produces a markedly superior quality. After 1900, the U.S. market grew in importance, quickly becoming the primary destination for Guatemalan coffee.

High-End Coffee and Foreign Earnings

Coffee remains one of Guatemala's most important exports, and up to 30 percent of the rural workforce is involved in coffee production, processing, and trade. Yet coffee production in Guatemala has changed dramatically since the 1990s. The large plantations traditionally produced, for the most part, "prime" and "extra prime" coffees. Despite the names, these relatively low altitude varieties (grown at 2,500'–3,500') are at the low end of the coffee value chain. As William Roseberry (1996) pointed out, U.S. tastes in coffee have shifted away from the commodity and to the singularized high end, what is called in the trade "specialty coffee." This coffee is grown at higher altitudes, the best above 4,500'.

The resulting shift in Guatemalan coffee production has been dramatic. Overall export volumes have dropped significantly and leveled off since the 1990s. At the same time, exports of the highest-quality SHB (strictly hard bean) washed Arabica have grown steeply and now make up the overwhelming majority of exported beans (see Figure 5.1). Thus, while overall coffee exports are lower, high-value beans make up a much larger percentage, resulting in total export earnings for coffee increasing steadily since the 2001 crash (see Figure 5.2).[4]

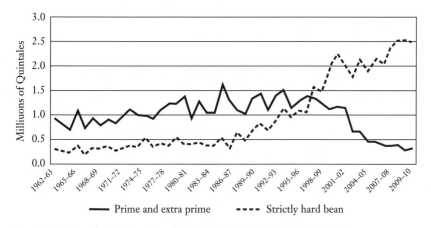

Figure 5.1: Volume of Guatemalan Coffee Exports by Grade, 1962–2010

(in millions of hundredweights). (Note the dramatic rise of SHB and the equally dramatic decline of Prime and Extra Prime.) Data courtesy of Anacafé.

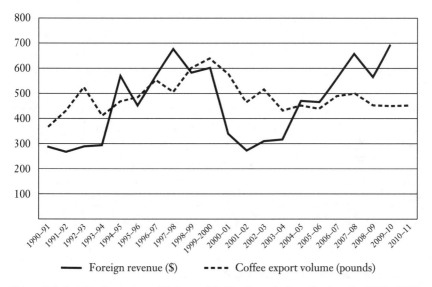

Figure 5.2: Foreign Revenue and Volume of Coffee Exports from Guatemala, 1990–2011

Coffee

There are two main species of coffee cultivated today, Arabica (*Coffea arabica*) and Robusta (*Coffea canephora*). As the name implies, Robusta is a heartier plant, and produces larger quantities at lower, more temperate altitudes. Its flavor, however, is considered inferior, more bitter and acidic and with a higher caffeine content. Arabica is grown in Central and South America and East Africa, and Robusta is grown in West Africa and Southeast Asia (Vietnam is the world's largest producer), though there are some major exceptions: for example, Brazil is the world's largest producer of Arabica and second largest producer of Robusta (Wild 2004).

Arabicas are marked by a much wider range of flavor, or "cup profile," as it is known in the industry. Grown at higher altitudes and usually under shade, the climatic and growing conditions produce a deeper, more concentrated flavor, with notes ranging from dark berries and chocolate to citrus (to employ the vocabulary developed around wine that is also used to describe high-end coffee). Arabicas are further graded based on the altitude of production; higher-altitude coffees have more concentrated flavor and are considered to be of higher quality. (See box for coffee types and growing altitudes.) Gourmet and specialty coffees are almost uniformly SHB Arabica, and even most major commodity brands (Folgers, Maxwell House, etc.) are Arabica, including SHB. Robusta is mostly used as filler in cheaper blends and in instant coffees.

Categories such as prime, extra prime, and strictly hard bean are used in the Guatemalan trade, although terms vary internationally. Strictly hard bean, for example, is also known as strictly high grown (SHG), and extra prime is referred to on the New York market as medium to good bean

---

Primary Arabica coffee variants in Guatemala
Bourbon, Caturra, Arabusta, Maragoype, Catuat, Típica

Altitudes for growing different grades of Arabica in Guatemala

Strictly Hard Bean (SHB)	4500'–circa 6500'
Hard Bean, Semi-Hard Bean	3500'–4500'
Prime/extra prime, etc:	2500'–3500'

(NY-MTGB). In Guatemala, exporters often speak of SHB coffees as being synonymous with what is called in the international trade "specialty coffee." While it is true that virtually all Guatemalan SHB winds up in specialty coffee, and that the overwhelming majority of specialty coffee sold in the world is SHB, the two are not definitionally synonymous; there are high-end specialty coffees that are not SHB, and a large percentage of the world's production of SHB goes into mass-market coffee brands.

The form of processing (wet or dry) also greatly affects quality. Most Robusta beans are dry-processed, which means that the cherry is simply laid out in the sun and the skin and meat are allowed to dry off the beans; the mild fermentation involved gives the beans a distinctive flavor. The higher-quality Arabica beans are usually wet-processed: the cherry is first floated in water to separate ripe and unripe fruits and to soften the skin and pulp; they are then de-pulped and soaked in water for twenty-four to forty-eight hours to remove the mucilage; after washing, they are dried (to 12 percent humidity) and sold as "parchment coffee" (the two beans of each cherry still covered by a final, thin layer of skin, or parchment) to exporters who remove the parchment and ship out "café oro" (green beans ready to roast).

The global metric for coffee prices is the New York coffee C futures contract price. Long traded on the New York Commodity Exchange (now ICE Futures), the C price, as it is known, is for quality washed Arabicas. The contracts are for container loads of exchange-grade green beans from nineteen countries of origin for delivery to one of eight licensed warehouses in the United States and Europe (New York, New Orleans, Houston, Bremen, Hamburg, Antwerp, Miami, and Barcelona).

Each producer country or region receives a premium or a discount from the C rate depending on quality; Colombian coffee regularly receives a 10–14 point premium. Guatemala is the sixth largest (as of 2010) producer of coffee in the world, even given its small size, and Guatemalan washed Arabicas receive a consistent premium over the C price, although not as great as the Colombian one. The final price paid to farmers in Guatemala can reach 20 percent or more of the C price in the case of Fair Trade and specialty coffees (Martinez-Torres 2006). In general, about 12 percent of the supermarket price and about 3 percent of the brewed cup price goes to growers.

The Coffee Market in the United States

Coffee is one of the world's most traded commodities. It is produced by 20 million farmers and workers, mostly in developing countries, and it is consumed by a majority of Americans and Europeans. Over 60 percent of the U.S. population drinks coffee on a given day (Luttinger and Dicum 2006).

The late 19th and early 20th centuries saw coffee become a staple of the middle and working classes in the United States and Europe, with market competition alternating between quality and price. Coffee consumption in the United States increased steadily from the late 19th century until the mid-1950s (although World War II shortages led many to turn to inferior substitutes). After the war, when the five-cent cup of coffee came to symbolize a new middle-class entitlement, the U.S. Congress used this as a populist rallying cry against high prices (Pendergrast 2010). Yet, starting in 1950, per capita coffee consumption in the United States began to decline (just as soft drink consumption took off), a trend that slowly continued for the next four decades. By 1993, declines in U.S. consumption had leveled off.

In the 1950s and 1960s, the market was dominated by a few big roasters: General Foods (Maxwell House), Standard Brands, Procter and Gamble (Folgers), Hills Brothers, and A&P made up 40 percent of market. By the early 1970s, over 50 percent of the market was controlled by General Mills and Procter and Gamble. During this time, competition focused increasingly on price (at the expense of quality). Starting in the 1950s, the blends of national brands started including more low-cost Robusta, and instant coffees (which used more Robusta) took off in popularity (Pendergrast 2010).

As the mass-market move toward lower prices and lower quality reached maturity, a counter-movement for high-quality "specialty" coffees began on the West Coast and in New York. This started in the late 1960s with Peet's and Zabar's, and was followed in the early 1970s by Starbucks. The specialty trend grew slowly through the 1970s, picking up steam in the 1980s and 1990s as smaller coffee shops opened around the country (and whole beans became available in supermarkets). In the early 2000s, Fair Trade coffees bolstered the specialty trend; Fair Trade consumption in the United States increased from 2 million pounds per year in 1999 to 45 million pounds per year in 2005, although it still constituted a small percentage of the overall market (Lutinger and Dicum 2006).

Specialty coffee companies reject the homogeneity of commodity coffee, selling higher quality in the cup as well as a connection to specific regions and growers. William Roseberry (1996), in his seminal article on the rise and meaning of specialty coffee in the United States, termed it "the beverage of postmodernism." The market moved to de-commodify coffee and singularize individual varieties and sources. Smaller coffee roasters and retailers began to distinguish coffees with designations of origin (e.g., Kona, Blue Mountain, Antigua) and grade (e.g., Kenyan AA), and to connect it with trends in natural foods and catchwords such as "organic," "whole," and "fresh." Such provenance branding was made possible by changes in the logistics chain that allowed for coffee to be sold in smaller batches (see Ponte 2002; Ticker 2010). It was accompanied by marketing that sought to create a felt connection between the consumer and the producer. Claims of authenticity were wed to notions of quality (Smith 2009), and such de-commodified coffee commanded a significant premium over New York C rates.

Roseberry (1996) describes how specialty coffee reflects post-Fordist patterns of consumption and production. The consumer's imagined link to places and producers creates a sense of intimacy and connection. But this sense can also be exploited, something we see in the rise of "styles" of coffee to substitute for true provenance ("Kona style," "Blue Mountain style"). Linking these connections to a "style" takes away the advantage local producers have, as coffee sellers don't have to wait for special provenanced coffees to arrive if they can label more readily available coffees as having the same "style."

By the early 1990s there were two main coffee-buying sectors. The first, which Robert Rice (2003) calls "industrial coffees," is the mass commodity coffee market dominated by a few international firms. Kraft (which owns Maxwell House and Jacobs among other brands), Procter and Gamble (led by their Folgers brand, now owned by Smucker's), Sara Lee, Nestlé, and Tchibo (from Germany) accounted for about half of all coffee purchases. Second, there was the much more diffuse specialty market, made up of thousands of small and medium-sized roasters and retailers.

Specialty coffee has been the growth segment in both volume and profits over the past twenty years. The specialty segment prefers the higher-priced washed Arabica varieties of coffee, and most specialty coffee comes from the strictly hard bean (SHB) classification, which has a richer, deeper taste profile than the prime and extra prime classifications. The higher altitudes required by SHB coffee in Guatemala are also the poorest areas of the country and formerly served as the primary sending communities for seasonal finca labor (and still do—less so in coffee, but in sugar and cotton).

Quotas and Quality: Anacafé

World coffee prices have always been volatile, responding to droughts and frosts as well as fluctuating consumer demand (see Figure 5.3). Fluctuating demand creates a volatile foreign revenue stream for commodity-producing countries, and favors large individual producers who can weather the drops.

Vulnerability to the volatile world market led coffee-producing countries to come together through the International Coffee Organization and ratify the 1962 International Coffee Agreement (ICA), which helped stabilize prices for struggling producer countries. (The United States supported the move in hopes that it would provide some immunization from the popular

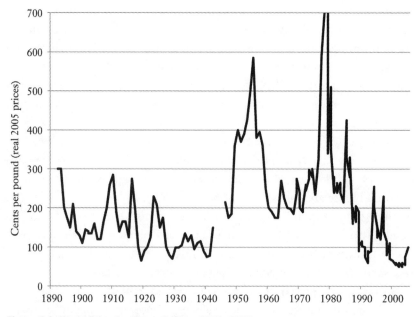

Figure 5.3: World Price for Green Coffee, 1890–2005

(based on Luttinger and Dicum 2006)

appeal of communism.) The ICA established a quota system by country to limit supply. Remarkably, the agreement brought together fifty producing countries (representing 99 percent of production) and twenty-five consuming countries (90 percent of the market). The quota system was in force until 1989.

Despite signing on to the ICA, the leadership of Anacafé, the Guatemalan national coffee producers' association, had a long history of ambivalence and even resistance to the quota system. In the late 1980s the board was composed mostly of life-long coffee growers and associated with the interests of the country's landed elite.[5] While they had long benefited from relative price stability in the bulk commodity market, they were never fully comfortable with the global producers' cartel, believing that it discounted Guatemalan quality. In interviews, former leaders also expressed a pronounced commitment to an Austrian-school inspired approach to free- market economics, opposed in principle to market regulation. Past presidents of Anacafé spoke proudly of the Guatemalan position as a lone voice for a free-market approach in international meetings. At the same time, board members also felt compelled at times to support market-stabilizing interventions, such as the issue of a government-backed coffee bond following the collapse of the ICA in 1989. In the 1990s, however, the Anacafé board unified around the free-market position, becoming a vocal opponent of quota systems (along with the United States) in the International Coffee Organization.

In 1993, prices dropped to their lowest point in almost twenty years, and the leadership of Anacafé had to confront the possibility that this time the drop was not just the latest fluctuation in prices but a step on a structural decline. Coffee consumption in the United States, the most important market, had steadily decreased since the early 1950s, even if specialty coffee sales offered a glimmer of hope in the dismal market. At the prices offered in the early 1990s (as low as $0.50 per pound) it was simply uneconomical to grow coffee—even the large growers could not survive unless prices were supported or subsidized.

Bill Hempstead, a past Anacafé president (1992–93) from a long line of German and English coffee producers, had attended the Specialty Coffee Association of America (SCAA) meetings in New Orleans in 1989 where he noted the rising interest in specialty coffees. Even though that was the first year the SCAA trade show met on its own and the trend was just emerging, as a history buff Hempstead knew that Guatemala's reputation for grow-

Anacafé's Eight Regions, Eight Cups

Acatenango Valley

Marked acidity, fragrant aroma, balanced body, clean lingering finish
4,300–6,500' altitude, 1,200–1,800 mm annual rain,
57–88°F temperature range, volcanic and pumice soils

Antigua

Well balanced, rich aroma, very sweet taste
5,000–5,600' altitude , 800–1,200 mm annual rain,
64–72°F temperature range, volcanic and pumice soils

Traditional Atitlán

Aromatic with citrus acidity and full body
5,000–5,600' altitude, 1,800–2,300 mm annual rain,
68–73°F temperature range, volcanic soils

Rainforest Cobán

Distinct fresh fruits, well-balanced body, pleasant aroma
4,300–5,000' altitude, 3,000–4,000 mm annual rain,
59–68°F temperature range, limestone and clay soils

Fraijanes Plateau

Bright, persistent acidity, aromatic, well-defined body
4,500–6,000' altitude, 1,500–3,000 mm annual rain,
54–79°F temperature range, volcanic and pumice soils

Highland Huehue

Intense acidity with full body and pleasant wine notes
5,000–6,500' altitude, 1,200–1,400 mm annual rain,
68–75°F temperature range, limestone soils

New Oriente

Well balanced and full-bodied with chocolate flavor
4,300–5,600' altitude, 1,800–2,000 mm annual rain,
64–77°F temperature range, metamorphic and clay soils

Volcanic San Marcos

Floral notes in aroma and taste, pronounced acidity, good body
4,300–6,000' altitude, 4,000–5,000 mm annual rain,
70–81°F temperature range, volcanic soils

SOURCE: *www.Anacafe.org.*

ing quality coffee stretched back to the 19th century. Hempstead became a strong proponent of this new specialty market, arguing that Guatemala should turn its focus to the quality segment and promote regionalization in branding.

Hempstead and others believed that Guatemala had the potential to be the main supplier of specialty coffee in the world. As Hempstead recalled, "We knew that Guatemalan growing regions are truly unique—it is not that way in other countries and that is our competitive advantage." They argued that coffee is not like oil and so cannot follow the cartel strategies of OPEC: coffee is a perishable product and it takes a long time to start up production.

In July 1995, Anacafé received the final report on a study it had commissioned. "The Coffee Chain Project" report recommended five regional coffees to promote. In a move that virtually all of the past presidents of Anacafé retell as an Ayn Rand–like story of the power of market forces, the board decided in 1995 to pursue a strategy of expanding into the growing specialty coffee segment. They did this through technical assistance that promoted high-end SHB coffees and a marketing strategy that delimited eight regional denominations of origin within Guatemala, each with its own cup profile (see box). It was not only the coffee that was different, though. Unlike the cafetalero's large fincas that produced high-yield prime and extra prime grade coffees, the growers who grew the SHB specialty coffee were mostly small-scale Mayan farmers and medium-sized ladino farmers in the highlands.

It seems odd that Anacafé supported a shift in emphasis that apparently ran counter to the material interests of the larger growers who held considerable sway in the association. It may be that the large producers came to see that the prime grade coffee they grew was not going to produce the returns it once did. Since this was the only kind of coffee they could grow on their current land holdings, they diversified to other crops and land uses. In hindsight it seems to have been a smart move to shift into rubber and cattle, but at the time the decision was full of risk and uncertainty. We could easily imagine the coffee oligarchy clamping down during the market shift and brutally protecting their declining market share. Or they could have ignored the small producers and focused Anacafé's technical and market support resources on the remaining prime coffee production. Instead, they turned the machinery of Anacafé to support the growing volume and profitability of the specialty coffee market.

Past and present leaders of Anacafé explain their decision not as an attempt to aid small famers but as an effort to follow the market where the market leads. "We just follow the market" was a phrase we heard again and again. More than just a business tactic, this deeply held laissez-faire position is at once anti-statist (and anti-regulation) and pro–free trade ("We should be able to sell to anyone we want," as one grower explained). Truth be told, they were not just following the market: their marketing, branding, and system of provenance fueled as well as followed Northern market trends toward SHB coffees.

While Kraft, Nestlé, Sara Lee, and Procter and Gamble controlled about 60 percent of the world market and 73 percent of the U.S. market (Martinez-Torres 2006; Renard 1999), by 2000 specialty coffees constituted about 10 percent of world coffee exports and approximately 15 percent of U.S. volume. Significantly, SHB coffees did not follow the C contract roller coaster. SHB prices continued to grow even when C contract prices were down.

A second international price collapse hit in 2001, brought about by increasing Vietnamese production, a bumper Brazilian crop, and declining demand (see Bacon, Méndez, and Gliessman 2008). In 2001, total Guatemalan coffee exports fell to $320 million from $600 million in 2000. Coffee prices dropped to historic lows of less than $0.50 per pound, far less than the cost of production. Anacafé reported that almost 1,000 coffee farms were abandoned following this price drop, and a large number were repossessed by banks (Lovell 2001: 171).

As a result of these price drops, many of the country's large coffee growers left the market, moving into rubber, macadamia, palm oil, and sugar cane production; some even sold off their land. Many of the younger generation of elite coffee-producing families have gone into finance or real estate or other non-farm pursuits. There have been a number of land invasions of the large fincas that went bust, and incidences of squatting. Banks foreclosed on coffee properties that were unable to make their payments. At the same time, more and more smallholding producers in Guatemala (those with less than five hectares under production) began growing SHB coffees for the burgeoning specialty market; by 2000, they represented 30 percent of total coffee production, up from 16 percent in 1979 (Lyon 2011; UNCTAD 2002). Today, we estimate that more than 50 percent of Guatemalan coffee production comes from smallholding producers.

In 2003, José Angel López was elected president of Anacafé. Unlike past leaders, he did not come from a traditional coffee family or one of the powerful private coffee associations. Indeed, he was an indigenous coffee grower from the small town of Jacaltenango. He was introduced to coffee by his father, who was active in the co-operative labor organization movement. And López himself had come up through the co-operative movement to sit on the Anacafé board.

As his tenure began, López faced a crucial decision. With the 2001 price bust, growers worried that this could be the final death blow for Guatemalan coffee. López was faced with the challenge to stick to the strategy of marketing regional specialty coffees mostly grown by smallholding producers to gain a high premium, or to reverse course and begin creating price supports, perhaps issuing bonds against future production, and pursue the Colombian route. Once again, Anacafé decided to "follow the market," and this meant an even greater commitment to the new high-quality producers. Today, the coffee industry is increasingly anchored by small-scale artisanal growers on one end, and a proliferation of quality roasters and brands. Brands like Starbucks and Green Mountain and microroasters are offering coffee in a dizzying variety of tastes, forms, and prices. Far from a commodity, coffee is increasingly distinguished by varietal, domain of origin, production method, preparation style, and social and labor practices.

Rapidly evolving specialty markets have kept coffee export value growing in Guatemala even as total volumes have decreased. In the past, the only price was the New York "C" price for commodity coffee. Now global Internet auctions are setting prices for microlots that can sometimes be hundreds of dollars a pound higher than the C price. Now the quality "in the cup" and certifications of various types translate into profitability even if the yield is very low.

Increasingly, coffee is sold directly to small roasters as distinctive varietals of strictly hard bean Arabica with domain-of-origin labeling. Buyers want to know not only what specific variety of coffee they are buying, but also the name of the farmer, the shade and orientation of the farm, and far more. Premiums are earned for organic, socially responsible, and environmentally sustainable practices. In an industry with a history that includes periods of forced labor, violence, and discrimination, coffee growers can choose from a number of opportunities to certify their labor practices, and to support community heath and development. These certifications, including Organic,

Fair Trade, and Rainforest Alliance, can add a real premium to the price the farmer receives for a crop(see also Berry 2001; Murray, Raynolds, and Taylor 2006).

Coffee production is labor-intensive, and global markets are always searching for cheaper labor. This is what led to the breathtaking rise of the Vietnamese coffee industry; Guatemala's labor cost for middle-range and low-end commodity coffee suddenly became more expensive relative to the new markets. The family-run smallholding producers are willing to self-exploit, relying on unpaid family labor to compete and get ahead. As Eric Wolf (1956: 262) observed more than fifty years ago in Puerto Rico, "If the peasant could rely on his subsistence crops, work harder and longer, and restrict his consumption requirements, he could compete."

Small Producers and High-Altitude Coffees

In the summer of 2011, Bart Victor and I led a team that conducted eighty-two in-depth interviews with new-entrant smallholding producers from the coffee-growing regions of Guatemala.[6] Our sample was drawn from an extensive database of producers maintained by Anacafé, the national coffee producers' association, which includes all registered coffee growers producing for export.[7]

We limited the sample to producers who, according to Anacafé records, had begun coffee cultivation for export within the previous fifteen years. We should note the focus on export here; most of those in our sample had grown coffee on their own land for personal consumption and some local sales more than fifteen years earlier. In addition, many in the sample had long family histories of work in coffee on the large fincas. We then selected farmers who had relatively small holdings. The definition of smallholder varied by the coffee-growing region. We oversampled in the Western Highlands, which was the primary focus of our study.[8] In these regions, a small holding was considered to be fewer than 2.2 hectares (50 cuerdas). In the Central/Eastern Highlands average holdings were significantly larger. Overall, 52 percent of our sample were cultivating one hectare or less (20 cuerdas), and 20 percent were cultivating more than 2.2 hectares.

A majority of our sample self-identified as indigenous (66 percent). In Huehuetenango, Quetzaltenango, Sololá, and other majority-indigenous areas, over 75 percent identified as indigenous, with most speaking a Mayan language as their native tongue. Significantly, smallholder coffee production is a family enterprise, with spouses and children providing important labor input. In family production, men tend to make most of the decisions, although there are a growing number of women taking on primary responsibility for coffee production. A surprising 94 percent of our sample was literate, well above the national average of 71 percent. They averaged 5.4 years of education, again higher than one would expect given the general demographics (the national average is 4.9 years, and it is significantly lower in rural areas).

Our interviews were conducted by five teams of two interviewers each; the interviewers were all either native Spanish or Mayan language speakers. We stressed depth over breadth in the interviews. Often they lasted two or three hours or more; they were conducted either at the farmers' homes or in their fields. Along with basic demographic information, the surveys collected data on new entrants' cultivation, labor, and coffee marketing practices. The in-depth interviews asked the respondents to relate their individual stories about choosing to begin cultivating coffee and the experienced and anticipated impact of coffee production on their lives. This qualitative approach allowed us to capture subjective aspirations as well as objective accomplishments.

The traditional large coffee producers frequently used the term "*cafetalero*" to describe themselves and to signify the primacy of coffee to their identity. A surprising majority of the new producers in our sample did not self-identify as cafetaleros. Just over 24 percent adopted the cafetalero moniker, and 51 percent called themselves "*agricultor*." This term reflects a different and more instrumental and utilitarian role of coffee as one among several sources of income for most families. Half of the families surveyed had other income-generating activities as well (ranging from weaving and occasional day labor to running a small store or tending someone else's fields).

This reframing of who grows coffee also represents a significant shift in ethnic relations and perceived opportunity structures. We found in our interviews that coffee exporting was once thought to be the exclusive domain of the elites, but had come to be seen as a viable market for small producers. Historically, there have been smallholding coffee growers (especially in the area around Antigua and Lake Atitlán), but they were minor contributors to total coffee production (see Williams 1994). One 21-year-old Q'eqchi' man (who had completed eighth grade) told us, "I learned about growing coffee from my father. As kids we used to play 'planting coffee.' I have been growing on my own for a few years now. Before there wasn't an opportunity for us indigenous people to plant our own coffee. It was just for the Germans." Several others likewise commented that they had taken up coffee production after "the Germans" (an often used shorthand for the coffee oligarchy that was established in the 19th century, many with German roots) had given up production.

All of the producers in our sample had begun exporting coffee in the previous fifteen years. However, many of the new producers we interviewed had entered the export coffee market gradually, and it was often hard for them to pinpoint the date when they began coffee production. In the early days, co-operatives working with Fair Trade and other certification regimes were able to pay significant premiums, stimulating new production and buffering global market slumps.

Government projects and international aid (especially through the U.S. Agency for International Development, USAID) have also played an important role in getting new producers into the market, and 81 percent of our sample had received some sort of financial assistance. Guatemala was an early player in the Fair Trade coffee movement, having worked with SOS Holland and its German partners to market "Indio-Kaffee aus Guatemala" (Indian coffee from Guatemala) in Germany and the Netherlands in the early 1970s. Still, it was not until the late 1990s that the Fair Trade market took off (U.S. consumption increased from about 2 million pounds per year to almost 45 million between 1999 and 2005). In 2000–01, when prices dropped to historic lows, Fair Trade premiums and a Starbucks program (which paid almost double the market price) helped sustain many farmers.[9] As demand rose steadily for high-quality washed Arabica SHB coffees in the early 2000s, prices went up substantially season after season. At market heights, prices for quality SHB exceed Fair Trade premiums, leading some growers to try to get out of their co-operative contracts and sell to intermediaries paying more.

Most new producers in our sample had previously maintained *milpa* (maize and beans subsistence plots), and many worked seasonally on coffee, sugar, and cotton plantations. Those who worked on coffee fincas learned the basic process of planting and caring for coffee. Often they kept a few coffee trees for decoration and some domestic consumption, but these were not seen as commercially promising. Especially in Huehuetenango, but also in other parts of the Western Highlands, a significant number had family members who had worked in the United States and sent home remittances. As demand began to rise in the 1990s for the high-elevation SHB coffees, they expanded their plots to devote more to coffee.

Manuel, a 55-year-old Mam Maya man from Huehuetenango, explained: "I used to just grow milpa and work on the fincas, but then I saw people here start making money from their own coffee, and I decided to take it up too. I still plant maize and beans for the family, but the coffee gives us more income to cover the expenses that maize production cannot cover." We heard variations on this story over and over again. Sergio, a 51-year-old K'iche' man, commented, "My parents just grew milpa. Nobody grew coffee; it wasn't our custom. We grew milpa and went to work on the coffee and cotton plantations for money. But now we can make money from coffee—I even used it to send my son to work in the United States."

Like Manuel and Sergio, the vast majority of our sample reported that coffee was not their only source of income and sustenance. They also maintained subsistence milpa plots and often other household or market crops. Many took on occasional day labor, and some continued to work on coffee fincas from time to time; a few were even professionals, such as school teachers, who produced coffee on the side (see also Goldín 2009).

Carlos, a 54-year-old farmer from Huehuetenango, explained, "At first we worked on the coffee farms, first with my father then on my own. We were poor, we didn't have anywhere else to work, anywhere to live, we did not have our own land to farm. Over time, we saved up some money from working on the fincas, and we were able to buy some land that we now grow coffee on. Around this time I had a patron who loaned me some money to buy half a cuerda of land. Now I have six cuerdas and a house. It is hard work, but I have been able to do it."

Starting very small, with just a few coffee plants, and expanding gradually is a risk-averse and non-capital-intensive strategy (although risks rise dramatically after a tipping point, when farmers have resources locked in to the crop for several years). As they expand, most farmers employ family labor, usually conceived in the mental accounting of costs as free labor. If they expand, they may hire temporary workers to help with the harvest. In our sample, small producers who hired workers employed two to ten workers, all of whom they hired locally.

María, a 32-year-old woman who worked with her husband on their six acres of coffee, observed, "Coffee is different from the other crops we plant around here. It is a form of self-employment that provides some income for people, sometimes enough to invest. When growers are very poor, they don't contract others for the harvest, the family just does it all. And this income stays in the community. Maize isn't very profitable, but coffee income lets us buy maize, or even maintain our milpa."

The majority of growers we interviewed owned the land on which they grew coffee. Significantly, this signals the economic capacity to purchase and maintain land as well as their commitment to coffee. Indeed, a number reported that they rented land for subsistence production and for producing other market crops (such as tomatoes or onions). There is, of course, a significant capital investment in coffee: it normally takes three to four years for trees to start producing, and then they maintain maximum production for up to fifteen years. Most new small producers hedged their bets by expanding production very gradually in step with overall increases in market demand. Once a sizable plot has been established, however, risk rises because one is more or less locked in to coffee for the medium term. In an expanding market, this is not a problem, but in a period of contraction, small producers are particularly vulnerable.

A number of farmers we interviewed used kinship metaphors in speaking about their coffee (see also Lyon 2011). The young plants were children that they needed to care for. And like children, they require long-term dedication before any returns are seen. Most said they were committed to coffee for the long term, even as they acknowledged that prices were likely to fall at some point. They vividly recalled the drop of 2000–01, when prices reached historic lows on the world market, below even basic production costs. It was then that many medium-sized and large producers left the market. Still, the small producers who had diversified income sources claimed that they could hold out during a price drop because coffee production is adaptable to variable inputs over several years. If prices are low, coffee can be left more or less unattended for a year or two without much harm done. Then, when prices rise, it can be cleaned up and harvested.

In fact, most of these small producers said that "coffee always sells," having experienced ten years of steady growth and rising prices after 2001. This attitude may reflect irrational exuberance (although it is usually tempered with an acknowledgment that prices might not always remain as high). It also reflects a pride in their product. One farmer remarked that the big fincas "don't care about quality, just producing as much as they can; we grow quality coffee," reflecting an appreciation that high-end markets are less price-sensitive.

Small producers sell either to a co-operative (if they belong), which has its own *beneficio* (wet mill processing plant), directly to a private beneficio (if they have access to a truck for hauling), or to an intermediary. Selling to a co-operative or beneficio is preferable, but many producers find themselves at the mercy of intermediaries. Some intermediaries are viewed positively, as helpful providers of advice and loans. Others are seen as predatory, loaning money against the harvest at extortionist rates and paying below-market rates. Such *coyotes* are viewed suspiciously, since their basis for earning a living (owning a truck or having connections) is seen as a less honest source of work.

Producers see being part of a co-operative or an association as a clear advantage; 72.4 percent of our sample belonged to an association, and most that did not said that they would like to. The co-operatives provide better terms for loans, are guaranteed buyers for production, and make the transfer of technical and market information more efficient. Some producers say that their co-operative operates too much like a private beneficio and complain of specific leadership and participation issues, but overall, co-operatives are seen as a huge advantage (see also Sick 1999; DeHart 2010).

Farmers normally get their price information from buyers (the co-operative, the beneficio, or the intermediary), which puts them at a disadvantage. Most also sell coffee in cherry form (the whole fruit), which, to ensure quality, should be processed within twenty-four hours or so. Some Huehuetenango farmers are able to process to the "parchment stage" (*pergamino*), which pays better and allows them to hold the product to seek a better price.

Debt is a pressing issue for small producers. Every respondent in our sample (100 percent) had taken out loans, and most did so almost annually. The majority of loans come from banks (especially Banrural, whose state-sponsored mission is to service farmers) and co-operative associations. Loans pay for fertilizer and other inputs as well as help tide families over until the harvest. But they are also viewed as a burden and a hindrance to getting ahead. These small farmers all worked constantly to pay off their debts.

The rise of small producers is largely seen as beneficial to surrounding communities. They are viewed as a positive alternative to plantation labor for day laborers and as a reliable source of business for local vendors. Workers report that conditions are generally better than on the large fincas. Many are paid a day rate, which is seen as more fair than the per quintal price. Workers report more casual and convivial working conditions. One man explained, "Before, when we worked on the finca, families got separated, but now we have the chance to be more together and more independent. You can see the benefits of this change, even those who don't have land, everybody now has better work conditions."

Coffee and the Good Life

Coffee is intimately linked to the desires and aspirations of the good life expressed by the smallholding farmers we interviewed. At one level, this is an end in itself: the meaningful project to expand and increase coffee production. More importantly, these farmers see coffee as a means to other ends, a way to achieve a better life as they themselves conceive it. Coffee production provides a path for upward mobility for small producers: it stokes aspirations and channels agency; its mode of production feeds into established family and community social networks; and it provides a sense of dignity through control over one's own means of production. At the same time, the benefits are by no means evenly spread, and those best able to take advantage of the new opportunities are not the poorest of the poor. Those with a higher level of education, some existing land holdings, and other sources of income are best positioned to reap the benefits of coffee production. Here we see the multiple possibilities of opportunity structures: the coffee market's new opportunities facilitating aspiration and agency for a large number of small growers, and at the same time the material limitations of abject poverty and lack of educational and economic opportunities frustrating the potential of those in severe poverty.

Coffee is seen not as a way to get rich, but as a significant source of income that can keep a family out of absolute poverty. For most small-scale growers, coffee income is not sufficient to sustain their families, but it is an important source of additional income, one strategy among several in the household economy. Virtually all of our sampled respondents produced at least part of that maize and beans they needed for their own subsistence. One famer noted that "with 1 quintal of coffee I can buy 5 quintales of maize." He also kept some milpa crops, recognizing that this equation can quickly turn upside down if coffee prices fall and maize prices continue upward. Over 54 percent grew other cash crops as well, and 51 percent had a significant non-farm source of income.

Miguel, a 41-year-old ladino farmer from Huehuetenango (with a sixth-grade education), observed, "We have to put food on the table, but we would also like other things, for our children to go to school, and for this it [coffee] isn't sufficient. So we feel constrained, and we are in a bad place if somebody in the family gets sick." Significantly, our respondents generally defined poverty as not having land and having to work on fincas.

There is dignity, many farmers told us, in working one's own land, being one's own boss; and they saw coffee as a potentially lucrative way to keep their own production and be financially independent. They viewed seasonal plantation labor as a form of dependency, fraught with the hardship of being separated from one's family, that they want to avoid if at all possible. They also preferred to hold wealth in land and saw coffee production as a way of expanding land holdings (or buying land for the first time).

Many of the coffee producers we talked to wanted to expand into other businesses. Perhaps taking the risk on coffee production reveals an entrepreneurial spirit that could be translated into other ventures. In this context, however, "entrepreneurial" connotes not so much speculative gain as economic security. Farmers say that their life is difficult, that they have to work hard, and that they feel vulnerable to market fluctuations, natural disasters, and family illnesses. They dream of making their lives marginally better in the short run and providing opportunities for their children in the longer run. They want their kids to stay in school, to get a high school degree, and, if they are really ambitious, to go to the university. They are realistic in their expectations of coffee, but value the possibilities it opens up, however limited.

In these ways, the farmers we interviewed overwhelmingly wanted to achieve *algo más* in their lives. They wanted their children to flourish, to have a better life and more opportunities than they did. They said they wanted to expand their land holdings, buy a truck, add on to their houses—

desires that, if a world away in some particulars, would not be unfamiliar to the German middle-class shopper. Yet they must pursue these dreams within the structure of a global market often beyond their control. As it turned out, our study was conducted just after world coffee prices peaked in 2011 (see Figure 5.4).

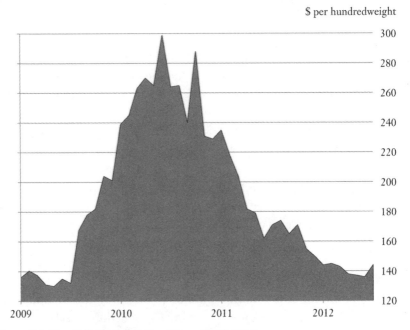

Figure 5.4: New York Market Coffee Prices, 2009–2012

CHAPTER 6

Agency, Opportunity, and Frustrated Freedom

The growth of the high-end, high-altitude coffee market has opened new opportunities for some Maya farmers and has increased the aspirational possibilities for many more. Working with rapidly changing and fickle foreign markets also presents new vulnerabilities for smallholding growers. Following the market height of mid-2011, commodity coffee prices dropped precipitously, reaching a low of just over $100 per hundredweight in late 2013, not enough for most farmers to cover production costs. Over this same period, farmers faced an epidemic of coffee rust fungus that threatened a significant portion of the country's overall crop. Then, with equal rapidity, the coffee rust threat receded (after wiping out almost 20 percent of production) and droughts in Brazil led the New York C price to rise to $180 in February 2014.

This chapter resulted from collaboration with Bart Victor. The notion of "frustrated freedom" was first presented in Victor et al. 2013.

Such market fluctuations can lead to disparities between levels of subjective agency and available opportunities. Comparative deficits of agency in relation to resources and opportunities produce what Amartya Sen calls "unfreedom," an inability to achieve one's capabilities. Bart Victor and I point to cases in which agency can exceed opportunity structures, thwarting aspirations and resulting in a condition we call "frustrated freedom." Among the coffee farmers in our 2011 surveys we found relatively high levels of agency and some degree of frustrated freedom, but farmers' aspiration combined with the expanding market opportunities at that time also resulted in high levels of subjective wellbeing.

Maya coffee farmers themselves talk about their aspirations, agency, and opportunities in ways that are broadly congruent with a capabilities approach to development. As laid out by Sen, Martha Nussbaum, and others, this approach argues that improving the material conditions of the poor is a means to a greater end, namely the ability to live a life that they themselves value. Such "development as freedom" involves promoting the capabilities and agency required to deploy material resources in intentional and strategic ways to create the life that one envisions.

The expanding high-end coffee market has created new opportunity structures for smallholding Maya farmers, a venue to exercise their agency and pursue their aspirations. Unlike the previous generations of coffee oligarchs, they do not identify as cafetaleros, but as farmers, plying their trade with another product. Coffee is not the end, but a means to other ends, what they hope will be a better life. In our interviews, producers viewed coffee as a useful resource and a means to other ends, but not a panacea. As one middle-aged producer commented, "Growing coffee hasn't allowed me to have all in my life that I wanted, but it moves me in that direction, and that is something."

Coffee producers construct their aspirations in the difficult circumstances in which they find themselves. In this context of limited opportunities, most farmers see coffee as a beneficial, if imperfect, addition to household economic strategies. Yet, importantly, agency and aspirations are constrained by what is seen as possible, the realm of what is achievable and conceivable, the space of opportunity structures. A valid critique of the capabilities approach is that "the life one values" is conceptually constrained by cultural norms and social forces external to the individual agent. This is to say that the capacity to aspire is not evenly distributed across a population; those with more wealth and more power aspire to different things, and on a grander scale, than the poor (Appadurai 2001). Further, aspirations and notions of the good life are often shaped by the very development efforts that seek to promote such capabilities in a feedback loop that recalls Foucault's notion of discipline (Biehl 2013; Li 2007). Liliana Goldín (2009) shows how diverse strategies pursued by rural Guatemalan households dialectically define economic ideologies and the realm of what is possible and desirable.

Coffee is seen by most farmers as an opportunity structure through which they can act and work toward ends that they value, even if those ends are conditioned and limited in the ways just noted. The farmers we interviewed value the income-generating potential of coffee, but see it as a means to larger ends, such as educating their children, buying more land, achieving a degree of financial security.

In this chapter, I suggest some implications of our coffee study for recent trends in development theory and practice, briefly covering the history of development efforts and the changes globalization has brought to the old paradigms. I then turn to the capabilities approach and its focus on achieving the good life. The interaction of different domains in contributing to wellbeing shows that, to be effective, agency must be combined with adequate structural opportunities.

Development and Dependency

We in the Northern Hemisphere have long depended on Southern producers to supply us with both exotic and, increasingly, mundane foodstuffs. The oft-told story of sugar illustrates a common trajectory. First prized for its distinction as a luxury good, with trade in England legally restricted to nobility, aspirational consumption of sugar expanded the market until, by the late 18th century, sugar (and tea) had become a staple of the English working poor's diet. Cheap and high in calories, sugar became, in the memorable words of Sidney Mintz (1985), a "proletarian hunger-killer" when combined with coffee or tea. All the while, this Western consumption fueled a system of slavery, exploitation, and extraction in the New World. Much the same happened with coffee, as I described in the previous chapter.

The other well-known component of this narrative is the ensuing dependency and underdevelopment of Southern regions. World system theories describe how capital and capital-intensive manufacturing have long been concentrated in the core countries of Western Europe and North America, part of a global economic system that renders peripheral economies dependent on the core and in competition with one another (Baran 1957; Cardoso and Faletto 1979 [1967]; Frank 1967; Wallerstein 1974). Such approaches reveal the structural logic of capitalism as simultaneously based on an expansion (of labor, capital, and consumer markets) and on a concentration of capital in the manufacturing and industrial economies of core countries. Feedback mechanisms built into the system act to restrict capital accumulation to the core while "developing underdevelopment" in the peripheral countries to ensure a continued cheap supply of raw materials and labor (Luxemburg 1913; Cardoso and Faletto 1979).

The history of Guatemala illustrates such dependency: it had a string of primary commodity export crops that provided the backbone of the economy during boom years until their respective markets collapsed, beginning with indigo and cochineal (used as dyes) and continuing up to today's somewhat more stable trade in coffee, sugar, bananas, and cotton. This resulted in what Alain de Janvry (1981) and Mark Moberg (1992) view as disarticulated economic structures: when the most productive sector of the economy is based on export production, producers do not depend on local consumer demand, which allows wages to be kept at a bare minimum, even below subsistence levels.

During the post–World War II period of international economic development, and reacting to the same patterns observed by dependency theorists, a consensus emerged from the UN Economic Commission for Latin America (ECLA) and other think tanks that developing economies needed more manufacturing and value-added production, but they were hindered by cheap imports and lack of local demand. To combat this, import substitution industrialization (ISI) policies were widely adopted in Guatemala and throughout Latin America, using tariff structures to stimulate demand for locally produced items.

ISI efforts did produce solid, if not spectacular, growth, and benefits were broadly distributed, if still skewed toward the elite classes. But they were also costly, and by the late 1970s and early 1980s were financed by spiraling debt. ISI efforts largely collapsed in the 1980s under the burden of debt, although Brazil stuck with the approach, which many would credit with its dramatic growth in the early 2000s. For Guatemala and much of the developing world, the 1980s ushered in a new era of neoliberal reforms (see Conroy, Murray, and Rosset 1996).

As a result of the neoliberal turn, there has been a dramatic restructuring of the global economic system, forcing us to reconsider many of the assumptions of classic theories. There is no broad agreement on what to call this new phase of globalization: Fredrik Jameson (1991) calls it "late capitalism," Scott Lash and John Urry (1987) prefer "the end of organized capitalism," and Jonathan Friedman (1994) sees it as a "post-dependency phase" of world capitalism. All agree that is a fundamentally new stage of capitalist development related to post-industrialization and post-Fordism in core countries and processes of transnationalization (especially dramatic declines in transportation and communication costs and the lowering of tariff barriers) affecting peripheral areas. In some ways, continuing patterns of dependency have marked the region for centuries. Yet the situation today is more complex and interwoven, with a different division of labor and different mechanisms of capital accumulation, than we found in classic world systems theory (Escobar 1994).

As the virtual collapsing of time-space distances allows for the creation of ever larger markets, the boundaries between core and peripheral areas become increasingly blurred. Today, industrial production—formerly the hallmark of developed economies—is rapidly being moved from core areas to peripheral regions, reversing the classic dependency pattern of modern global commodity flows. No longer are raw materials simply imported from peripheral countries and processed in core areas, where exchange value accumulates. Increasingly assembly if not complete production of consumer goods destined for sale in both core and peripheral countries is carried out in "peripheral" regions. Emblematic of this shift, perhaps, was the 2005 purchase by China's Lenovo (which is one-third owned by the Chinese Academy of Sciences) of venerable IBM's personal computer business.

Transnationalism offers the possibility of more direct articulation between peripheral economic formations and global markets, unmediated by state-level, elite-dominated market structures. Friedman argues that the world system is characterized by alternating periods of hegemonic expansion from a few powerful centers and subsequent periods of fragmentation and hegemonic contraction. During "stable hegemonic phases" the global political economy largely conforms to the predictions of world system theory. In contrast, during periods of core hegemonic contraction, "new small and rapidly expanding centers emerge, outcompeting central production, leading eventually to a situation in which the center becomes increasingly the consumer of the products of its own exported capital" (Friedman 1994: 169).

One aspect of new value chain regimes is the *maquiladora* industry in Guatemala. Mostly owned by Koreans and notorious for harsh working conditions, these factories assemble clothing (including many familiar brand names) for export mostly to the United States (Armbruster-Sandoval 1999). Their employees are overwhelmingly young single women, many of whom are indigenous (Avancso 1994). Surprisingly, and perhaps indicative of how aspirations are adapted to circumstances, Goldín (2009) finds that most of the *maquila* workers see their jobs as unfulfilling in themselves, but as steps toward a better (often understood to be more independent) future, unencumbered by traditional patriarchal norms.

It is also in this globalized space that Maya farmers have found new opportunities. For broccoli famers, lower transportation costs, greater access to communication, and free-trade agreements have allowed them to successfully compete with California farmers—feeding the growing U.S. appetite for healthy foods while retaining control over their means of production, especially their land. These same factors, along with changing consumer tastes for quality and provenance, have created a new market for small producers of SHB coffee.

Income, Freedom, and Wellbeing

Increasing income and access to material resources are necessary but insufficient conditions for improving the wellbeing of those in poverty. We have long used GDP, household income, and absolute poverty lines to measure development, and, by extension, overall wellbeing or quality of life. Yet research has also shown that income and material resources have a complicated relationship with wellbeing. Studies have found that "links between material resources and subjective wellbeing are weak" in developing country contexts (Müller 2010: 255; see also McGregor 2007; Gough and McGregor 2007; Camfield, Choudhury, and Devine 2007; Easterlin, 2001). This is true not just for the poor. The economic and psychological literature on happiness in the developed world has also found non-linear relationships between differences in wealth and differences in personal wellbeing (see Krueger 2009; Kahneman 2011; Layard 2005; Deaton 2007).

The capabilities approach offers a theoretical explanation for these findings. In this view, human development depends not only on real opportunities (including material resources and opportunity structures), but also on the ability to envision and pursue goals that people value (agency) (see Sen 2002; Alkire 2005; Clark 2009; Foster 2011; Nussbaum 2011). Wellbeing is thus seen to result from the interaction between resources and agency: it is through agency that actors are able to employ objective material resources and opportunity structures to achieve the life that they desire.

This perspective at once expands the determinants of poverty from average GDP or income alone and, significantly, respects the aspirations and desires of "the poor" themselves (recognizing how complicated that category is). In Sen's approach, capabilities are conceived of as providing a space for what is possible for individuals to do or to be. The goal of development is to increase capabilities, to ensure that people have the freedom to choose their own life path and the power to effectively pursue their goals (Sen 1999; Foster 2011). Freedom of speech, for example, requires the capabilities of literacy and technology, and the freedom of self-determination requires a whole range of capabilities that allow people to achieve those things and states of being that they themselves see as valuable (see Alkire 2008).

Conventional welfare economics holds that more income gives people more choice, which they will then use to pursue their preferences and utilities. While there was and still is considerable debate over what levels of absolute or relative income are deficient enough for individuals or families to be labeled poor, income has served as both the measure of poverty and the focus of development interventions. In recent years, this basic understanding has been the subject of significant critique. Sen (1999) demonstrates that income differences among the poor have a limited relationship with differences in the lived conditions of poverty. This is to say, lived poverty is not merely an absence of wealth; nor is its alleviation merely a question of an increase in income. The ability to act on what one values, or "what a person can do in line with his or her conception of the good" (Sen 1985: 206), contributes directly and necessarily to wellbeing and freedom. In Sen's view, an absence of agency as well as a deficit of material resources can produce the condition he labels "unfreedom."

In a parallel literature, research in happiness psychology and economics has also taken on the relationship between income and wellbeing, focusing particularly on developed country contexts. Richard Easterlin (2001) famously observed the apparent paradox that within countries wealthier people are on average happier than poorer ones, but between countries there is little relationship between per capita income and average happiness. Numerous studies in happiness psychology and economics have demonstrated that differences in income have a limited and non-linear relationship with differences in individual happiness or life satisfaction. Daniel Gilbert (2006), Richard Layard (2005), and others stress the importance of non-material aspects of wellbeing (stable marriage, employment, social networks, and health are all associated with happiness; unhappiness is associated with divorce, unemployment, and economic instability). In a study of Latin America, Carol Graham and Eduardo Lora (2009) found that friends and family were most important to the happiness of the poor, but that work and health mattered most to the affluent.

Like the development literature, the happiness literature has paid careful attention to structural opportunity. One reason increases in wealth may have a diminishing positive impact on wellbeing is that there is often not an equivalent increase in agentive capacity. That is, people may have more opportunity space than they are capable of converting into their own wellbeing.

For example, in studies of British civil servants (hardly a disadvantaged group), those who describe themselves as having low levels of empowerment actually report lower levels of health and wellbeing than their more empowered peers (Marmot and Wilkinson 2001). This is a condition comparable to Sen's "unfreedom" in that it is characterized by a mismatch between opportunity space and level of empowerment. However it is experienced at levels of relative wellbeing that can hardly be described as poverty.

Graham suggests that unhappiness may result from a kind of surfeit or excess agency: "The process of acquiring agency may in and of itself produce short-term unhappiness. And, if prospects of a more fulfilling life are raised but the opportunity to live that life does not materialize, one can surely imagine lasting unhappiness as a result" (Graham 2011: 47).[1] Graham and Lora (2009) document the "paradox of unhappy growth": any sort of uncertainty is detrimental to happiness; this often results in a negative correlation between economic growth and happiness. From this observation one might expect an experienced excess in agency to actually diminish one's sense of wellbeing if the limitations of the resource and opportunity space one occupies limit the full realization of that agency.

Sen is critical of the perspective of happiness underlying utility models in traditional welfare economics (1997, 2002; see also Clark 2009). He observes that in terms of "the mental metric of utility" people tend to adapt their aspirations to the context of what is perceived as possible and realistic (see also Elster 1983). He states that "a person's deprivation, then, may not at all show up in the metrics of pleasure, desire fulfillment, etc., even though he or she may be quite unable to be adequately nourished, decently clothed, minimally educated and so on" (Sen 1997: 45). This is to say that the reduced (or "disciplined," to use the Foucauldian term) desires of the severely deprived in terms of agency and capability are not the same as the "confident and demanding desires of the better placed" (Sen 1997: 11).

Moving beyond income measures allows the capabilities approach to give due consideration to life satisfaction and subjective wellbeing (Alkire 2002). Granted, such things are often missed in revealed preference models: we cannot rely on "the revealed preference approach as a guide to well-being if people's abilities, behavior and choices are shaped by the experience of poverty" (Clark 2009: 34; see also Foster 2011). Yet by the same token, as Carol Graham (2011) argues, happiness (if broadly conceived as subjective wellbeing) is fundamental to understanding capabilities. The goal of human development, argue many happiness scholars, should be to increase people's own assessment of their wellbeing. This is true not just for the developing world. Joseph Stiglitz, Amartya Sen, and Jean-Paul Fitoussi (2010) make the case that policy in France and the developed world should focus on increasing quality of life, which is understood to include broad measures of objective and subjective wellbeing.

Yet well-being is a rather elusive state when it comes to measurement, and for many subjective wellbeing (especially life evaluation, not just hedonic happiness) serves as a solid signal of overall quality of life. Stiglitz, Sen, and Fitoussi (2010: 18) write that "quantitative measures of these subjective aspects hold the promise of delivering not just a good measure of quality of life per se, but also a better understanding of its determinants, reaching beyond people's income and material conditions." (Significantly, they go on to note that "proponents of the capabilities approach also emphasize that subjective states are not the only things that matter, and that expanding people's opportunities is important itself, even if this does not show up in greater subjective well-being" [p. 64]).

Agency

The capabilities approach to development emphasizes the importance of individual and collective capacity to convert objective levels of resources and opportunities into the lives people would choose for themselves. Thus, for Sen, wellbeing requires an alignment of both subjective agency and objective resources and opportunity. Importantly, Sen sees agency as intrinsically motivated. That is, substantive freedom entails making choices that are consistent with one's values and not simply the result of mechanical self-interest or extrinsic reward seeking (see also Laidlaw 2002). In this light, we may understand agency as a psychological state of being and not simply a measure of achieved wealth or status.

Sabina Alkire (2008) shows that it is largely assumed that agency contributes directly to wellbeing, since pursuing one's own goals would, ipso facto, increase one's (subjective) wellbeing. Thus the capabilities approach to development stresses the importance of freedom to choose one's life path—the exercise of agency—in a manner than enhances overall wellbeing. Despite this centrality, agency remains an elusive analytic construct. Composed of psychological traits such as confidence, will, intention, autonomy, and aspiration, agency is a subjective concept that interacts in complex and mutually constitutive ways with material resources, opportunity structures, and life histories.

Murat Kotan (2010: 370) defines agency as "the ability to exert power so as to influence the state of the world, [and] do so in a purposeful way and in line with self-established objectives." Note that here (as in Sen's definition above), the importance of realized effectiveness is unclear: exerting power so as to influence the world does not necessarily mean that the world is so influenced and changed. In this vein, Alkire (2008: 4) distinguishes between effective power (the ability to achieve chosen ends) and control (the ability to make choices and control procedures).

Edward Deci and Richard Ryan (1980) identify two key components of agency: (1) competence and efficacy; and (2) autonomy, the extent to which one perceives the right or freedom to choose. Importantly, autonomy is not identical to individualism. That is, autonomy can be a shared or collective freedom in which one internalizes a group's preferences as one's own. This quality of autonomy allows for a robustness of the agency construct across cultural variations in collectivism and individualism (Alkire 2008).

While the literature presents a plethora of definitions, here I consider agency to be subjective agency, the internal capacity and psycho-social power of individuals to make decisions. Such subjective agency itself is insufficient to realize effective change: there also must be adequate resources and opportunity structures with which to act. Thus in our model subjective agency acts on and through available material resources (including income) and socio-political opportunity structures.

Opportunity Structures

Opportunity structures are the socio-political structures and formal and informal institutional climate in which agency operates and that affect its efficacy (Alsop, Bertelsen, and Holland 2006; Ibrahim and Alkire 2007). Opportunity structures encompass critical resources (Abadian 1996) and social support and engagement (Ryan and Deci 2001); we may usefully distinguish between personal agency and available resource opportunities, both of which factor into subjective wellbeing. Ruth Alsop, Mette Frost Bertelsen, and Jeremy Holland (2006: 13) observe that "an actor may be able to choose options, but the effective realization of those choices will largely depend upon the institutional context within which the actors live and work. The opportunity structure comprises these institutions that govern people's behavior and that influence the success or failure of the choices that they make."

James Foster (2011: 687) defines opportunity freedom as "the extent to which a set of options offers a decision maker real opportunities to achieve." Foster notes that economic models of choice tend to focus on outcomes, which leaves unexamined the ways in which choices are constrained and compromised by structural conditions. He provides a model that accounts for the quantity and quality of unchosen alternatives as an indicator of opportunity freedom.

Solava Ibrahim and Sabina Alkire (2007: 9) observe that opportunity structures are necessary as the "preconditions for effective agency." Thus a capability model must account for the effective freedom to choose and the structural conditions and resources outside of a single individual's control that limit the range of functioning and possibilities. As Deepa Narayan (2005) points out, it is not just the psychological but also the human and material resources a person can call upon in achieving his or her goals that can lead to empowered action. In many ways, this is an iteration of the long-standing debate in the social sciences over agency and structure—the range of the ability to act and structural constraints on action.

Poverty and Frustrated Freedom

Several efforts have been made to integrate agency, resources and opportunity structures into multidimensional measures of poverty and wellbeing (see Narayan 2005). Notable is the model developed by the Oxford Poverty and Human Development Initiative (OPHI) discussed in the Introduction (see Alkire and Foster 2011). In multidimensional analyses of wellbeing, the constitutive elements are often seen as additive or substitutive. In fact, an ethnographic approach leads us to see the various dimensions as complexly interrelated, and often valued relative to another. *Relative* levels of agency, resources, and opportunity structures produce particular subjectivities and ways of acting in the world, not just any one dimension acting alone.

From a capabilities perspective, the conditions of poverty and wellbeing may be understood as freedom and unfreedom. Here, freedom refers to the ability to lead the life one values, unfreedom to its opposite. In the multidimensional approach, researchers usually distinguish at least two conditions of poverty. One we may call "absolute deprivation," marked by inadequate material resources for subsistence. The other, in which we find at least minimally adequate resources and yet a deficit of agency and opportunity structures, is what Sen focused on as unfreedom. Sen and others hypothesize that one of the most insidious deficits of poverty is an insufficiency of the agency to convert resources into lived differences. The substantive freedom of capabilities is produced when agency effectively mobilizes resources and opportunities. Thus we can identify three categories of poverty and wellbeing: substantive freedom, absolute deprivation, and unfreedom.

Research that Bart Victor and I have carried out suggests a fourth condition that we call "frustrated freedom" (Victor et al. 2013). In this condition, a person's agency is effectively greater than the available resources and opportunity structures; that is to say, individuals possess the subjective agency to achieve more than their material resources and opportunity structure can

Plate 11: *Reinas de Tecpán*

Maya women's traditional dress, known as *traje*, consists of a woven blouse (*huipil*) and skirt (*corte*). Each community has its own distinctive style of traje, although these days many young women mix designs from various communities. Traje, of course, like Western dress, has always been a medium for fashion trends (Hendrickson 1995), and over the past fifteen years the fashion cycle has been accelerating. Raxche' Rodríguez, a cultural activist and social entrepreneur from Tecpán, has developed a popular windbreaker style jacket using traje fabric. Raxche's jacket is popular among ethnically conscious younger men, but for the most part males under 50 or so do not wear traditional dress except on special occasions, such as the crowning ceremony for the town's queens.

In Tecpán, there are two beauty contests held during the town's annual fiesta, one for the Maya candidates (the *Reina Indígena*) and one for the ladinas (simply the *Reina*). When I first moved to Tecpán (as a boy from southern Alabama) I was taken aback by this segregation, but my Maya friends in Tecpán did not seem to mind, and even saw the indigenous pageant as a chance to express themselves away from the ladinos. Here are the two queens and their escorts; on the left, in traditional dress, is Heidi Lux. (Photo courtesy of Heidi Lux.)

enable. In such a condition, opportunity and resource deficits frustrate their perceived capacity to successfully make the decisions and choices that they believe would enhance their wellbeing.

James Ferguson (1999) provides a clear example of frustrated freedom in his study of the copper boom in Zambia and its aftermath. Ferguson shows how rapid economic growth expands the range of capabilities and expectations of agency as important, internalized motivational forces; the aspirations window of ordinary Zambians opened wide and provided new points of reference for dreams of the future. After the bust, these dreams became unviable; perceived and previously achieved agency was no longer effective, leading to decreases in wellbeing based on unsatisfied aspirational capabilities (see also DeHart 2010).

To investigate the relationships between agency, opportunity structures, and wellbeing, in 2010 Bart Victor, Alfredo Vergara, and I led a team that conducted a large-scale population survey in the Zambézia province of Mozambique. We collected our data as part of the monitoring and evaluation of a USAID-funded initiative known as Strengthening Communities through Integrated Programming (SCIP). Zambézia is a poor province in a poor country. The major elements contributing to the vulnerability of its people are the lack of social infrastructure, poor health and sanitation, food insecurity (low levels of food production, frequent food shortages, lack of alternative sources of income, and poor access to markets), and the spread of diseases, especially HIV/AIDS and malaria (Victor et al. 2014).

Based on a large random sample from Zambézia province, we looked at the relationship of agency and wellbeing measures in the context of acute poverty. We discovered that increases in both resources and agency are related to increased wellbeing only to a certain point. In the context of this Mozambique study, the objective, absolute level of resources is severely limited, which tightly bounds levels of health, income, education, and safety. In such conditions, we find that higher levels of agency may be associated with decreases in wellbeing. This is to say, subjective wellbeing improves with self-reported agency up to a point, after which increases in agency are associated with an apparent decrease in subjective wellbeing. We argue that the turning point marks when the limitations of opportunity structures kick in, after which increases in subjective individual agency raise people's level of frustration when external conditions prevent them from realizing their ambitions (Victor et al. 2013).

Coffee, Aspirations, and Wellbeing

Our sample of Guatemalan coffee farmers had much higher levels of well-being and subjective life satisfaction than the Mozambique sample. Just over 67 percent of the Guatemalan farmers reported being satisfied or very satisfied with their lives overall. We also found very high levels of subjective agency: ranking their belief in agency on a 1–10 scale, the average among our sampled coffee farmers was 7.87. At the same time, we found a more mixed picture in looking at realized agency, the ability to achieve one's aspirations. Only 28.2 percent of our sample reported "always" or "almost always" being able to successfully implement their decisions, and 46.2 percent reported "never" or "almost never" (see Figures 6.1 and 6.2).

Based on the quantitative data we collected, we found that (1) subjective agency, (2) opportunity structures, and (3) family and social support were the best predictors of overall wellbeing. In our qualitative data, there was a marked valued placed on fairness and dignity, especially as expressed in controlling one's means of production, and on the larger moral projects of the lives and visions for the futures.

These farmers' assessment of their own situation echoes key elements of the capabilities approach to development as outlined above. As Sen,

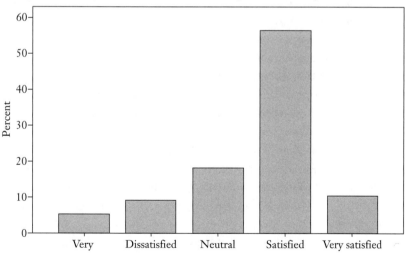

Taking into account your life as a whole, how would you characterize your satisfaction?

Figure 6.1: Life Satisfaction among Guatemalan Coffee Farmers

How often are you able to freely make decisions that impact your life?

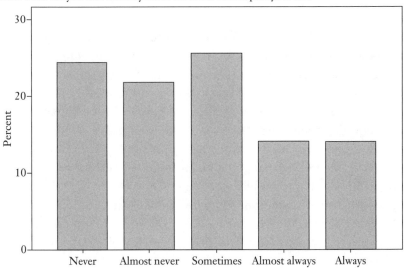

Figure 6.2: A Measure of Agency among Guatemalan Coffee Farmers

Nussbaum, Alkire, and others predict, agency and material resources are essential elements in the freedom to construct the life that one values. Sen argued that low levels of agency deprived persons of the benefits of their resources and opportunities and resulted in a deprivation that he termed "unfreedom." Less attention has been paid to the complex dynamic between aspirations, structural opportunity and agency. What we found in the Mozambique sample, and to a lesser extent among Guatemalan coffee farmers, was a situation in which people's aspirations and agency effectively exceed opportunities and resources.

The coffee farmers were striving for something more, something better out of life, and saw themselves as capable, held back by lack of access to credit, educational opportunities, and political influence, as well as by the enduring legacies of structural discrimination (recall the young man who said coffee was only for the Germans to grow, not the Maya). Coffee is an imperfect vehicle for economic development, but it allows producers to retain control over their means of production, to have a degree of control over their destiny that they value. Indeed, they do not believe that a lack of ability or agency holds them back, but a lack of opportunity. Said one young farmer, "If we had the opportunity we could be more successful, but we don't have the opportunity."

Still, for the majority of Guatemalan coffee farmers, the experience of frustrated freedom was mitigated by the dramatic upward trajectory of the market, with its aspirational promise of ever greater returns. These producers viewed the coffee market as a mechanism, a tool, a technology, a way of mobilizing available resources toward desired ends. These ends do not generally extend to the sorts of radical structural changes most would argue that Guatemala needs for sustainable human development. Rather, it is a means to achieve *algo más* (something more, something better) given the actual context of limited opportunity and material resources.

The farmers we interviewed overwhelmingly saw coffee as a useful means to pursue a better life, to realize their aspirations for the good life. Their goals and stated preferences are limited by their cultural and social horizons; more radical futures are certainly imaginable. We can and should dream of such futures, and we must respect as legitimate the hopes and dreams of the subjects of our study. It is, after all, their aspirations and agency that help define what the good life can mean.

CHAPTER 7

Experiments in Fairness and Dignity

Among smallholding coffee growers and broccoli farmers in Guatemala, there is often a felt tension between self-interest and social obligations, between individual advancement and the common good. This is discussed in the language of moral projects and dignity: just what is fair and just? Local moral codes value just rewards for hard work and accept a significant degree of income inequality as a result. Yet they also harshly condemn ill-gotten gains, as well as those who get rich too quickly and do not help family and neighbors get ahead too.

In Tecpán, a common subject of gossip is the nefarious means some individuals employ to get rich quick by making Faustian pacts with extraworldly demons. Stories told about *coyotes* (the intermediaries in the coffee trade) fold together not only the fears of economic exploitation but also the

The research and analysis reported in this chapter were conducted with Avery Dickins de Girón, and sections borrow heavily from Fischer and Dickins de Girón 2014.

imaginings of transnational flows of opportunity and potential excess. These stories reveal the persistence of a moral economy based on fairness, corporate labor over individual gains, and modesty. This moral model intensifies at the margins of the global economy as local producers are brought into relations with the global marketplace, where they become aware that they do not benefit in the same ways that those higher up the value chain do (Fischer and Benson 2006).

Like the German shoppers, Maya coffee and broccoli farmers are constantly negotiating a balance between material self-interest and moral projects implicated in the good life. The German sense of solidarity may be more abstract and the Maya sense of fairness more rooted in local communities, but they share a sense of social obligation and a vision of a better life.

As we saw in Chapter 2, the methodological individualism of economics often ignores the cultural and institutional contexts of decisions—the fact that choices are delimited by structural conditions. Granted, there is a mathematical beauty to utility functions that neatly condense human behavior to a drive to maximize returns in the pursuit of certain preferences. But from an ethnographic perspective, such models fail to account for the complex, often contradictory, motivations stemming from moral values, cultural identities, and all the messy realities of quotidian experience that do not lend themselves to coding as tidy variables. In theory, affective motivations may be treated as a type of preference, but as we have seen, rational-choice methodologies privilege "revealed" preferences over "stated" preferences.

While mainstream neoclassical economics has mostly ignored ethnographic critiques of self-interest, the burgeoning subfields of behavioral and experimental economics are leading a soft revolution in the discipline, drawing on social psychology and game theory to account for widespread "deviations" from rational-choice expectations. Experimental games and scenarios gauge actual behavior against rational-choice assumptions, taking into account proximate knowledge and context-dependent decisions, risk aversion and status quo biases, and cooperative as well as competitive motivations (see, e.g., Smith 1999; Thaler 1992; Shiller 2005; Camerer 2003; Akerloff and Kranton 2011; Ariely 2010).

In this chapter, I turn to experimental methodologies, in the form of the Ultimatum Game, to examine the rationalities of cooperation and competition in two Maya communities in Guatemala. The Ultimatum Game offers a robust experimental method for documenting the limits of self-interest and rationality in actual behavior and the competing pulls of competition and cooperation in the context of anonymous game play (see Güth, Schmittberger, and Schwarze 1982; Camerer and Thaler 1995; Roth et al. 1991; Thaler 1992).

An Ultimatum

> *Let's play a game. In the field, we would play with real money, but here I will have to ask you to suspend disbelief and pretend that I have just given you $100 in ten $10 bills. In this Ultimatum Game, you have one move and one move only. You will offer a percentage of your $100 to an anonymous player with whom you have been partnered. That player, in turn, also has but one move: she can accept your offer, and you both split the money as per the offer (if you offered $30, she would get $30 and you would get $70), or she can reject the offer and you have to return the money to me. What would you offer?*

In the Ultimatum Game, two players are anonymously paired with each other and a sum of money (x) is given in cash to Player A. Player A's sole move is to offer Player B a portion (y) of the total x. Knowing the amount (x) that Player A has received, Player B's one move is to either accept or reject the offer. If Player B accepts, he keeps the money offered (y) and Player A keeps the rest ($x–y$). If Player B rejects the offer, the money is returned to the main pot and neither player receives anything. Thus the game consists entirely of Player A making an offer and Player B either accepting or rejecting that offer.

To maximize material gain, the most rational move for Player A is to offer the smallest unit of account (10 percent if playing with ten bills) and for Player B to accept the offer (since any amount will have more utility than zero, which is the alternative). In fact, we find that, across cultures, the modal offer is overwhelmingly 50 percent of the total (x) and that the average offer is usually between 40 percent and 50 percent of the total. Hessel Oosterbeek and colleagues (2004) conducted a meta-analysis of thirty-two Ultimatum Game experiments from around the world, finding the overall average offer to be 40 percent of the total (and the rejection rate 16 percent), independent of the size of the pie.

Here I report the results of several rounds of the Ultimatum Game that Avery Dickins de Girón, Pakal B'alam, Ixchel Espantzay, Marvin Tecun, and I played in the Kaqchikel Maya town of Tecpán and the Q'eqchi' Maya community of Chisec. Players made unusually high offers in Tecpán, suggesting that they favor a high degree of cooperation; in Chisec, people made relatively low offers and more aggressively competitive moves. Our results are consistent with the hypothesis advanced by Joseph Henrich et al. (2004), Jean Ensminger (1999, 2002), and others that greater market integration results in more cooperative game playing. Tecpán is a booming market town tightly linked to the national economy while Chisec is more remote, marginalized, and impoverished. Although market integration may show a strong correlation with cooperative game behavior, it offers only an incomplete explanation of comparative degrees of cooperation and competition (see Chibnik 2005, 2011). Equally important for understanding the Ultimatum Game results from Tecpán and Chisec are moral conceptions of equality, dignity, and fairness, socio-economic differences between individuals and communities, and local histories of violence and activism (Fischer and Dickins de Girón 2014).

Experimental Methods and the Prisoner's Dilemma

The prisoner's dilemma, an iconic scenario in experimental economics, captures the fundamental tension in solving collective action problems: balancing individual self-interest with a common good. Based on Rand Corporation experiments first conducted in 1950, the classic prisoner's dilemma considers two individuals arrested for a crime that the authorities are sure they committed but for which there is insufficient evidence to convict unless one of them confesses (see Luce and Raiffa 1957, Flood 1958; see also von Neumann and Morgenstern 1944). The prisoners are placed in separate rooms for interrogation and cannot communicate with each other. Each prisoner has the choice to deny her involvement in the crime or to confess. Each prisoner is told that, if neither confesses, both will be convicted of a lesser crime (and serve two years each in jail). If both confess, they will be convicted, but with a sentencing consideration that will have them serve four years each. If one confesses but the other does not, the one who confesses will go free in exchange for her testimony, and the other (who denied involvement) will receive the maximum sentence of five years (see Luce and Raiffa 1957: 94–95; Bicchieri 1993).

Table 7.1: The Prisoner's Dilemma: Outcomes of Different Strategic Choices

Player A	Player B	
	Cooperates	Defects
	Prison time received	
Cooperates with fellow prisoner	A: 2 years / B: 2 years	A: 5 years / B: 0 years
Defects to police	A: 0 years / B: 5 years	A: 4 years / /B: 4 years

In reading Table 7.1, keep in mind that cooperation here is between the two prisoners; to defect is to confess to the police. From Player A's perspective there are two choices (defect or cooperate), and the outcome of each depends on the unknown actions of Player B. Let us look at Player A's choices:

If Player B cooperates, Player A can also cooperate (and get two years in jail) or defect (and serve no time)

If Player B defects, Player A can cooperate (and serve five years) or defect (and serve four years)

Player A's most rational choice is to always defect (zero versus two years or four versus five years in jail), as is Player B's—an example of John Nash's (1951) subgame equilibrium. Yet this solution is suboptimal for the game as a whole if we consider the two criminals together as a team. If both players cooperated with each other by not confessing, the overall sentence would be shortest: four years of total jail time versus five or eight years in the other solutions. In this light, the pareto-optimal solution–the point beyond which the game becomes zero-sum, with all of one player's gains taken at the expense of the other player–is for both to cooperate. The prisoner's dilemma illustrates the collective action problem we discussed in Chapter 2: how self-interest can work against a collective good, how cooperation can be individually irrational and yet collectively rational, and how a pareto-optimal solution requires individuals to trust each other enough to be willing to accept sacrifice.

The Ultimatum Game: Cross-cultural Results

The Ultimatum Game applies the hypothetical dilemma of competitive versus cooperative behavior to an experimental context in which there are real material stakes. Average offer sizes place a monetary value on players' preferences for cooperation and competition—higher offers reflect greater cooperation. Rejection rates similarly value the utility of punishing non-cooperative behavior. Results from the Ultimatum Game played around the world offer a powerful critique of narrowly economic conceptions of self-interests and rationality. Comparing figures from published studies, average offers range from 26 percent of the total (among the Machiguenga of Peru) to 57 percent (among the Lamalera of Indonesia); rejection rates vary between 0 and 29 percent (see Table 7.2). In between these extremes, we find great variability in game strategies, belying any presumption of universal rationality.

Perhaps the most significant finding to emerge from these studies is that most modal offers across cultures tend to be 50 percent of the total, suggesting, if anything, a widespread (perhaps universal?) bias toward cooperation. The deviation from rational expectations (offers of the smallest unit of play and rejection rates of 0) is striking. The most common reason given for higher-than-minimum offers is the risk of having the offer rejected—a rational choice when taking into account the irrationality of the other player, who might not accept a low offer. Rejection rates, when seen from the perspective of "opportunity costs" (the value of the road not taken), measure the economic value of punishing other players for having offered a minimum percentage (or in economic terms, for acting rationally). Rejecting an offer is equivalent to paying that same amount to punish the other player for not acting fairly.

Table 7.2: Ultimatum Game Results in Different Cultures

	Portion of total pot offered		
Location of players	Mean	Mode	Rate of rejection
Lamalera	.57	.50	n/a
Tecpán (Maya)	**.51**	**.50**	**.05**
Ache	.48	.40	.00
Pittsburgh	.47	.50	.22
Developed country average	.44	.50	n/a
Shona	.44	.50	.08
Chisec (Maya)	**.43**	**.40**	**.29**
Tokyo	.42	.50	.24
Germany	.37	.50	.10
Mapuche	.34	.50	.07
Machiguenga	.26	.15	.05

SOURCES: Comparative data from Roth et al. (1991); Oosterbeek, Sloof, and de Kuilen (2004); and Henrich et al. (2004: 20); developed country average from Henrich et al. (2001); see also Hoffman et al. (1994). n/a = not available.

Results from Ultimatum Games may vary in different experimental contexts. In face-to-face play, when players are known to each other, they are more likely to demonstrate cooperative behavior by making higher offers than they are when the other players are anonymous (see Hoffman, McCabe, and Smith 1994). In experiments in which the same subjects play multiple rounds of the Ultimatum Game, average offers tend to decrease as players presumably learn to be more rational through experience. Finally, the size of the pot to be split may affect offer size, although here there are practical limitations to testing this (it quickly becomes too expensive to play with real money and too hypothetical if one does not). A few studies suggest that stake size does not significantly affect offer size (see Hoffman, McCabe, and Smith 1994), or, where it does, acts to move offers toward a 50-50 division (see Cameron 1999).

To control for these experimental context variables, and thus isolate sociocultural and economic influences on Ultimatum Game behavior, a project led by Joseph Henrich (with Robert Boyd and Jean Ensminger) conducted anonymous Ultimatum Games using a common protocol in a total of sixteen small-scale societies around the world. The stakes were benchmarked with a local day's wage. Reporting on the results, Henrich et al. (2004) found positive correlations of market integration, anonymity, social complexity, and settlement size with cooperative behavior in games. This research and related studies suggest that market integration (paradoxically) conditions greater levels of trust and cooperation, leading to more equitable offers (Henrich et al. 2004; Ensminger 2004). This may be explained by the fact that market economies require a great deal of trust between strangers (trust in a common currency, trust that a vendor accurately represents a product, trust that one has access to accurate information).

At the same time, there is evidence that other social and cultural factors play a key role in cooperative behavior. Michael Chibnik (2005) argues that attempts to isolate a single key predictor oversimplifies the cultural context of particular economic decisions. In this vein, Michael Gurven (2004) demonstrates that it is not market exposure but village membership that influences offer size (at least among the Tsimane' of Bolivia); and Richard McElreath (2004) finds significant generational differences (cf. Henrich and Smith 2004).

Francisco Gil-White (2004) documented in-group and out-group variation in offers between different ethnic groups. Out-group offers were actually higher between Mongols and Kazakhs in Western Mongolia. His subjects attributed this to a greater uncertainty over rejection levels of the group they know less well; being risk-averse and cognizant of differential cultural norms of equity, they made higher offers to ensure acceptance. In contrast, John Patton (2004) found differences in game behavior due to political-economic differences rather than enculturation among the Achuar and Quichua residents of a single village in Ecuador.

Brian Paciotti and Craig Hadley (2003) note that while individuals within ethnic groups have the capacity to act altruistically, local social norms govern how this is actually realized. Frank Marlowe (2004: 187) surprisingly found offers to be very low (33 percent) among the Hazda, despite the Hazda norms of "extreme egalitarianism, with a strong sharing ethic." At the same time, Kim Hill and Michael Gurven's (2004) work with the Ache of Paraguay suggests a causal relationship between strong norms of sharing and the high average offers (48 percent) and large number of hyper-fair (>50 percent) offers. Michael Alvard (2004) offers a similar analysis for the highest reported average offers (57 percent) he recorded among Lamalera (Indonesia) whalers, whose subsistence base rests on high levels of cooperation (working alone proves to be very inefficient in whale hunting).

Such results give rise to the idea that there may be a human propensity toward reciprocity and fairness and an aversion to unfair inequalities. Steven Pinker (2008), Jonathan Haidt (2007), and others include fairness on their short lists of universal moral values (along with not harming others, group loyalty, respect for authority, and purity). Frans De Waal (2009) reports that inequity aversion is widely found among our closest primate relatives. A number of researchers link altruistic behavior in experimental games to an evolutionary advantage to cooperation and reciprocity (e.g., Camerer and Thaler 1995; Fehr and Gächter 1998; Henrich and Boyd 2001). Whatever its ultimate origins, notions of fairness and dignity are found everywhere, expressed through myriad cultural variations.

The Contexts of Play

Our study compares two rounds of Ultimatum Game experiments. The first was conducted in 2003 with Kaqchikel Maya participants from Tecpán, Guatemala, and the second was carried out in 2004 with Q'eqchi' Maya participants from Chisec. These are two very different Maya communities: one a progressive commercial center with a long history of integration into the national political economy, and the other a struggling migrant community on the margins of national life. We call on these circumstances to explain the distinct Ultimatum Game strategies recorded in each town.

Located along the Pan-American Highway about eighty kilometers west of Guatemala City, Tecpán is a relatively affluent Maya town with approximately 10,000 residents. The local economy depends heavily on agriculture—subsistence milpa plots of maize and beans and export production of broccoli and snow peas (Hamilton and Fischer 2003). But its commercial base sets Tecpán apart from neighboring indigenous communities. Tecpán is home to a large regional market, which takes over the town center on Thursdays, and a thriving manufacturing sector. The areas of greatest growth and opportunity are in sweater production and nontraditional agriculture, both of which favor small producers through low barriers to market access and the synergistic network effects of concentrated production (see Thomas 2011; Fischer and Benson 2006). As a result, we find a strong indigenous bourgeois class that has long supported ethnic consciousness and the value of education. It is increasingly common for Tecpaneco youths to complete their secondary education and go on to attend university in Guatemala City. Our surveys found the average level of education to be 8.6 years, extremely high for a Maya community, and less than 3 percent of indigenous respondents were monolingual Kaqchikel speakers.

Tecpán has a reputation in Guatemala as an especially progressive place, materially, ideologically, and culturally. There is a widespread sense of common purpose among Kaqchikel residents based on the notion of a Tecpaneco exceptionalism—that this is no ordinary Maya community. Tecpán is the seat of the prehispanic Kaqchikel empire, the first capital of Guatemala; long integrated into national life, Tecpanecos proudly proclaim theirs to be a *pueblo vanguardista* (see Hendrickson 1995; Fischer and Hendrickson 2002). A disproportionate number of Maya leaders spearheading the country's pan-Maya movement come from Tecpán, a fact reflected in local organizations to promote Maya culture and the Kaqchikel language.

Located in the relatively remote department of Alta Verapaz in north-central Guatemala, Chisec serves as an urban market center for scores of surrounding villages and hamlets. The municipal population of about 8,000 is composed mostly of Q'eqchi' Maya; most families rely on milpa agriculture

Plate 12: Bohemios Internet Café

We often think of places like Guatemala as remote, marginalized, and disconnected. Although located along the Pan-American Highway, by cosmopolitan standards Tecpán is remote. But cell phones and the Internet have opened the town up to global connections.

When the town's first Internet café ("Bohemios," pictured above) opened in the late 1990s it was soon flooded by high school kids exploring the wonders of the World Wide Web. Once, in 2001, while checking my email, I surreptitiously glanced around to see what the teenagers were looking at, and was startled by the graphic pornographic photo the young man across from me had on his screen. Jostled out of a moment of ironic romanticism (it's 2001 and I'm surfing the web with Maya kids!), I realized that I would not have been surprised by this scene at my university library, and that in many ways these youth are no different from teens in Nashville. Today, many have their own cell phone—ever more have smartphones—and all except the very poorest households have some sort of prepaid service. In 2012, the World Bank estimated that the country has 137 cell phones for every 100 inhabitants.

Neoliberal market openings in Guatemala (as elsewhere) have wrought good and bad. Cheap U.S. corn coming into Guatemala in the early 2000s damaged domestic markets and threatened local production (although by 2013 the demand for ethanol had pushed U.S. corn prices up). On the other hand, after Guatemala privatized the state telephone monopoly, Internet and telephone access rapidly came within the reach of most, with cellular services leapfrogging several generations of technology.

for their subsistence, and a sizable portion also grow small plots of cardamom (which makes its way up through layers of middlemen to be exported to the Middle East) and keep a few head of cattle. The town is home to a number of hardware stores, restaurants, and other small businesses, although the commercial sector is only a fraction of the size of Tecpán's. Indeed, Chisec is considered to be a relatively affluent community for the area, but in comparison with Tecpán the poverty is striking. The Chisec region has been historically marginalized from national politics and economics (see King 1974; Wilson 1991: 36) and neglected by the international development programs that have had a stronger presence in the highlands around Tecpán.

This isolation is reflected in low education levels and high rates of monolingualism, illiteracy, and poverty. Q'eqchi' families in Chisec typically live in wooden homes with earthen floors and thatch roofs; homes located in the central part of town have electricity, but those on the periphery have no electricity or drainage systems. The participants in our study in Chisec had attended an average of 1.76 years of school, less than a second-grade education; 57 percent had never attended school, and 61 percent were monolingual Q'eqchi' speakers. The Q'eqchi' of Chisec and the surrounded area are an immigrant population, having been forced out of their highland homelands over the past hundred and fifty years by the expansion of coffee plantations and land scarcity. In 1981, at the height of Guatemala's civil war, Chisec was converted by the army into a "model development village" and populated by hundreds of families forced to resettle from their remote hamlets into a more easily controlled urban environment.

Despite Chisec's greater poverty, lower levels of education, and overall marginalization, respondents there were much more optimistic than those in Tecpán about the economic and political future of Guatemala (see Table 7.3). More Chisecos saw a positive economic future for themselves and their children than in Tecpán (69 versus 51 percent), but Tecpanecos had significantly lower opinions of both the local and the national governments. And while only 34 percent of Chisecos believed that postwar democracy in Guatemala was working "well" or "very well," a mere 3 percent of Tecpaneco respondents agreed. Yet the optimism of the Chisecos does not translate into greater willingness to cooperate, as we found in the results of our Ultimatum Games.

We attribute the optimism in Chisec to the historical lack of development in the region. The presence of humanitarian aid organizations has

Table 7.3: Survey Results from Tecpán and Chisec

Community characteristics and opinions	Tecpán (2003, n = 76)	Chisec (2004, n = 70)
Average years of education	8.6	1.8
Catholic (self-identified)	49%	43%
Kaqchikel or Q'eqchi' monolingual	2.5%	61%
Community socio-economic status	High	Low
Community market integration	High	Low
See positive economic future for themselves	51%	69%
Negative opinion of national government	78%	37%
Negative opinion of municipal government	72%	46%
Democracy working "well" or "very well"	3%	34%

increased dramatically in recent years, largely due to the construction of a paved road completed in 2002. In discussion groups with game participants, many individuals described themselves as having little knowledge, education, or skills. They expressed enthusiasm for the arrival of development programs in the region, implying that in their current situation they have nothing to lose and everything to gain. There is a palpable sense in Chisec that things are changing for the better.

Rules of the Game

Borrowing from established methodologies (Güth, Schmittberger, and Schwarze 1982; Camerer and Fehr 2004; Camerer 2003; Smith 2000; Kagel and Roth 1995), we played Ultimatum Games in Tecpán and Chisec, using a common protocol. Local assistants hung posters, made announcements in municipal meetings, and used word of mouth to recruit participants. Although these methods did not produce random samples, we strove for representativeness by recruiting participants from across sectors of the local Indian populations (Chisec's population is over 91 percent indigenous, and Tecpán's is about 70 percent). Only adults over 18 years of age were allowed to participate, but no eligible volunteers were refused. The average age of participants was 34 in Tecpán and 37 in Chisec (with an age range of 18–80 for all participants). In Tecpán, 61 percent of the sample were male, 41 percent in Chisec. In total, seventy-six Tecpanecos and seventy Chisecos played the game. Volunteers were interviewed in the month before the actual experiments took place and the games were conducted over several days in both towns. Each participant was paid a small stipend for his or her time, and players kept any earnings from the game.

The pot size for the Ultimatum Games we conducted was 10 quetzales (approximately $1.25). This relatively small stake is equal to the lowest day wage for unskilled domestic or agricultural labor in both Tecpán and Chisec. (Purchasing power is about the same in both Tecpán and Chisec, with lower overhead costs in Chisec offset by higher transportation costs.) For some players, the amount involved was significant, and for others it was not; and we must consider the possibility that 10 quetzales was not enough to invoke more rational behavior on the part of more affluent players. But this itself is revealing: perhaps a certain affluence engenders generosity (and perhaps too much affluence mutes it).

In both towns we rented three rooms in a house close to the center, where games were played with groups of between eight and twenty individuals at a time. Upon entering the location, participants picked a slip of paper from a bag that placed them in one of two groups (A or B) and assigned them a number. The two groups were kept in separate rooms throughout the game and were anonymously paired based on their randomly selected numbers (A1 with B1, A2 with B2, and so on). The game was explained to both groups in Spanish and Kaqchikel or Q'eqchi, followed by questions and answers. Immediately before each participant played the game, investigators explained the rules to each player individually and asked her to respond to hypothetical game scenarios (e.g., If you offer 3 quetzales and the offer is accepted, how many quetzales do you keep?). Whenever examples were given, a range of hypotheticals was used (e.g., offers of 3, 5, and 7) to avoid influencing participants' perceptions of our expectations.

We used 1 quetzal coins to tangibly demonstrate the structure of the game. We asked each participant A to go through several trial runs in which he made an offer and then explained the possible outcomes to us until we were sure he understood. We repeated the demonstrations and trial runs a sufficient number of times so that particular examples would not affect the individual's strategy in the actual game through imitation. Similar hypothetical trial runs were conducted with each Player B, who could accept or reject the offer made by player A.

During the games, local assistants acted as intermediaries between the two anonymously paired players. Offer-making and the subsequent acceptance or rejection were made by players one-on-one with one of the investigators who had checked the player's understanding of the game and gave the person a chance to ask questions. Once all offers had been accepted or rejected and accordingly disbursed, we brought all of the players together and held a group discussion to debrief the participants and to hear their comments and observations regarding the game.

Results

The most surprising finding was that Tecpán's average offer was 51 percent of the total (x), which put it among the highest recorded anywhere in the world (see Table 7.2 for comparisons), while in Chisec the average offer was 42 percent (see Table 7.4). In both communities, the modal offer was 50 percent of x, but in Tecpán 76 percent offered half the pot, while in Chisec only 17 percent offered half. Hyper-fair offers (those of more than 50 percent of x) made up 16 percent of offers in Tecpán and only 11 percent in Chisec. More significantly, 69 percent of offers in Chisec were below the midpoint, whereas only 8 percent of offers were below the midpoint in Tecpán. The high percentage of offers below 5 made by players in Chisec (69 percent) suggests that the participants in Chisec were playing a more aggressive (and rationally maximizing) game.

Yet in Chisec the rejection rate was much higher (29.4 percent) than in Tecpán (5.3 percent), a presumptively irrational strategy (any percentage

Table 7.4: Ultimatum Game Results from Tecpán and Chisec

Offers (in quetzales)[a]	Tecpán	Chisec
Average offer	5.1	4.2
Mode	5	5
Minimum acceptable offer	4.3	3.7
Income-maximizing offer (IMO)	4.85	4.67
Average offer minus IMO	0.25	–0.47
Rejections	5.3%	29.4%

a. There was a pot of 10 quetzales (approximately $1.25) available in each game of x offers greater material utility than nothing) but consistent with the characterization of Chisecos employing especially aggressive strategies in the Ultimatum Game. Rejection rates are interesting because they place a monetary value on punishing another player for what is perceived as unfair behavior. To reject an offer of 3 quetzales is equivalent to paying 3 quetzales in order to deny the other player 7 quetzales. Optimal income-maximizing rational behavior would result in no rejections (any amount is better than none). The rationality of lower offers in Chisec than in Tecpán is seemingly offset by the presumptive irrationality of Chisec's high rejection rate. Yet the overall rejection rate in Chisec is a bit misleading. Disaggregating the 29 percent rejection rate, we found that in Chisec 58 percent of offers below the median were accepted (versus 37 percent in Tecpán). Thus, although we found a higher rejection rate in Chisec than in Tecpán, players in Chisec were actually more likely to accept a low offer (i.e., less than half of the pot size) than players in Tecpán. Although Chisec participants played more aggressively, they were willing to accept lower offers.

Here we encounter the conundrum that Player A may be acting rationally to maximize income given the anticipated irrationality of Player B (expressed in a willingness to reject an offer seen as insultingly low). To account for this, we calculate the income-maximizing offer (IMO) (see Paciotti and Hadley 2003; Camerer and Fehr 2004). The IMO takes into account the probability that an offer at a given level will be accepted. The IMO is determined by ranking the results of each possible offer size (1, 2, 3, 4, 5, etc.) multiplied by 1 minus the percentage of players who said they would reject that offer. (Before revealing the actual offers, we asked each Player B to specify the minimum amount that they would accept, which allowed us to determine the probability of rejection for all possible offer amounts.) The IMO in Tecpán was 4.85 and in Chisec 4.67—very close. But when we compared this with actual offers (average offer minus IMO), we found that the average offer in Tecpán was higher than the IMO (0.25), and in Chisec it was significantly lower (–0.47). Again Chisecos played much more aggressively in both offers and rejections.

Correlations between offer size and education level was different in the towns—and here we must note that education is highly correlated with socioeconomic status. In Tecpán, players who offered less than half of the total (x) had a significantly higher level of average education (11.3 years versus 8.6 years). This figure is skewed by the low number of respondents offering less than half (n = 3), and hides the fact they many of the higher offers were made by individuals with higher education levels. In fact, among those with more than ten years of education, the modal offer was 50 percent of the pot, and the average offer was 47 percent. Thus most of the more educated players favored cooperative behavior, while a significant minority pursued a risky income-maximizing strategy. In Chisec, we found an inverse relationship between education and non-midpoint offers: participants who offered more than 50 percent of the total had a much higher average education (6.2 years) than those who offered the midpoint (4.6 years) or below (1.2 years). Participants in Chisec with a higher education came from more affluent families. In discussions following the game, they explained their hyper-fair offers in terms of fairness: the size of the pot was not seen as significantly large to fight over, and it was likely that their partnered player needed the money more than they did.

Men were more likely to make hyper-fair offers in both towns. All of the hyper-fair offers in Tecpán were made by men, and four of the five hyper-fair offers in Chisec were made by men. This pattern is likely related to women's concern with household finances. In both towns, hyper-fair offers also tended to be made by younger individuals. The difference was more pronounced in Chisec, where all of the hyper-fair offers were made by individuals in their 30s. Religion did not make a significant difference in either town; midpoint and non-midpoint offers were relatively evenly split between Catholics and Protestants.

Fairness, Local Histories, and Moral Values

Our findings of hyper-fair average offers in Tecpán and significantly lower offers in Chisec are consistent with the hypothesis that market integration encourages cooperation between anonymous partners (see Henrich et al. 2004). Yet this correlation by itself only partly explains the higher average offer size in Tecpán. Following Chibnik (2005), we argue that other sociocultural contextual influences were also at play. In the cases of Tecpán and Chisec, these included personal income and general community affluence (which are hard to separate from market integration), moral values suspicious of inequalities (and particular conceptions of what constitute fair gains), and the different ways violence, ethnic activism, and the world market had converged in the recent histories of the two towns.

It may be simply that higher general community affluence and personal wealth (usually associated with degree of market integration) encourages more cooperative behavior: in this case, Tecpanecos could afford to be more generous and cooperative whereas the absolute poverty of Chisecos compelled the pursuit of more immediate self-interest. In Tecpán, a number of cultural traditions reinforce moral values of reciprocity and cooperation—communal harvesting, ritual exchanges of sweet-rolls on Maundy Thursday, collective obligations for the town fiesta, and so on. These customs should not be romanticized as just a subaltern anti-capitalist stance; most Tecpanecos value just rewards for hard work and want to better their own material circumstances. At the same time, the Tecpaneco vernacular of capitalist meritocracy (valuing hard work and the fruits of affluence that are honestly come by) is tempered by deep suspicion of those who get too rich too quickly and are stingy with their resources. Morality tales are told about greedy individuals' Faustian pacts with the devil, hidden chests of gold, and connections to the drug trade.

Tecpán is also home to a number of national leaders of the pan-Maya movement, which seeks to raise the ethnic consciousness of Guatemala's indigenous peoples in pursuit of political recognition and material concessions from the state (see Fischer and Brown 1996; Warren 1998). The movement builds on a long local history of Maya cultural activism and social cohesion based on a common sense of Kaqchikel identity and Tecpaneco exceptionalism (Fischer 2001). Local activists celebrate reciprocal and cooperative cultural traditions, and the salience of these ideals certainly influenced the higher average offers.[1] When questioned after the games about why they offered what they did, players who offered 50 percent or more of the total told us that they imagined their partner needed the money as much as or more than they did, and in this light they did not feel right taking more than half. Most players who offered less that 50 percent similarly reported that they felt they probably needed the money more than their partner and thus felt morally justified in making a lower offer (and a few invoked a clear income-maximizing rationality to justify low offers). For these reasons, Tecpanecos were inequality-averse players in the Ultimatum Game.

Paradoxically, because of the town's affluence, Tecpanecos could afford to pursue inequality-averse cultural norms. But for Chisecos, this strategy was tempered by their trying economic circumstances; their offers tended more toward the rationality of self-interest-maximizing returns. Although the subsample sizes are very small, the data suggest that, even within communities, higher-income individuals tend to exhibit more generosity. Henrich et al. (2004) found that the individual attribute of relative wealth did not predict offers once group-level variables (ethno-linguistic group traits) were factored in. At the same time, Henrich and Smith (2004) also found that the generally better-off cash-croppers among the Machiguenga (in the Amazon region of Peru) tended to make higher offers, although as the authors point out, this could also be consistent with the greater market integration hypothesis.

In comparison with Tecpán, social cohesion in Chisec is weaker, which helps explain the Chisecos' more aggressive game playing (and lesser degree of cooperation). In contrast to Tecpanecos' strong identity and pride rooted in their ties to their community's history, Q'eqchi' families living in lowland Alta Verapaz are migrants. In the late 19th century, many Q'eqchi' were forced to leave their highland homeland around Cobán after foreign investors rapidly moved in and converted much of the fertile land there into coffee plantations (Kahn 2001; Siebers 1999; King 1974). They settled in lowland regions of Alta Verapaz, Izabal, El Petén, and Belize, and this process of migration continued into the 20th century because of population growth and land scarcity. Further displacement occurred during Guatemala's civil war, which reached its height in the early 1980s. At that time, the army established "model villages" in order to control guerrilla activity among primarily indigenous groups living in rural areas. Smaller *aldeas* (villages) were destroyed and their inhabitants moved to these settlements where they were subjected to "ideological instruction" and interrogations, which has had a long-lasting impact on trust (Siebers 1999). Chisec was one of the model villages, and current residents describe being moved from their small, relatively insular communities to Chisec. (The population of Chisec grew from 651 in 1973 to 1,005 in 1981, and to 5,158 by 1994.) In the early 2000s, many families in Chisec had lived there for only one or two generations, not long enough to develop strong ties to others. Model villages had fragmented community identity and cohesion by mixing people from various settlements. Similarly, the absence of long-standing civic organizations in Chisec, exacerbated by low educational levels, also diminished trust and cooperation associated with overall social cohesion. In addition to the effects of migration and resettlement, there is no strong sense of Q'eqchi' solidarity based on ethnic identity. Although a pan-Q'eqchi' awareness has emerged in Cobán (the highland homeland of the Q'eqchi', and now departmental capital), most Q'eqchi' identify themselves in terms of their community rather than ethnic group, whether Maya or Q'eqchi' (see Siebers 1999; Wilson 1995). In this context, Chisecos displayed a tactical pragmatism in playing the Ultimatum Game that is closer to rational expectations than the cooperative bias found in Tecpán.

Self-Interest, Cooperation, and the Good Life

Deirdre McCloskey has remarked that economists are very good at explaining competition through mathematical formula and theoretical modeling but that they are dismal at explaining cooperation (McCloskey 2002). She was speaking of the neoclassical tradition that rose to dominance in the field (and in the public policy arena) in the post–World War II era, reflecting the discipline's steady 20th-century turn toward mathematics and scientific modeling (as opposed to philosophic interpretation and narrative argumentation). The formal modeling of the neoclassical tradition forces economists to rely on a number of key axioms: rationality, self-interest (the pursuit of "preferences"), and equilibrium. Human beings are generally assumed to be, in the aggregate, rationally calculating actors.

The prisoner's dilemma reveals the constraints of enlightened self-interest—often individual optimization comes at the expense of collective well-being. In turn, results from the Ultimatum Game and other economic experiments show that individuals often do not act self-interestedly (as least not by strict definitions). This comes as no surprise to anthropologists, who have long noted different cultural logics of economic rationality (Malinowski 1922; Boas 1909; Sahlins 1972; Gupta 1998; Ferguson 1999; Kearney 1996; see also Polanyi 1944; Veblen 1899). For many economists, however, it is a heretical idea that people often cooperate at the expense of their immediate material self-interest (see Shiller 2005). To understand this behavior, in Tecpán and elsewhere, we must look to the bases and mutual benefits (material as well as symbolic, psychological, social, and otherwise) for cooperation.

By using real money, experimental methods such as the Ultimatum Game allow us to get at our interlocutors' future-oriented intentions by revealing their preferences. In the cases of Tecpán and Chisec, we found that economic affluence and the social context of community solidarity (or lack thereof) are key factors, along with market integration, in understanding differences in cooperative behavior.

While the boundaries of fairness varied between these two communities, it is significant that in both we found strong norms for what is considered "fair" and a willingness to pay to punish unfair behavior. Such informal social norms can have a powerful effect on individual behavior in relatively cohesive communities, discouraging free riding (see Ostrom 1990). Indeed, they are in many ways equivalent to the more institutionalized relations we described for Germany, also concerned with fairness (and what it means for solidarity). They are both ways of keeping the potential arms race of positional values in check (Frank 2011), as BMW did in linking executive pay to wages on the shop floor. Fairness and the sense of dignity and respect it implies are important elements of subjective wellbeing and notions of the good life in our Guatemalan and German examples.

CHAPTER 8

Narco-Violence, Security, and Development

If Job were a country, it would have to be Guatemala. Certainly there are other countries in worse shape—Haiti comes to mind, and Somalia and Rwanda and Afghanistan and all the rest—but rarely do we see the convergence of so many different sorts of disasters. Guatemala is a world apart from the comfortable stability of Germany. This little country (the size of Tennessee) suffers plagues of biblical proportions so frequently that they become almost mundane—a seismic tremor that would send San Francisco office workers scurrying hardly merits acknowledgment—and they threaten the stability of an already fragile state.

Geography matters in Guatemala, as witnessed by the ever-present risk of natural disasters. But the biggest threats are political, not seismic. Its geographic location (combined with a weak state) makes it an ideal transshipment point for Colombian cocaine. It is estimated that over 80 percent of cocaine destined for the United States travels through Guatemala. Guatemala competes with El Salvador and Honduras as the most violent place on

Plate 13: Volcano: Ominous or Beautiful?

Geography plays an important role in Guatemala's tumult; it is, literally, a turbulent country. Its terrain ranges from expanses of lowland rainforest in the north (once home to Classic Maya civilization, now the base for cocaine trafficking) to the dramatic peaks and valleys of the fertile highlands (the most densely populated part of the country, home to most of the country's majority Maya population). The highland landscape is beautiful, the stuff of postcards and calendar photos, but it is a fragile beauty; George Lovell calls it "a beauty that hurts." Seismic instability gives rise to the picturesque landscape, and the lush valleys are shadowed by active volcanoes and lie on top of major fault lines. And, looking a bit beyond the verdant fields and colorful dress of the natives, we find crushing poverty and an epidemic of childhood malnutrition.

From 2010 to 2012 alone, Guatemala suffered a major volcanic eruption, earthquakes, tropical storms, and landslides that killed hundreds, left thousands homeless, and inflicted untold damage on roads and infrastructure.

earth—and taken together, this transshipment triangle dwarfs even Afghanistan and Iraq in the number of intentional homicides. Guatemala City ranks with Ciudad Juárez among the world's most deadly cities. In 2010, the murder rate in Guatemala City was 108 per 100,000; this was twice the rate for Baghdad; the comparable figures for New York and Berlin are 6.5 and 1.5. More than one in every thousand people in Guatemala City is killed every year—and virtually no one is prosecuted. A rate this high ripples quickly through the population, touching everyone in some way. It is a whole new category of non-war violence, the level of terror we see in places like northern Mexico (with not dissimilar causes). Its implications are felt throughout the city (see O'Neill, Thomas, and Offit 2011; Offit 2008). For a fortunate few, the upside is a building boom, with new luxury high-rises filling the Guatemala City skyline, giving a verticality to the city's stark inequalities (O'Neill and Fogarty-Valenzuela 2013).

In March 2010, the national police chief, Baltazar González, was arrested along with the head of the anti-narcotics agency, on charges of helping drug traffickers. Six months earlier, González's predecessor had been arrested on similar charges. And in March 2014, former Guatemalan president Alfonso Portillo was convicted by a U.S. federal court of money-laundering charges.

Recognizing that Guatemala was in real danger of becoming a narco-state, in 2007 the country's government, which usually guards its sovereignty jealously, legally empowered a UN-sponsored commission of international jurists to initiate and carry out investigations and to help prepare cases to be presented through the national courts. The International Commission against Impunity in Guatemala (CICIG), which targets criminal networks that pervade parts of the justice system and provides assistance with reestablishing the rule of law, has successfully pushed forward a number of high-profile cases.

Still, the violence continues. On June 10, 2010, four severed heads were found in plastic bags in prominent spots around Guatemala City, from the national congress to an upscale shopping center. A note attached to one incongruously called for an end to impunity for corrupt government officials. The note attached to another attacked prison officials for new rules governing prisoners' visits and communication, threatening to hold the entire Ministry of Justice responsible for such perceived abuses of authority. The severed heads seemed to send a forceful, no-uncertain-terms message. Yet notes are usually not attached to body parts; and when translated into such blunt violence, the intended messages are often hard to read. Indeed, it is the ambiguity of their attribution and intent that is especially terrorizing.

This is nothing new for Guatemala; the country has long suffered endemic violence. The period in the 1970s and 1980s know as *"la violencia"* was especially brutal, marked by massacres, kidnapping, torture, and pervasive everyday terror. The UN commission charged with documenting the effects of the civil war concluded that it constituted a case of genocide, with the military intentionally targeting the Maya population for extermination (see Lovell 2001; Nelson 1999; Hinton and O'Neill 2009). The charge of genocide is a controversial one, with many Guatemalans (mostly non-Indians) arguing that communities were targeted because of their (perceived) support of revolutionaries and not because of their race or ethnicity; it just happened that most (but not all) of those were Maya communities. Even some sympathetic lawyers think that crimes against humanity is a more appropriate charge. Whatever the nomenclature, far too many innocent people were killed, often in especially brutal and cruel ways.

Every two years, the Latin American Public Opinion Project (LAPOP), run by Mitchell Seligson, conducts large, representative surveys in Guatemala and throughout Latin America. The LAPOP data show that a clear majority of Guatemalans see security as the country's primary problem (see also Goldstein 2010). They also point to the overall fragility of the Guatemalan state.[1] One question in the 2012 survey asked about trust in institutions. At the top of the respondents' list were: 1. the Catholic Church, 2. evangelical churches, 3. the military, and 4. the media. At the bottom (the least trusted) were: 17. the Supreme Court, 18. the national congress, 19. political parties, and 20. the national police. The state is seen as being so dysfunctional that popular support for a military coup to put things back in order has risen to 47 percent. And this in a country that suffered brutally under military dictators not so long ago.

In fact, in 2012 General Otto Perez Molina assumed the presidency, elected at the head of the Patriot Party and under the slogan *"mano dura"* (iron fist) for his stance against crime. During Guatemala's violence of the early 1980s, Perez Molina commanded one of the key areas of conflict and later went on to lead military intelligence operations. He is a man who knows something about *mano dura*.

In this book's chapters on Guatemala I have focused on the individual aspirations and collective desires of Maya farmers and how these inform notions of wellbeing. But institutions also matter greatly, as they do in Germany. In Germany an elaborate legal and regulatory structure encourages and enforces certain collective goods. In Guatemala, the state is largely absent, but community norms enforce notions of fairness.

El General

General Efraín Ríos Montt talks to God. To hear him tell it, they are good buddies—two old, privileged white guys sharing their disgust at the state of affairs in the world today, from the rise in crime and corruption to the decline in family and faith. Ríos Montt's God speaks in Old Testament tones, calling for vengeance rather than forgiveness, the need for discipline more than compassion. And it was this God who told the former military dictator and born-again evangelical Christian to run for president in Guatemala's 2003 elections.[2]

The legality of Ríos Montt's candidacy was contested throughout the election. A quaint section tucked away in Article 186 of the Guatemalan Constitution bars those who have participated in coups from being president. Because a military junta brought Ríos Montt to power in 1982, the Supreme Electoral Tribunal ruled in June 2003 that he was ineligible to run for president, a decision that was at first upheld by Guatemala's Constitutional Court. Ríos Montt, however, continued to campaign, confident that he would prevail. On July 24, "Black Thursday" as it was called, the Ríos Montt campaign organized demonstrations that shut down Guatemala City and caused extensive property damage. Thousands of rural supporters were bused into the capital city and armed by campaign workers with machetes, sticks, tires, and gasoline; organizers, with cell phones held up to their black ski masks, directed the protestors toward targeted courthouses, government buildings, and private businesses, a number of which were looted while police looked on, unwilling to intervene. As smoke from burning cars and buildings filled the Guatemala City skyline, Ríos Montt announced to the press that he would not be able to control his supporters, that the people must be heard and their will heeded. Following this blatant flexing of muscle, the Constitutional Court overruled itself and, citing international accords, voted 4 to 3 that retroactively applying the 1985 Constitution to Ríos Montt's 1982 actions would violate his human rights.

One would hope that wearing the mantle of human rights victim would be uncomfortable for *el General* (as he likes to be called). Various human rights monitors, from Amnesty International to the U.S. State Department, hold him largely responsible for the torture and death of tens of thousands of noncombatants during his 1982–83 reign at the height of Guatemala's long civil war against Marxist insurgents. Because the victims were overwhelmingly rural Maya Indians (who make up about half of the country's population), a UN Truth Commission declared the violence a case of genocide. But politics can make for unlikely bedfellows, and in 2003 it was poor, rural, Maya peasants–the very targets of his scorched-earth campaign two decades ago—who formed the base of Ríos Montt's popular support. As the majority leader of the national congress, Ríos Montt had cultivated this allegiance by pushing through huge subsidies for fertilizer and increases in the minimum wage, and making large payments to those who served in the country's notorious civil patrols of the early 1980s.

I saw Ríos Montt speak one summer Saturday afternoon in 2003 in Xenimajuyu, a Maya village outside of Tecpán. In the local Kaqchikel language, Xenimajuyu means "at the foot of the mountain," and true to its name a dramatic peak rises over the village, overshadowing the distant volcanoes. Before the arrival of the Spaniards in 1524, the mountain served as an outpost of Iximche', the nearby capital of the Kaqchikel Maya empire. Climbing up its preposterously steep slopes, one sees why—the mountaintop offers a strategically unencumbered view for dozens of miles around. Today, the ground is littered with potsherds and broken obsidian blades churned up by Maya farmers as they colonize the last remaining lands around town for their small plots. In contrast to its environs, Xenimajuyu appears somewhat drab: a few cinder-block buildings (the school, the health center, some small churches), along with wood plank and adobe houses, line one of the village's two dirt roads; kids play in the street, women dressed in their vivid handwoven blouses go about their daily chores, and men can be seen walking to and from their fields of corn and beans much as their ancestors did for millennia.

On the day of the rally, over a thousand people gathered in a large field on the edge of the village. I was surprised at the turnout—both because of Ríos Montt's reputation as an iron-fisted dictator and because the sole publicity for the event consisted of a few members of Ríos Montt's advance team going around that same morning to recruit supporters. I had heard about the rally only a couple of hours before it was to begin at noon, and made it to the site right at 12:00—which turned out to be about two hours early by Guatemalan time. Under the glaring, high-altitude sun (before the rainy season's afternoon clouds had formed), I milled among the crowd as inconspicuously as possible for a blond gringo. Several people I talked to had come to the rally because they were promised information about the next installment of payments the government was promising to men (or their widows) who had served in the army-led Civil Auto-Defense Patrols (PACs) during the country's civil war in the early 1980s.

The PACs were a bad idea to start with–villagers were forced into paramilitary service and charged with protecting their towns from "subversives"; they were often given quotas of suspects to hand over to the local military garrison for "questioning." Many of those suspects never returned from the interrogations, their bodies showing up days or weeks later by the side of the road, perhaps missing a hand or covered in cigarette burns. During Guatemala's civil war, PACs were responsible for thousands of extra-judicial killings (as the Guatemalan legal code delicately phrases it) and worked with the army to instill a quotidian terror in Guatemalans that we can scarcely imagine, even in this age of terrorist threats. Yet the civil patrollers were also victims, forced into their position under the threat of persecution and death themselves. Poor Maya farmers were forced to turn on their neighbors and friends, also poor Maya farmers, in this hot spot of the Cold War. It is for this suffering that the Guatemalan congress, led by Ríos Montt (who, twenty years earlier, oversaw the expansion of PACs and sanctioned their atrocities), authorized compensating former civil patrollers with cash payments. The payments are to be disbursed in three parts. The first payout of 5,000 quetzales per claim (about $640, a year's income for a poor farmer) was made in April 2010. Over 600,000 applications were filed, but only 250,000 names appear in the official, but incomplete, government registry of patrollers who are eligible for payment.

This was Ríos Montt's fourth attempt at the presidency. In 1974 he lost an election under suspicious circumstances. While early results had given him a decisive lead, television and radio broadcasts mysteriously stopped on the night of the vote count. By the next morning, when broadcasting resumed, his rival, General Kjell Laugerud, had apparently pulled ahead to win the presidency. Fearing for his life, Ríos Montt fled to California, where he made contact with Pat Robertson's Church of the Word. Born again as an evangelical protestant, Ríos Montt came to believe that it was God's will that he lead Guatemala in the battle against communism that threatened his land. He returned to Guatemala to head a 1982 coup that overthrew another military dictator, General Romeo Lucas García. Ríos Montt's reign as head of state lasted only eighteen months, but it was the bloodiest year and a half in the country's ongoing civil war. Tens of thousands of civilians were killed, often in horrific ways: pregnant women were eviscerated, children were swung by the legs to shatter their skulls against walls, men were castrated and decapitated. In scenes reminiscent of the Holocaust, victims frequently had to dig their own mass graves before being executed. Whole villages were bombed and fields burned to the ground, forcing hundreds of thousands to flee into the jungle or to the anonymity of Guatemala City's slums. By 1983, Ríos Montt's megalomaniacal excesses became too much for even the hardened army brass, and he was overthrown and replaced by a reformist general who oversaw a transition, at least a nominal one, to democracy in 1986.

In 1989, Ríos Montt mounted a campaign for president, but his candidacy was blocked by the electoral tribunal and the constitutional court. He went on to found a new political party, the Guatemalan Republican Front (FRG). Courts again barred Ríos Montt from the 1994 FRG presidential ticket, but he was elected to the national congress. In 1998 the FRG ran Alfonso Portillo as a stand-in for Ríos Montt in the presidential elections. Portillo, who as a young leftist living in exile in Mexico had killed two men in a 1982 political dispute, was able to spin scandals about his past in his favor (calling himself "a man who can defend himself to defend our country") to win a five-year term that ended in January 2004.

The FRG government (which held the presidency, a majority in congress, and great sway over the judiciary) was troubled by corruption scandals involving shockingly large amounts of money (hundreds of millions of dollars) even for a system long accustomed to a high level of graft. The commission set up to investigate the Panamanian bank accounts of senior officials was led by Ríos Montt's daughter (Congresswoman Zury Ríos) and his niece. Ríos Montt, who campaigned on a platform of greater security (to combat the wave of crime that has swept in the country in the years following "demilitarization") and an end to corruption, found himself in a position of having to distance himself from Portillo and other officials of his own party. Arguably the most powerful man in the country, el General was running as the underdog, fighting corruption and the entrenched oligarchy.

Ríos Montt arrived in Xenimajuyu in a red helicopter, accompanied by a fanfare of firecrackers and campaign songs ("My mommy votes for Ríos Montt, my daddy votes for Ríos Montt . . ."). Like private jets in the United States, helicopters are de rigueur for serious Guatemalan presidential aspirants, allowing them to travel the campaign trail above rather than on the country's poor roads. Just outside of Xenimajuyu, the Pan-American Highway–the country's primary transportation artery–is a poorly paved two-lane road that looks like a county highway in rural Alabama.

Then a spry 77, el General roused the crowds with the fervor of an evangelical pastor. Even knowing of his brutal past, I found myself captivated by his impassioned sermon about the country's many ills and the straightforward solutions he proposed. He railed against corruption: "I am not a rich man. I started out with three little quetzales, and I am where I am today because of my hard work. But I am not rich." He inveighed against political patronage: "Who does your mayor work for? Who does your congressman work for? Who does the president of the Republic work for? You, that's right. And so why should you have to enter their offices with your head bowed and hat in hand to beg for a little favor? This is wrong. You are their boss." And he preached against infidelity and loose morals: "I have been married to the same woman for almost fifty years. A man should have just one wife, just one woman. If any candidate–even the FRG candidate for mayor of your town—cheats on his wife, I urge you not to vote for them." At this last remark, the mayoral candidate, who was on the dais, looked sheepish, and a wave of muted giggles passed through the crowd.

El General took no note and moved on to embrace Pedro Palma, a former guerrilla leader, holding his hand tight while declaring, "The past is behind us and we must leave it there. We must move forward. Together." The contrasting appearance of the two men was striking: Ríos Montt wore a cheap, slightly ill-fitting gray suit, looking like a humble man who had dressed up for a special occasion; Palma, in contrast, sported black designer jeans and a stiffly pressed Guayabera shirt, looking like a dandy who had dressed down for a trip to the countryside. Palma, who lived for years in the jungle fighting the Guatemalan army, appeared unbothered by the irony of running for congress on the ticket of his former mortal enemy.

Pointing to one side of the stage, Ríos Montt stated, "There is the plantation of yesteryear," and pointing to the other side, "There is the nation of tomorrow." He said that Guatemala is walking this treacherous path from plantation to nation while dark forces try to pull it away from the straight and narrow. Yet Guatemala should fear no evil—el General has his eye out for evil, and like the national patriarch he seeks to be ("I am Guatemala," he is fond of saying), he says he will guide his Guatemalan family to safety. This will not be easy, Ríos Montt admits, but he claims to have the moral fortitude and the "*mano dura*" to see it through. Like the protagonist of Miguel Angel Asturias's novel *El Señor Presidente*, Ríos Montt is a man fighting demons of surrealistic proportions, but his demons are of a particular fundamentalist variety.

During his speech, Ríos Montt repeatedly mentioned the PAC payments—pointing out that the opposition candidates were opposed to them and that the FRG was the only party that would ensure the next round of payments. At one point, Ríos Montt's daughter Zury took the microphone and declared the sitting opposition congressman from the region a traitor for walking out on the congressional debate over PAC payments.

The day after his visit to Xenimajuyu, Ríos Montt made an ill-timed campaign stop in Rabinal, a Maya town in the K'iche' region. Forensic anthropologists had been working for some time in Rabinal, excavating clandestine graves and identifying victims' bodies in order to document what happened there during the violence and to bring some sense of closure to still-grieving families who never knew for sure the fate of their "disappeared" loved ones. On the day Ríos Montt arrived in Rabinal, several bodies were being reburied in marked graves. The presence of the man many hold responsible for these deaths was too much for some townspeople, and they arrived at the rally with a coffin painted black and began to jeer at Ríos Montt. Not heeding the advice of his security team, Ríos Montt took the stage to try to calm the crowd, but he was met with a barrage of bottles, sticks, and rocks. After getting hit on the head with a stone, Ríos Montt retreated to his helicopter, holding a handkerchief to his bleeding forehead. The reasoned editorials of the national press that followed pointed out that it was foolish for Ríos Montt to have gone to Rabinal that day, but they also condemned the protestors for using tactics of intimidation in a free election. But who can really blame them?

In the end, Ríos Montt was disqualified from the election and has since suffered a whirlwind reversal of fortune. In 2012 he was arraigned on charges of genocide by a brave Guatemalan court. Despite several dramatic political machinations, and against most odds, Ríos Montt was tried in 2013 in front of a panel of three judges and convicted on charges of ordering genocidal attacks on the Ixil Maya population. The first head of state to be tried for genocide by his own country's courts, Ríos Montt was sentenced to eighty years in prison (50 for genocide, 30 for crimes against humanity). The verdict was subsequently set aside by the Constitutional Court on technical issues.

New Violence

After peace accords were signed in 1996, the military retreated from its historically heavy-handed role in national politics. The size of the army was reduced from close to 60,000 in the mid-1980s to less than 15,000, and key intelligence units were disbanded. The resulting power vacuum in Guatemalan national politics has only partly been filled with political parties.

The real new power rests with what Hal Brands calls an "unholy trinity" of organized criminal organizations: the narco-traffickers (the most powerful group being the Zetas, based in Mexico), international street gangs (the largest and strongest in Guatemala being MS-13, based in El Salvador), and the ominously named "Hidden Powers" (Los Poderes Ocultos), mafia-like groups formed from corrupt military officer fraternities.

The U.S. Drug Enforcement Administration (DEA) estimates that over 80 percent of Colombian cocaine bound for the United States is transshipped through Guatemala. U.S. air and sea defenses have made direct importation too risky, and Mexico's aggressive air surveillance in recent years has pushed illicit air traffic south to Guatemala. It turns out that Guatemala was a good choice, with its weak state, corrupt institutions, and huge expanses of lowland forest that are largely uninhabited and lightly governed.

Guatemala had a corrupt system to begin with, but adding drug money has exacerbated the problem to almost terminal proportions in the judicial system. The Zetas (the violent break-off group from the Gulf cartel made up largely of former elite Mexican soldiers) and other trafficking gangs are exceptionally well organized. The Zetas have reportedly recruited former Kaibiles, Guatemala's elite troops, who orchestrated terror campaigns during the civil war, to provide on-the-ground expertise. The narcos—the big players at least—are better funded, better organized, and better armed than the state. They effectively control large swaths of Guatemalan territory.

The minor drug lords who live in the little jungle towns near airstrips stand in for the government. They pave roads, buy uniforms for the soccer team, and are widely respected, if also feared. Their justice is much more swift and efficient than that of the state, but one doesn't want to get on their bad side. The result is a sort of Pablo Escobar phenomenon—a benevolent but vicious patron is backed up by untold cocaine riches.

With the Zetas has come Mexican-style violence. A sense of impunity is so widespread, especially among the police and military, that the stories that do make the news seem almost beyond belief. For example, on February 19, 2007, three El Salvadoran representatives to the Central American Parliament (PARLACEN) were murdered along with their driver en route to PARLACEN meetings in Guatemala City. Their charred bodies were found on a remote farm after their car had disappeared from a police motorcade. To soothe international tensions and ensure an impartial investigation, the next day President Oscar Berger asked the FBI to help investigate. As it turns out, the head of the national police's organized crime unit had a GPS device in his official car, and that car was at the scene of the murders when they were committed. And so, in a rare display of prosecutorial speed, on February 22, just three days after the murders, he and three of his officers were arrested.

Then four days after the arrests, on February 25, the police officers, who reportedly had confessed (claiming they thought the representatives were drug dealers), were killed inside the maximum-security prison that housed them. A group of armed men in ski masks walked into the prison (through at least seven locked gates) and executed them. The other prisoners then rioted, demanding access to the press to proclaim their innocence after prison officials initially blamed the murders on other inmates.

And so it goes—they keep killing until the investigation stops. Mexican-style.

The organized crime groups most connected to the government are what Susan Peacock and Adriana Beltrán (2003) call the "hidden powers." With names such as La Cofradía and El Sindicato, these groups evolved out of military fraternities and include both active and former offers from intelligence and the notorious Estado Mayor Presidencial (Presidential Guard). They have close ties to the state and a vested interest in thwarting any investigations into past human rights abuses. They are often the *"desconocidos"* (unknowns) police refer to as the perpetrators of political violence. They specialize in white-collar or New York mafia sorts of crimes: kickbacks, extortion, tax evasion—although they do have ties to the narco-groups and even to the street gangs.

Plate 14: No Guns, No Smoking

The sign in front of an upscale restaurant used the familiar red circle and backslash to forbid guns and smoking. Such signs are not uncommon in Guatemala, but one admonition is taken seriously and the other often ignored. And therein lies a paradox of this complicated place: there is no smoking but plenty of shooting in a country that is crumbling while it is flourishing. Violence is rampant and impunity reigns; all the while, several social indicators are up: infant mortality has declined and education levels have improved. And oddly, it is much easier to slip a gun into a bar than to sneak a cigarette.

Starting in February 2009, Guatemala banned smoking inside bars and restaurants. One would have thought—and indeed I did—that in the context of such lawlessness and violence, such a prohibition would have little impact. But lo and behold, it has and is widely enforced. A cynic might say it is because smoking in bars would be an ideal target for *mordidas* (bribes), thus encouraging police to vigorously enforce the regulation, if for private as much as public gain. But it also shows how quickly new ideas can take root, and how advances in public goods are being made even as crime grows.

Emblematic of the hidden powers' reach is the 1998 murder of Bishop Juan Gerardi. Gerardi headed the Catholic Church's historical memory commission charged with investigating *la violencia* in Guatemala. Two days after he released the report (*Guatemala: Nunca Más*), he was brutally murdered in the sacristy, just down the street from the Estado Mayor Presidencial headquarters. It was a clear message to those who want to lay specific blame for war crimes (see Goldman 2007).

And finally there are the international street gangs such as MS-13 and Barrio 18, most of which are El Salvadoran in origin, who specialize in street drugs, robbery, and extortion. One of their prime targets for extortion in Guatemala has been bus drivers. It is estimated that gangs have 14,000 members in Guatemala, the largest by far being MS-13 (aka the Salvatruchas). Like the large narco-traffickers, their organization charts could come from a Fortune 500 company. MS-13 is led by a team of international executive-level gang leaders; reporting to them are local leaders who are in charge of sections devoted to money laundering, smuggling, extortion, and intelligence/propaganda/enforcement. These gangs are highly organized; they plan strategically and brutally enforce compliance. At the highest levels, they have contact and occasionally forge short-term tactical alliances with the narcos and the hidden powers.

Along with all of this organized crime is a lot of disorganized crime as well. The activities of the less well organized groups and individuals not only heighten the sense of pervasive violence and the terror it instills; they also provide a thin but useful cover for organized crimes and political assassinations, as there always exists the possibility that the murder of a drug case prosecutor or human rights advocate was just a robbery gone bad.

Private security guards now outnumber police in Guatemala by five to one (see Dickins de Girón 2011). It is a tragedy that even upper-middle-class families who can afford it feel the need for bodyguards. Still, they are the fortunate. For most, having a car, much less a driver or bodyguard, is impossible, and so people rely on buses for most if not all of their transportation. And buses are prime targets for extortion and violence. As a result, there is a palpable sense of fear in Guatemalan daily life. Fear is fueled, certainly, by the gruesome newspaper stories; and it spreads virally via people's personal stories of robbery or kidnapping or murder of family and neighbors.

Plate 15: Tinted Windows

The most poignant examples of the violence in Guatemala for me are the most mundane—the little, often taken for granted, ways in which violence defines cultural norms. Take automobile window tinting, for example, which is booming. The most sought-after shades are so opaque they look like black polished metal and they cover all the windows, even the front windshield. At night, you can glimpse drivers leaning in over the steering wheel as they try to see out. There is a new anti-robbery version—an extra-thick and strong layer of film that helps prevent windows from breaking, buying a few crucial seconds to get away while a crook hammers on your windshield.

Dark windows make for dangerous driving, but potential thieves have no idea how much firepower might be inside. The first thing most visitors to Guatemala notice is the ubiquity of guns. Guns, guns everywhere. Armed guards are not only in front of banks but in office buildings, neighborhood pharmacies, and on coke trucks. Alfredo, a middle-class businessman I know, carries a gun daily for protection—to get past the metal detectors in office buildings he has a pocket full of decoys: a ring of keys, a metal lighter, and finally a knife, which satisfies all but the most vigilant guards and leaves him with his 9mm handgun.

For Alfredo and his peers, such weapons provide a sense of protection against the violence sweeping the streets. The daily newspapers are filled with gruesome tales of the slaughter, and everyone has their own stories to tell, every life having been touched.

The Guatemalan Paradox

Still, Guatemala does amazingly well considering the conditions. Violence notwithstanding, a number of social indicators have been improving since the late 1980s. As of this writing, in 2014, the country's economy looks stable for the short term; it is propped up with drug money, but that shows no sign of stopping anytime soon. The schools function—more or less—and average years of education are on the rise. Life expectancy is increasing. Incomes are growing slightly. Indeed, by the metrics the United Nations Development Programme uses, Guatemala is making significant gains in overall human development. But serious lingering inequality is not improving.

Here we find one of Guatemala's many paradoxes: the hope and inspiration that is as much a part of daily life as the violence and poverty. Diane Nelson describes the appeal of Omnilife, a direct-sales pyramid marketing company that peddles nutritional supplements. For some in Joyabaj, a community hit hard by the violence of the 1980s, Omnilife has become a source of hope and a means to get ahead. She write that "while apparently falling prey to Omnilife's sophisticated manipulation of indigeneity, consumer sparkle, and self-help affirmation, they don't seem any more conned by it than the rest of us caught in late capital's meshes of commodified subjectivization, military optics, and the boom in affective labor. They say they participate in Omnilife because they deeply enjoy helping people. They understand themselves to be supporting their communities, re-building networks torn brutally apart by the war, and finding a way to survive and to give their children a home, food, and education in a scary globalized economy, although perhaps not in a form they would have chosen under other circumstances" (Nelson 2013: 304).

We have seen the modest successes of smallholding coffee farmers, and Figure 8.1 shows the country slowly improving on a number of key development indicators, including education and health. The UNDP's Guatemala office has mapped the Human Development Index (HDI) by municipality and found a striking correlation with proximity to a major road (Figure 8.2).

Yet Guatemala still teeters on the brink. However, the scary future for Guatemala probably does not involve a full failure of the state. What is more likely, and worse, is that the quasi-narco-state status quo will be maintained. But such an arrangement actually puts the country's institutions on a downward spiral by further undermining the legitimacy of the government

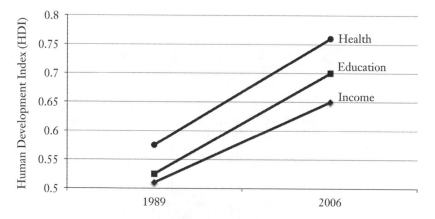

Figure 8.1: Guatemalan Human Development Index (HDI) by Component, 1989–2006
(based on data from Linda Asutrias and UNDP-Guatemala)

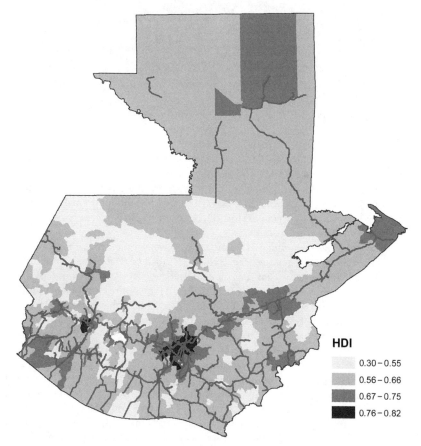

HDI

	0.30 – 0.55
	0.56 – 0.66
	0.67 – 0.75
	0.76 – 0.82

Figure 8.2: Roads and Human Development
(courtesy of UNDP-Guatemala and Gustavo Arriola Quan)

Plate 16: Transmetro Station

Riding buses in Guatemala City can be dangerous. In 2010 a bus driver was killed on average every other day, making made it the country's most deadly profession. If that is not bad enough, the gangs attacking buses for failure to pay the escalating extortion charges have turned to lobbing grenades at offending vehicles. As a target of extortion, buses are ideal. The drivers and their assistants carry wads of cash.

But things are changing, led by the introduction of the Transmetro, a bus rapid transit (BRT) system, in 2007. Often described as an above-ground subway, BRT is a bus system that runs on dedicated lanes and makes stops only at fixed stations. First developed in Curitiba, Brazil (1974), the idea took off with Bogota's advanced TransMilenio (2008). In Guatemala, the stations require that a prepaid card be swiped for entry (eliminating cash on the buses), and there are security personnel in the stations and on the buses. BRT systems are promoted for reducing traffic congestion and speeding bus travel—and in Guatemala they have the significant benefit of being safe. The Transmetro program has proven popular among commuters.

The mayor of my home city of Nashville is currently (2014) pushing forward a BRT system ("the AMP") for the city's main thoroughfare. Cleveland, Pittsburg, and a growing number of cities in the United States are turning to BRT as a feasible and affordable way to expand rapid transit without the subway infrastructure.

and of democratic representation and fostering a lack of trust that reverberates throughout society.

Some suggest that Guatemala needs a military coup. LAPOP's public opinion polls show a widespread distrust of democracy, and the military is one of the country's most trusted institutions. Even a number of my left-leaning Guatemalan friends, still leery of past human rights abuses, say the situation is dire enough now that they might support a coup to restore order. It is this level of discontent that fueled Perez Molina's election in 2011.

Others suggest a "Colombian solution," an all-out war on traffickers and gangs. Given Mexico's experience, and Guatemala's limited resources, it is not at all clear that Guatemala could win such a war. And mounting a major internal military action would be unconscionable given the brutality and human rights abuses of military action during the civil conflict.

A Colombian solution would also require more taxes. Guatemala currently has one of the lowest rates of tax collection (as a percentage of GNP) of any country in the hemisphere. The result is a vicious cycle in which the underfunding and ineffectiveness of many state services gives rise to corruption. Ineffectiveness and corruption are then given as the primary reasons people of means in Guatemala avoid taxes so aggressively. One affluent businessman told me, "I'd happily pay my share if it were going to be put to good use, but I don't want to feed the corruption."

And so it goes in Guatemala. The impressive improvements in social indicators will mean little if the country's corrosive violence continues apace. The greatest danger for Guatemala is a continuation of the current trajectory, with moderate improvements in health and education placating concerns about physical security and the lack of legal recourse against drug traffickers and organized criminals. This may well prove to be the model of a new, more sustainable form of narco-state.

Despite all of this, Guatemala's scores on LAPOP's insecurity index fell significantly between 2004 and 2010. I suspect that the decline reflects people's adaptation to a new norm, as crime rates have continued to increase significantly. Equally surprising, Guatemala scores relatively well on measures of subjective wellbeing. As in Germany, institutions matter, but fortunately for Guatemala, they are not *all* that matters.

Conclusion

The Good Life and Positive Anthropology

The Südstadt supermarkets in Hannover, Germany, are a world away from the coffee farms of Huehuetenango, Guatemala. It would seem to follow that the daily lives and mundane concerns of Maya farmers have little to do with those of middle-class European consumers, except, perhaps, to start the long supply chain that provisions an occasional pound of coffee. The preceding chapters have shown how different lives are in these two places. Poverty and insecurity make the stakes much higher in Guatemala: it is hard to compare worries over the corn crop and one's ability to put food on the table with concerns about the moral provenance of eggs. Nonetheless, intertwined with chasmic differences, we also find common concerns, themes in which visions of the good life overlap and converge.

For purposes of measurement, it is tempting to think about the good life exclusively in terms of income and material standards of living such as health and security. These are crucial elements of wellbeing in both Germany and Guatemala, even if they have different meanings in the two contexts. In Germany, average income is over eight times that in Guatemala, life expectancy is almost a decade longer, and the violent crime rate is so low as to be almost unimaginable from the Guatemalan perspective. Yet the felt impact of income deprivation is highly positional, experienced relative to the norms and averages of one's social milieu. Thus Germans' absolute affluence in comparison with that of Maya farmers means little for their quotidian happiness. Both rural Maya farmers and urban German consumers are concerned with having "enough"—they just differ greatly in what enough is. The same is true, although to a lesser extent, for health and security: both are highly valued, but what is considered adequate differs from place to place.

Philosophers and psychologists usually define "the good life" as one that people themselves value and find meaningful. The goal of this book has been to ground such an understanding in ethnographic detail, looking at the substance of what constitutes the good life in radically different places, among different peoples and cultures. The examples provided here have shown the importance of aspiration and agency—a sense of control over one's own destiny—for both Maya coffee farmers and German supermarket shoppers, even if what they aspire to differs in form and substance. Opportunity structures and institutional arrangements are just as important in German social democracy as they are in a Guatemala torn by narco-violence. Notions of dignity and fairness inform the choices involved in German ethical consumption just as they do in Maya economic calculations.

Throughout this book I have highlighted the importance of larger life purposes to conceptions of wellbeing, and the morally ambiguous role of markets as a means of achieving the good life. Although "moral" is often used in a normative, prescriptive sense, the conception of moral projects presented here is descriptive and ethnographic: we have looked at what people value, what matters deeply to them. We have seen how German moral discourses around "solidarity" frame both consumer choices and industrial relations. We have seen how the desires of Maya famers for a better life are tempered by the moral values of fairness and social obligation. The moral valences vary, but the sense of being part of a larger, meaningful project is central to wellbeing in both contexts.

Such grassroots visions of the good life can and should provide the basis for thinking about institutional arrangements. Following Andrew Sayer

(2004), we may see the study of moral economy as both a positive study and a normative one. That is to say, based on an empirical understanding of the values that already permeate economic relations, we can construct models and policies that nurture those values and cultivate common goods. For both theory and policy, it is important to look at exactly what the good life means in different places.

Seeing markets as social contrivances (from a positivist perspective) liberates us to structure them as we see fit (in a normative sense). An empirical understanding of human behavior as driven by social commitments and culturally contextualized moral projects as much as by materially maximizing self-interest opens the possibility for conceptualizing different sorts of collective ends and better futures. This points us toward Arjun Appadurai's (2013) ethics of possibility and opens the door for a positive anthropology.

First, let us review the measures of subjective wellbeing in Germany and Guatemala and then draw some conclusions about wellbeing more generally.

German and Guatemalan Happiness and Wellbeing

If we asked German egg buyers or Maya coffee farmers "Are you happy right now?" most would probably say yes. There would certainly be variations in expression: a common northern German working-class response to "How's it going?" is *Muss, ja*—roughly, "Well, it has to." Similarly, a Maya woman in Guatemala might respond to the same query by saying *Luchando por la vida*—"Just fighting for life." And an American might simply say "Fine." Still, by and large, on a daily basis, at any given moment, most folks in Germany, Guatemala, and around the world say they are reasonably happy.

A lot depends on the phrasing of the question. Indeed, we often get different answers if we ask not about hedonic happiness but about overall wellbeing and life satisfaction (that is, satisfaction with one's ability to construct a good life as one envisions it). Such life-satisfaction questions are sensitive to conceptions of the good life (*eudaemonia*) in a way that measures of hedonic happiness miss. Seen over a longer time horizon (the course of a life rather than just a moment's snapshot), we find significant differences in people's life satisfaction that correlate with income, social networks, and political structures (Kahneman and Deaton 2010; Di Tella and McCulloch 2008).

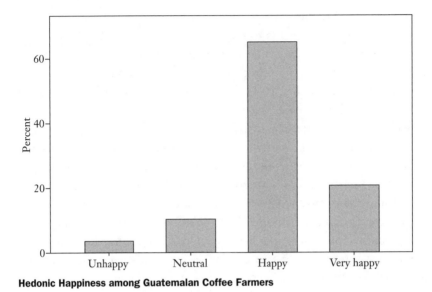

Hedonic Happiness among Guatemalan Coffee Farmers

This makes sense: we adjust our daily expectations to what is "reasonable" for us and our circumstances, and adapt our daily contentment and hedonic happiness to that norm. But when we look back (or forward) over the broad sweep of possibilities, at what was obtainable and what was not on our life path, we are struck more by what could have been. And the more income one has, the smaller the universe of what-could-have-beens.

Measuring eudaimonic wellbeing is difficult. Virtually all approaches use multidimensional measures combined into a single index, but the variables included and the weights given to each differ significantly. How much weight should be given to subjective wellbeing? To health or physical security? (The OECD website oecdbetterlifeindex.org/ allows you to choose your own variable combinations to compose an index that reflects your own vision of a better life.)

Indices of self-reported life-satisfaction are often used as a practical (from a measurement standpoint) indicator of overall wellbeing (see box). While revealing, such measures also have their drawbacks. Presumably, they condense many of the variables that contribute to wellbeing and the good life, but their culturally embedded nature (with differing norms and value systems) makes comparisons between countries complicated (see Jiménez 2007).

Surveys of Self-Reported Life Satisfaction

World Values Survey of Subjective Wellbeing (1995–2007)[a]

United States	rank: 16th
Guatemala	17th
Western Germany	35th
Eastern Germany	49th

Latin American Public Opinion Project, Life Satisfaction in the Americas (2010)[b]

Guatemala:	rank: 13th
United States:	18th

OECD Better Life Index (2010)[c]

United States: 70 percent satisfied or very satisfied with their lives; rank: 13th among OECD countries; 76 percent had mostly positive feelings on a given day

Germany: 56 percent satisfied or very satisfied with their lives; rank: 20th; 72 percent had mostly positive feelings on a given day

Gallup Wellbeing Index (2010)[d]

United States:	Thriving: 56 percent;
	Struggling: 41 percent;
	Suffering: 3 percent;
	hedonic happiness index: 71.9
Germany:	Thriving: 42 percent;
	Struggling: 54 percent;
	Suffering: 5 percent;
	hedonic happiness index: 77.4
Guatemala:	Thriving: 33 percent;
	Struggling: 49 percent;
	Suffering: 18 percent;
	hedonic happiness index: 74.6

World Database of Happiness Life Satisfaction Index (2009)[e]

United States	7.4 (out of 10); rank: 21st
Guatemala:	7.2; 25th
Germany:	7.1; 30th

Satisfaction with Life Index (2006)[f]

United States	rank: 23rd
Germany:	35th
Guatemala:	43rd

a. Subjective wellbeing here is composed of happiness and life satisfaction, equally weighted (see www.worldvaluessurvey.org).
b. See Corral 2011 and www.vanderbilt.edu/lapop.
c. See www.oecdbetterlifeindex.org.
d. See www.thrive.gallup.com.
e. Ruut Veenhoven's World Database of Happiness, www.worlddatabaseofhappiness.eur.nl.
f. Adrian White's (2007) metastudy results available at www.wikipedia.org/wiki/

From the rankings, the most glaring result is that the United States shows the highest levels of life satisfaction in all except the LAPOP index. Germany edges out Guatemala for second place, but the World Values Survey and the World Database of Happiness both rank Guatemala higher. Notice that the World Values Survey separates eastern and western Germany; this is significant because, although eastern German incomes increased dramatically after the 1991 reunification, wellbeing levels have not gone up. In 2006, unemployment was still above 18 percent, and in some areas it topped 25 percent. Germany's generous social benefits and massive investment in the former East Germany have raised incomes, but, as we have seen, wellbeing depends on more than just income.

The OECD, LAPOP, and Gallup measures of life evaluation and satisfaction come closest to the broad sense of wellbeing used in this book. They ask subjects to rate their overall life satisfaction on a ladder scale, with 0 being the worst and 10 being the best possible life one can imagine. The Gallup poll is the only one of these three that covers both Guatemala and Germany.

Gallup reports wellbeing in three categories that combine current life evaluation and where one expects to be in five years; the responses get at both subjective wellbeing and people's aspirations and desires. Those who placed themselves at 7 or higher on the 0–10 scale (and 8 or higher for where they expect to be in five years) are labeled "Thriving." Those who placed themselves at 5–7 (and no higher in five years) are labeled "Struggling"; people who ranked themselves lower are "Suffering."

By this measure, the United States scores much higher than Guatemala and significantly higher than Germany. Comparing Guatemala and Germany, we find significantly lower levels of "thriving" and higher levels of "suffering" in Guatemala. Given Germany's strong economy and wide social net, we might expect Germans to be more satisfied with their lives, and I think we can attribute a significant portion of the dissatisfaction captured in such quick surveys to a cultural propensity toward moderation and modesty in expressions of happiness. One might also argue that such expressed dissatisfaction has led to the social and legal infrastructure of German stakeholding and to the calls to impose ceilings on executive salaries and to turn off Blackberry servers after hours.

Qualitative Elements of Wellbeing

A lot gets lost in translating the lived experiences of wellbeing and deprivation (joy and pain, hopes and fears) into the numerical metrics of such rankings. From an anthropological perspective, what is lost is often what is most important: a subjective understanding of what people value, what their view of the good life is and could be, the pathways they see for realizing their aspirations. The subjective aspects of wellbeing are fundamentally different from the more objective and material factors (such as income and health), even if those material conditions partially determine the horizons of one's aspirations.

Looking at conceptions of wellbeing and the good life in Germany and Guatemala, I have focused on several key dimensions: aspiration and opportunity; dignity and fairness; and commitment to larger purposes.

ASPIRATION AND OPPORTUNITY

Aspiration, a hope for the future informed by ideas about the good life, gives direction to agency—the power to act and the sense of having control over one's own destiny. Both are core elements of wellbeing in affluent as well as economically deprived contexts. Appadurai (2013) describes this as the "capacity to aspire," which he links to a politics of hope.

In this book, we have looked at the moral aspirations of German supermarket shoppers and the ways that ethical consumption links such aspirations to the material act of buying a product. Their preferences, based on the sometimes competing ideals of social solidarity and personal thrift, and their visions of the future lead them to exert their purchasing power to promote certain sorts of market relations.

We have also seen how Maya famers envision a better future, aspiring to something more for themselves and their children. In rural Guatemala, such aspirations involve increasing incomes—to pay for children's education, to buy land to provide economic security, to expand the range of what is possible—but are no less morally driven.

Yet people's choices are not always their own. Even in free markets, the range of choice is dictated not only by supply and demand but also by manipulative marketing, corporate collusion (implicit and explicit), and government regulation. The range of morally provenanced eggs in the Südstadt Edeka supermarket has been carefully chosen by a supply chain more industrial and corporate than many consumers are likely to imagine. And the cheap eggs from chickens housed in battery cages are no longer available, that option having been eliminated by government regulation.

This is to say that aspiration—the will—is alone insufficient to effect change; it must also have a way, the space to operate among a range of substantive opportunities. This involves market access, freedom from discriminatory social norms, access to education and legal rights, and the full range of institutional structures that define what is possible for an individual. Michael Jackson (2011: 184) observes that "a sense of hope, a sense of a way out, is crucial to the ability to endure. Equally crucial is a sense that one is able to act on the situation that is acting on you—that one can give as much as one can get."

In Guatemala, the market for high-end, high-altitude coffees has opened up new opportunity structures for smallholding Maya farmers and provided a new source of hope. They have no illusions that the opportunities of this new market are perfect or even fair; and yet they overwhelmingly value the choice and the expanded range of agency in their quest to construct a better future. Aspiration, agency, and opportunity do not always go hand in hand. Amartya Sen has written about "unfreedom," the condition of a deficit of agency in relation to resources and opportunities, a particularly pernicious form of underdevelopment. But agency can also exceed opportunity structures, especially in this age of globalized communication and development efforts focused on empowerment, and result in "frustrated freedom."

DIGNITY AND FAIRNESS

One's sense of self and individual wellbeing is deeply linked to others, dependent on social relations and perceptions. In both Guatemala and Germany, this is closely related to notions of dignity and fairness. Exactly what constitutes dignity and fairness varies among cultures and individuals, but it is always a function of a positional value: "fair" is based on the relative position of A to B, and dignity is based on respect expressed through social relations.

In capitalist labor markets, work is a key vector of identity and dignity. For many, work offers the opportunity to cultivate the practical skills and knowledge embedded in local experience that give dignity to a practice. As for fairness, several studies have also shown that people are very sensitive to relative economic positions, meaning that value comes more from relative standing than from absolute levels (see Johansson-Steman, Carlsson, and Daruvala, 2002; and Solnick and Hemenway, 1998).

For German consumers, fairness and dignity are conceptually linked to notions of solidarity and a sense of social obligation. These ideas find expression in the large market for *öko* and Fair Trade products, with consumers interested in both frugality and fairness along the commodity chain. Notions of dignity and fair working conditions also come into play in the highly regulated German labor market. The German labor/capital system of co-determination is built around legal and institutional arrangements that give formal power to, and promote dignity among, workers. The apprentice system and the professionalism instilled in the training of waiters and store clerks as well as carpenters and cobblers, combined with relatively high wages, cultivates a sense of dignity across a wide range of jobs in Germany.

Guatemalan coffee farmers also place a high value on notions of fairness and dignity. In many Maya communities, powerful local social norms enforce notions of fairness and propriety. In playing the Ultimatum Game, Maya farmers were willing to pay a significant premium in order to punish others whom they perceived as playing unfairly. All the same, the coffee farmers in our sample demonstrated a tolerance for income inequality as long as those who do well are seen as treating others with fairness and generosity. Overwhelmingly, they saw a dignity in owning their own land, being able to sell export crops for a profit, and working to achieve a better life.

COMMITMENT TO LARGER PURPOSES

Life satisfaction also depends on doing something meaningful with one's life—having aspirations and hope, which imply the values with which we vest our very notions of self. While very different in particulars, having a purpose that is larger than one's immediate material self-interest provides a crucial sense of meaning for German shoppers and Maya farmers alike.

German consumers expressed ideals of solidarity and visions of the future through a concern with moral provenance and the ecological impact of their purchases. Maya coffee farmers aspired to a better future (*algo más*) for themselves and their communities, balancing a desire for self-interested advancement with prosocial and long-term commitments to a moral community. For both groups, commitment to a larger purpose converges with the capability to aspire, the opportunity structures to facilitate agency, and a social sense of dignity and fairness.

Certainly, material prosperity can provide the time, and ideological justification, for a greater range of higher pursuits. Yet, for all but the most severely deprived, lives are filled with numerous meaningful projects. These range from providing for the family to political and religious commitments to mastering a skill or craft. Characterizing meaningful projects as moral endeavors does not mean that we have to agree with their goals: religious extremism, joining a racial hate group, mastery of a video game—these are also practices of devotion to a larger purpose.

Management researchers have shown that, for employees, believing that they have a larger purpose (are part of something greater) is even more important for wellbeing than is income. Robert Frank (2010) finds that the more morally satisfying a job is, on average, the less it pays. We could see this finding as meaning either (1) that employers must pay a premium for employees who will compromise their morals, or (2) that some jobs provide compensation that satisfies in non-financial ways.

Gordon Mathews (2009: 167) writes of the importance of the Japanese term *ikigai*, meaning "that which most makes one's life worth living." Sometimes understood as "self-realization" and sometimes as "commitment to the group," *ikigai* captures the tension of private gain and public good that we found under different names in Guatemala and Germany.

. . .

Thus: we may see overall wellbeing and the good life as composed of several key domains. First, there are objective material conditions as measured by income, health, and physical security. Second, there are the more subjective factors of agency, fairness and dignity, and meaningful life projects. Third, there are the intermediary and more instrumental social elements of opportunity structures and family and community networks. In this system, we find a complex interrelationship between the elements of wellbeing, both subjective and objective. Given such mutual constitution—that wellbeing is born of myriad interactions—what is most important varies from circumstance to circumstance.

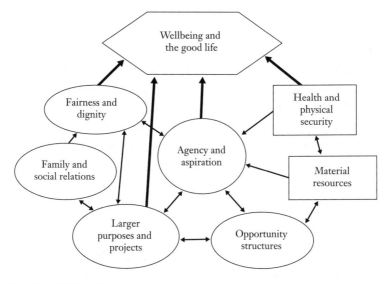

Components of Wellbeing

Markets as Technologies

The market constitutes a key venue through which people pursue the projects of their lives and their visions of the good life. Public discourse on both sides of the Atlantic tends to portray markets in binary moral terms.[1] Yet our German consumers and Guatemalan farmers do not see markets as inherently good or bad, but as mechanisms—tools, apparatuses—to achieve various ends. Markets can be subversively democratic (as in Adam Smith's vision), and they can fail us, morally and economically (as the financial crisis of 2008 reminds us). The market for organic produce or Fair Trade coffee is seen—at both ends of the commodity chain—as an imperfect yet important means of striving for a better life.

There is a great deal at stake in understanding social and moral dimensions of markets. A view of the market as somehow natural, or at least inevitable, makes it an attractive arbiter of value—and not just monetary value, but political and social and moral values as well. As Wolfgang Streeck (2009) has observed, we have become willing to disavow tough political decisions onto the market—the market's efficiency serving as a substitute ethical metric.[2]

Andrew Carnegie (1899) argued that markets exist outside of the moral realm—as simply brutal ways to make money, they can have no moral meaning. In contrast, our German shoppers and Maya farmers see markets as a venue in which to pursue moral projects. Following their view, we may understand markets as mechanisms: technologies that can and do fail, imperfect (though often efficient) means of achieving other ends. Seemingly free markets have long enforced a structural racism in Guatemala (Nelson 2009); they also have facilitated openings for Maya smallholding farmers. Seeing markets as social constructions, as means to ends that we decide upon politically, opens the possibility of new sorts of market restructuring and regulation, of adjusting the balance between private gain and public good.

Goals, Moral Projects, and Virtues

Economic decisions are informed by moral projects.* Moralities are aspirational, looking to the way things should be; they are internalized views of excellence and worth that are also improvised by individuals as they construct their identities and strive for the good life. This does not mean that every action is "moral"—selfishly hedonistic indulgence, for example, also plays a role. But, when viewed over the expanse of a lifetime, certain values tend to orient people's engagement with the world. These are to a degree idiosyncratic, although they are also culturally informed and reference salient social norms.

We may discuss these aspirations in terms of virtues and behaviors that are linked to aspects of personhood and its social production. Virtues orient (without determining) the aspirational process of coming to identify oneself in a certain way. A conception of virtues thus aids in understanding the cooperative pursuit of common goals that characterizes moral projects. Aristotle found virtues in the happy medium, eschewing extremes for the balance of courage, temperance, liberality, magnificence, good temper, friendliness, modesty, and so on. The Aristotelian good life is brought about by virtuous living, with virtue (*arete*) understood as human excellence.[3]

---

* Anthropologists would agree with economists that we all pursue goals, although anthropologists are more concerned with the variability of ends. Such goals may be rationally (i.e., most efficiently) pursued from an economic perspective, but not necessarily. There are systematic psychological "distortions" of our ability to make rational decisions (e.g., overvaluing the present and discounting the future), social impediments to rationality (such as in access to information), and cultural and moral inflections of rationality.

Alasdair MacIntyre (1984) argues that virtue is excellence within a practice whose satisfaction is internal to that practice. This is in contrast to activity driven by "external goods," the fame and fortune that may or may not come from such excellence. This perspective considers it much more fulfilling to hang one's aspirational fortunes on internal goods than on external rewards. MacIntyre acknowledges that institutions are necessary to facilitate practices but also that institutions are always in danger of becoming corrupted, subordinating the pursuit of internal goods to that for external goods.[4]

We can see MacIntyrian virtue at work in German forms of stakeholding, especially in the greater professional dignity associated with a wide range of blue-collar trades. Similarly, Guatemalan coffee farmers take pride in the quality of their coffees and the dignity their hard work commands.

John Ruskin (1862) was also concerned with the virtues inherent in practices (as professions). Noting that society values the soldier over the merchant, Ruskin asserts that "this is right." He writes that what is really worth working for is worth dying for. He enumerates the professions of soldier, pastor, physician, lawyer, and merchant: "And the duty of all of these men is, on due occasion, to die for [their calling]. The Soldier, rather than leave his post in battle. The Physician, rather than leave his post in plague. The Pastor, rather than teach Falsehood. The lawyer, rather than countenance Injustice. The Merchant—what is his 'due occasion' of death?"

Ruskin postulates that wealth can be good or bad. The value of wealth "depends on the moral sign attached to it, just as sternly as that of a mathematical quantity depends on the algebraic sign attached to it." Wealth accumulated from a just moral source is real wealth; ill-gotten gains are "illth." Ruskin was thinking of moral absolutes, but his idea of illth fits with our culturally contextualized understanding: from BMW employee concerns with executive compensation to Maya farmers' suspicions of those who do too well. In both cases, cultural norms of fairness and dignity—what is just—define the parameters of illth.

Practical Wisdom and Institutions

Barry Schwartz and Kenneth Sharpe in their (2010) *Practical Wisdom* make a strong case for revaluing the Aristotelian virtue of *phronesis*, or practical wisdom. They explain that practical wisdom is not a list of rules but a state of mind, a perspective built through experience. Elsewhere, Schwartz writes, "It is distressing that modern social trends are conspiring to make wisdom ever more difficult to cultivate" by "substituting financial incentives for motivation to do the right thing."[5] He concludes that "market incentives and bureaucratic rules may be an appropriate short-term response to greedy doctors or unimaginative teachers, but in the long term, they only make doctors greedier and teachers less imaginative."

Lynn Stout (2010) argues in *Cultivating Conscience* that financial incentives often undermine the very moral basis of work and vocation in a way that is both inefficient and contributes to dissatisfaction. We all know that specific rules can have unintended consequences, but it is surprising how rules themselves can sometimes undermine the common good they are meant to ensure. Robert Frank (2011) shows how such incentive structures fuel the arms race for positional goods in ways that heighten inequality and erode the social bonds that provide the grounding for a common morality.

Institutional frameworks also condition the expression of moral positions. Caitlin Zaloom's study of commodity traders shows that the market itself is seen as an ethical arbiter, punishing and disciplining those who exceed its mandates: "The market is the [Chicago Board of Trade] traders' moral authority . . . it is both the single truth and the arbiter of a trader's work" (2006: 139). This is very different from artisanal morality of work, or indeed for most professions outside of the financial industry. Richard Sennett's (2008) study of skilled work that requires years of training and practice focuses on the intrinsic rewards that come with such practices (see also Kondo's (1990) look at the construction of identity and craft in a Japanese chocolate factory). In contrast, Robert Jackall (1988) finds that company bureaucracies instill their own ethics that are different from the outside-of-work moral positions of executives, and that within this milieu self-interested opportunism becomes habituated through repeated social interaction; and Michael Brown (2010) shows how this sort of bureaucratic regime shapes aspirations and moral projects.

Toward a Positive Anthropology

Cultural anthropology has long, and rightly, prided itself on its critical stance, the study of exceptions and hidden commonalities that disrupt dominant conceptions of the world, making sure that social constructions are not misconstrued as being natural or predetermined. I suggest that now we might more fully embrace the constructive possibilities of a positive anthropology.[6] To fully enter into public discourse, to exert the influence that most of us think we should have, it will be necessary to offer answers as well as pose critical questions. Anthropologists shy away from prescriptive stances for good reasons. Ethnography, in building up knowledge through a dialectical engagement with individuals and communities, continually counters the sorts of generalizations that answering the big questions of public discourse implies: the complexity we observe through the microscopic ethnographic lens resists the essentializing broad strokes required for much punditry. John Comaroff (2010) observes that over the past thirty years anthropology has increasingly retreated to the local, so denying its relevance to broad political, economic, and cultural debates.

And yet. And yet. Perhaps we could, even should, try to offer positive alternatives, contextualized in a way that avoids moral judgment—non-prescriptive, non-definitive options that might inspire other ways of looking at issues, an anthropology of best practices. Arjun Appadurai (2013: 299–300) calls on us to advocate an "ethics of possibility" that is "grounded in the view that a genuinely democratic politics cannot be based on the avalanche of numbers—about population, poverty, profit, and predation—that threaten to kill all street-level optimism about life and the world. Rather it must build on an ethics of possibility, which can offer a more inclusive platform for improving the planetary quality of life and can accommodate a plurality of visions of the good life."

Such an anthropology offers a positive complement to our critical stance. In addition to documenting structural inequalities, it would look at cultural norms and social structures that seem to work well and from which lessons could be extrapolated (and sometimes even more or less directly adopted). This could be something as concrete as a technique to induce more polite driving (as has worked in Bogota) or something as ethereally cultural as attitudes toward "fairness" (which we looked at in the cases of Germany and Guatemala).

Documenting best practices brings up the prickly question of what "better" is, but a positive anthropology could be essentially ecumenical (taking what folks involved in a particular practice consider better, and this might be more or less transferable to other practices and contexts). It may also be the case that we could make claims based on understanding collective desires about what "better" for our own contexts and society could be.

A positive anthropology would contribute more readily to public discourses about what the good life should look like, documenting cultural norms, social structures, and institutional arrangements that seem to promote wellbeing in their specific contexts. These could form a vast social toolkit, not unlike the Chicago Boys' more parsimonious market liberalization techniques for spurring economic growth. Critique would continue to be central to the enterprise, but complemented by attention to positive alternatives as well. Keith Hart, Jean-Louis Laville, and Antonio Cattani (2010) provide an example of what this might look like in their review of varieties of markets and economies and call for a new "human economics." There is already a form of positive economics in the capabilities approach to development studies and in the behavioral approach to policy nudges.

The policies of *buen vivir* in Latin America offer another example. Based on the Kichwa concept of *sumak kawsay*, *buen vivir* encompasses the broad, multidimensional understanding of wellbeing expounded in this book with a particular emphasis on environmental rights, dignity, and community cohesion. While *buen vivir* indexes a range of heterogeneous positions, it has provided a broad ethical basis for industrial policy and social programs in Bolivia and Ecuador (Gudynas 2011). Their consistency and efficacy have been critiqued, but *buen vivir* policies have managed to change the terms of debate over social goods and the good life in these two countries.[7]

If we take "the good life" (as variously and broadly conceived) as our shared end, it allows us to look at the economy and markets in new ways. An economist would most likely say that we have to give the most weight to what people actually do—that this "revealed" preference is the true preference. And yet, as I have argued, we should also take seriously stated preferences, how people say they would like things to be. Stated preferences may be more attuned to overall life satisfaction, in comparison with revealed preferences. If this is the case, it sheds new light on the role of smart regulations. It suggests that we sometimes need structure and flexible constraints to be our best (Thaler and Sunstein 2008; Frank 2011), and that there are ways we can structure the economy and our lives to best promote the common good.[8]

. . .

Ethnography is always comparative, if only implicitly so. We ethnographers focus on differences or surprising similarities between the people we study and our own culture. Implicit, and sometimes explicit, in such comparisons is a critique of our own culture, the demonstration of other possibilities found in the ways "they" do things. My argument is that there are important lessons to be learned from the German and Guatemalan cases: lessons for theories of economic behavior, moral values, and cultural norms, but also more practical lessons to help us rethink our own economic relations, variety of capitalism, and moral obligations in the marketplace. This is not to say that Germans or Guatemalans do things better (or worse) than others; it is clearly not that simple. But the German and Guatemalan examples do confront us with other possibilities (other ways of organizing markets, for example) and forces us to recognize the contrivance of what seems so natural to us as cultural insiders. And this contributes to a needed political discourse of possibilities grounded in what Charles Taylor (2005) terms "philosophical anthropology."

Although rapidly changing, German political economic institutions of co-determination support a particular form of stakeholding that balances individual self-interests with collective goods. Such stakeholding can be seen not only in national policy but also in on-the-ground consumer behavior. Our Hannover sample shows that, across income groups, consumers put a high value on the moral provenance of goods and the ways these contribute to a common good. I have shown how values are called upon to justify consumer decisions in a process as much moral and emotional as it is calculatingly rational. Such stakeholding constitutes a form of imaged (and usually unarticulated) moral community that informs the ways that (ever-contingent) identities emerge from the ongoing process of identification. This process of identification is aspirational and oriented around recognized moral virtues (which may or may not be tied to a polity or a profession). Widely held German notions of stakeholding create imagined moral communities in which sympathy and commitment balance narrow self-interest; the culture and practice of German stakeholding conditions and reinforces institutional structures.

Our look at the desires and aspirations of Maya coffee farmers adds an ethnographic and cultural dimension to the capabilities approach to human development. In this view, material conditions are simply a means toward an end: that the true goal of development should be the freedom of people to live lives that they themselves value. Development thus depends on the ability to envision and pursue goals that people value (agency) and real opportunities to achieve these goals (including material resources and opportunity structures). In our Guatemalan case, a number of external factors (including changing consumer tastes, established market relations, trends toward direct sourcing) have created a particular opportunity structure in the form of the coffee market. The desires of smallholding coffee farmers engage this imperfect structure (filled with trade-offs and its own set of incentives) in pursuit of the better life that they envision from their current circumstances.

In both cases, life projects were driven by certain values and a desire to live the good life. In some ways, then, the two populations are not so different: the Germans are living in an affluent market economy trying to become better people and live better lives; the Guatemalans are living in a quasi-narco-state trying to become better people and live better lives. These folks improvise and adapt and sometimes act against their own "better judgment" and their own values. And their values can well include improving their own financial situation and material circumstances. We may all want to be better off (according to that elusively relative standard), but we also want to be part of larger, meaningful projects.

It takes more than income to produce wellbeing, and policy makers would do well to consider the positive findings of anthropology and on-the-ground visions of the good life in working toward the ends for which we all labor.

Notes

1. This endeavor points us toward what Keith Hart, Jean-Louis Laville, and Antonio David Cattani (2010) call *The Human Economy*. See also Melania Calestani (2013) on the value of ethnography in studying wellbeing and Thin (2012) on policy implications. Gordon Mathews and Carolina Izquerdo (2009) present a useful survey of wellbeing across cultures and reach a number of conclusions for which I find support in the present study. Alberto Corsín Jiménez (2007) presents several insightful anthropological approaches to wellbeing, ethics, and the political imagination. Robert and Edward Skidelsky (2012) make a compelling case for revaluing the good life while reclaiming economics' roots as a moral science.

2. There is a growing body of social psychology research on these types of happiness; for example, see Waterman, Schwartz, and Conti 2006; Kahneman, Diener, and Schwartz 2003.

3. My research and this formulation are deeply influenced by the capabilities approach of Amartya Sen (1999), Sabina Alkire (2002), and James Foster (Alkire and Foster 2009). I should also note that the World Bank project *Voices of the Poor* adopts a similar perspective, with remarkable results for development policy (see Narayan 2000).

4. Although not in so many words, anthropologists have long observed this dynamic at play. Arjun Appadurai (1996, 2004) calls attention to the motivational force of hopes and dreams, and Melania Calestani (2013) assesses the role of faith and aspiration in the context of development projects. James Ferguson (1999) describes the tragedy of unrequited aspirations fed by the hope of development, and Anna Tsing (2004) looks at the frictions produced between unequal realities and universalizing aspirations of prosperity, knowledge, and freedom. Tania Li (2007) and Neil Thin (2012) both point to the ways aspirations and desires are managed and disciplined, channeling agency in particular directions. Jens Beckert (2011) writes of the power of daydreams and imaginations of the future in the construction of consumer identities, and Peter Benson and I (2006) have made a similar argument for the role of understanding desire in producer identities (see also Moore 2011).

5. Bart Victor coined the term "frustrated freedom," and I review our joint research on the topic in Chapter 6.

6. Indeed, many studies have shown that family, education, social ties, and other factors are all closely related to life satisfaction (Layard 2005; Gilbert 2006; Veenhoven 2000; Graham 2011; Thin 2012). Alan Krueger (2005: 14) observes that "worker satisfaction depends at least as much on social aspects of work, and having a sense of meaning and interest in work, as it does on material rewards." Dolan, White, and Peasgood (2008) find that strong corollaries of subjective wellbeing include health, meaningful employment, degree of social contact, and having a spouse or partner. Carik Graham and Eduardo Lora (2009) find that friends and family matter more to the happiness of the poor in Latin America, while work and health matter more to the wealthy (see also Mathews and Izquierdo 2009).

7. Margarita Corral (working with the Vanderbilt Latin American Opinion Project) reports on a large-scale comparative study of life satisfaction across Latin America. She finds a close association between national economic development (as reflected in income) and evaluations of overall life satisfaction (http://www.vanderbilt.edu/lapop/insights/I0858en.pdf).

8. Easterlin's new research tracks rising Chinese middle-class individuals over many years and finds no significant increase in wellbeing as income levels rise.

9. See Laidlaw 2002 for a more nuanced analysis of ethics, agency and freedom.

10. References to Aristotle here are to his *Nicomachean Ethics* (circa 350 BCE) as translated by W. D. Ross and available at http://classics.mit.edu/Aristotle/nicomachaen.html.

11. Alberto Corsín Jiménez (2007: 180) observes that the study of wellbeing "throws into relief how difficult it is to talk about social life and human virtues simultaneously."

12. John Kenneth Galbraith (1998 [1958]: 215) presciently observed, "In the United States, as in other western countries, we have for long had a respected secular priesthood whose function it has been to rise above questions of religious ethics, kindness and compassion and show how these might have to be sacrificed on the altar of the greater good. That larger good, invariably, was more efficient production." As Galbraith makes clear, this is not just a matter of economics but one of morality (see also Fourcade and Healy 2007: 304; Carrier 1997; Fullbrook 2004; Stiglitz 1993).

13. Behavioral economics is working to redefine the limits of rationality, and document systematic "biases" that subvert rationality (see work by Thaler 1992; Ariely 2008; and others) and a growing group of academic economists works on issues that touch on the role of cultural values and moral concerns. For example, George Akerlof examines the ways identity affects commitment and performance within organizations (see Akerlof and Kranton 2005). Robert Frank (1988 and elsewhere) documents how economic decisions are informed by a sense of identity and narrative life history. Daniel Kahneman and Richard Thaler (1991) champion experimental methods and behavioral observation to show how psychology influences

rationality. And this list goes on. On the margins of the discipline is a vibrant heterodox economics movement and a vocal minority calling for a "post-autistic" approach (to use the 2000 rallying cry of rebellious French students) that moves beyond the "uncontrolled use" of mathematics and better engages with empirical realities (see www.paecon.net).

14. The discovery of mirror neurons that induce feelings of sympathy and empathy for others (Rizzolatti and Sinigaglia 2008) sheds new light on Smith's hypothesis regarding human nature.

15. Even neoclassical economics inevitably introduces moral premises into its models and explanations; the methodological individualism of rational choice theory is itself quite parochial and moralistic (McCloskey 1998: 47). In fact, the free-market model is itself a kind of morality that embodies assumptions about who deserves what and what kinds of citizenship are valuable to the national product and national future. For all its claims to moral agnosticism, such extreme economistic thinking has itself become a form of theology (Nelson 2001), laden with unchecked cultural assumptions and confident about making the world in its own secular image and converting fables about behavior's natural causes into everyday common sense.

16. See Hart and Hann 2011; Graeber 2001; Goldin 2009. Indeed, the idea of intentionally looking at economic issues through the lens of moral considerations goes back to the foundations of modern economics. Far from promoting an everyone-for-themselves ethos, Adam Smith was a virtue theorist who was keenly interested in questions of justice and regarded moral considerations as a cornerstone of political economy; he was aware of the potentially corrosive effects of the market on solidarity and community (see also Bellah et al. 1992; Gudeman 2008).

17. See Aspers and Beckert 2011; Colloredo-Mansfeld 1999. Monica DeHart (2010) reminds us that moral frameworks do not emerge from some romantic consensus but are worked out through often conflictual practice (see also Lucero 2008). Preference bundles can capture moral preferences (if morals are what matter most to people, then this is captured in preferences). Kedron Thomas (2012) shows how this plays out in different moral conceptions of intellectual property rights among small-scale capitalist Maya garment producers. As these studies show, individual morality and the collective best interest are not always aligned, giving rise to collective action issues and free-rider problems.

CHAPTER ONE: VALUES AND PRICES

1. Germany registers the religion of taxpayers and collects church tithes with regular income taxes; to avoid paying, one may unregister or refuse to register a religion. Unregistering has become increasingly popular, provoking occasional calls to disallow church marriages between unregistered couples. A 2002 Pew Research Institute survey found that only 32 percent of Germans think it is necessary to believe in God to be moral and have good values.

2. They were designed by the artist Gunter Demnig.

3. Our sampling strategy was simply to ask every sixteenth passerby to consent to an interview, with counting starting at the end of the previous interview or rejection of the request (approximately 35 percent refused).

4. Some previous market surveys in Germany have found that low prices are the most important factor for consumers; in one GfK report 50 percent of their sample reported that price was more important than any other consideration (GfK 2005).

5. It is interesting to compare such intense skepticism toward nationalism tempered by the obligations of a secular social contract between residents of the former East and those in the West (see Berdahl 1999; Borneman 1992).

6. Positive and negative externalities occur when an exchange between two parties affects a third party that is not directly involved in the exchange.

7. The Fair Trade market certainly has its own set of problems, from being a marketing diversion for some to the differential distributions of profits resulting from the moral premiums consumers pay. My concern here is not with the objective qualities of Fair Trade but with consumer perceptions of Fair Trade and its symbolic role in representing economically just relations of production.

CHAPTER TWO: WORD, DEED, AND PREFERENCES

1. National sales figures are from the GfK-Haushaltpanel; see www.animal -health-online.de/lme/2009/09/10/mehr-eier-im-juli-gekauft/3788/.

2. Although Easterlin (2001), Layard (2005), and others have pointed out that income above a certain level does not seem to affect hedonic happiness proportionately, new research does show that income plays a significant role in overall life satisfaction (see Kahneman and Deaton 2010).

3. This also speaks to the notion of "aspirations" as a sort of capability (in the Amartya Sen sense) as captured by Arjun Appadurai (2004) and Debraj Ray (2006). Jens Beckert (2010) writes about the power of daydreams and imaginations of the future in the construction of consumer identities, and elsewhere Edward F. Fischer and Peter Benson (2006) made a similar argument for the role of understanding desire in producer identities.

Dominic Boyer (2005: 17) presents this as a tension between *Geist* (spirit) and *System*, between creative subjectivity and external forms: "dialectical social knowledge emerges in the tension between the knowing subject and the compromising forces and conditions of epistemic context." For our present purposes, we may map such a tension onto the dialectic engagement of individual agency and institutional structures.

Such tensions also emerge from German notions of *Bildung*. *Bildung* may be translated as "education" or "formation" but connotes the realization of potential, of self-formation, of making oneself into an image (*Bild*) of how one should be. This process of becoming, in the Hegelian tradition, involves an individual's realization from within being writ large in the world (see Boyer 2005). In a case study of Berlin police officers, Andreas Glaeser (2000) observes the dialectic construction of the self through interactions with others (and others' projections), the way individuals strive to be the sort of person they want to be and how this is informed by the sort of person others may want one to be. (Glaeser also points out the value placed on sincerity and authenticity in changing conceptions and presentations of the self.)

CHAPTER THREE: MORAL PROVENANCE AND LARGER PURPOSES

1. From *The Eighteenth Brumaire of Louis Bonaparte*: "Men make their own history, but they do not make it as they please; they do not make it under self-selected circumstances, but under circumstances existing already, given and transmitted from the past. The tradition of all dead generations weighs like a nightmare on the brains of the living." Marx's works are all in the public domain and available online; I have used the versions in the Marx/Engels Archive at www.marxists.org.

2. Ara Norenzayan and Azim Shariff (2006) report on experiments in which subjects play the "dictator game" (unilaterally deciding how an amount of money should be split with another player); those primed with religious or civic words tend to be much more generous in their offers to others. In this light, it seems likely that invoking an idea of the commons might also act to prompt generosity (on the philanthropic side) or a willingness to pay a premium for externalities that benefit "the commons" (on the market side). The discourses about "solidarity" among the German sample reflected the same tendencies.

3. Quotes from Adam Smith's *Wealth of Nations* come from the open version available online at http://en.wikisource.org/wiki/The_Wealth_of_Nations.

4. Quotes from Marx's (1887) *Capital* come from the open source version available online at https://www.marxists.org/archive/marx/works/1867-c1/.

CHAPTER FOUR: SOLIDARITY, DIGNITY, AND OPPORTUNITY

1. My discussion here relies heavily on the work of Wolfgang Streeck (1997, 2009), Kathleen Thelen (2001, 2004), and Lowell Turner (1998). I focus on the mid-2000s, the period of my fieldwork, but it is important to keep in mind that this snapshot developed out of a particular history; the Germans I write about are not naturally either morally social or socially moral. Bismarckian anticipations of the social market attempted to co-opt class dissent and unrest; the postwar manifestations were reactions to the horrors the previous system produced; and then there is the issue of East German socialism and the efforts to reunify after 1991. Sartre noted (as Peter Mancina pointed out to me) that moralities all have histories, and that a foul smell always accompanies their genesis.

2. Dyson and Padgett (1995: 116) define the Rhineland model of capitalism as a coordinated, managed, and stakeholder-driven system in which the state promotes and mandates "non-market cooperation in areas like finance, labor markets, and welfare, which supported the efficient, long-term functioning of the market economy." Strong employer and labor associations are balanced by a strong central

bank; corporate government relies on principles of co-determination; and the economy is technology driven and export-oriented. Busch (2005: 132) stresses the key
element of cooperation and the strong role of associations. He characterizes Rhenish capitalism as a feedback system anchored in bank-oriented corporate finance,
cooperative industrial relations, intertwined firm relations, and a highly specialized
training system.

3. Individual taxes are likewise relatively high. Under Gerhard Schröder, the top
income tax rate fell from 51 percent to 42 percent, but by 2008 it had gone back up
to 45 percent. The value-added tax (VAT) is 16 percent; unemployment insurance
is 6.5 percent (half paid by employers), and social insurance is up to 20 percent;
television and radio tax is €17/month; the list of taxes is long, including a temporary
(but by now long-standing) "solidarity" tax to support development in the former
East Germany. The government burden has grown dramatically since reunification,
which has cost upwards of €1 trillion a year. The high tax burden is routinely criti-
cized by German business and the conservative Christian Democratic Union (CDU)
for hindering Germany's competitiveness in global labor markets. The issue of Turkish guest workers—and the issue of immigration as a whole—invokes the darker side
of solidarity and stakeholding, namely that it often involves some form of exclusion,
as seen most dramatically in the rise of a radical right and neo-Nazi organizations
(especially in the former East).

4. Responding to the weakening of social ties following unification and the rise
of the "Turkish question," the government instituted a media campaign in 2005 to
stir up stakeholding. Ads declaring *"Du bist Deutschland!"* (You are Germany!) portrayed a wide range of German citizens today, seeking to bolster a sense of common
purpose among them. The potential payoffs are great, because such sentiment not
only can produce cultural change but can minimize free-loading, diminish a sense of
entitlement (which is a product of the success of the past functioning of the stakeholding system), and otherwise reduce material strains on the system.

5. I began my German research with the intention of studying works councils at
Volkswagen. VW had offered access for the study, but just as I was about to begin in
late 2005, a scandal erupted around the works councils, closing access for me.

CHAPTER FIVE: PROVENANCE AND VALUES

1. The coffee was purchased by YT Infinite, which does business as Brian's Coffee (see www.brianscoffee.com).

2. The objective qualities of coffee are, of course, learned. I have long liked coffee, and the PJs coffeeshop in New Orleans introduced me to specialty coffees in the
early 1990s. But it is really only since I have read several books on the subject and
taken a coffee cupping course that I learned to (crudely) make the distinctions that
are recognized by the experts, the tasters whose judgment determines price. See also
Weissman 2008; Bourdieu 1984.

3. Native to East Africa, coffee was first consumed and traded on a large scale

in the Middle East in the 15th and 16th centuries; the first coffee shop opened in Constantinople in 1554 (Luttinger and Dicum 2006). By the 17th century, coffee consumption had spread to Europe, and was followed by an expansion of coffee production to the European colonies by the 18th century. Indeed, production rose hand in hand with the rise of slave labor and plantations in the Caribbean Antilles. By 1788, St. Domingue (Haiti) supplied half of the world's coffee (Pendergrast 2010).

4. For comparison, see Sick 1999 and Smith 2009 on the different market shifts in Costa Rica and Panama.

5. Anacafé is a member of CACIF, the country's agricultural and industrial chamber of commerce; Guatemalan insiders often use "CACIF" as shorthand for oligarchical interests.

6. Tatiana Paz, Luis Velásquez, Carlos Pérez-Brito, Ixchel Espantzay, Pakal B'alam, and Felipe Girón helped develop the survey questions; Paz and Velásquez finalized the survey design and a training module; and Paz, Velásquez, Espantzay, B'alam, and Girón administered the surveys in the field with the assistance of Ana Liggia Samayoa, Ixkik Zapil, María Fernanda Villagrán, Elizabeth Pellecer, and Tere Aguilar.

7. Because of the nature of the database used, virtually all producers we interviewed had had previous contact with Anacafé, many having attended technical assistance workshops.

8. For our purposes, the Western Highlands include the departments of Huehuetenango, Alta Verapaz, El Quiché, Quetzaltenango, Sololá, and Suchitepéquez; the Central/Eastern Highlands include Sacatepéquez, Guatemala, Santa Rosa, Jalapa, Chiquimula, and Zacapa.

9. There is an often-noted fundamental paradox of Fair Trade: efforts to reform markets toward social justice end; but working through and depending on those same markets continues (Jaffee 2007; Reichman 2011; Lyon 2011; Carrier 2010).

CHAPTER SIX: AGENCY, OPPORTUNITY, AND FRUSTRATED FREEDOM

1. Carol Graham also looks at the paradox of "happy peasants and frustrated achievers." Her happy peasants fall into a category that Sen cautions is a misleading form of adaptation to circumstances. Graham suggests that this results from one possible adaptation to poverty: privileging hedonic happiness over life satisfaction. Indeed, there is broad agreement that "the absence of agency severely limits well-being, broadly defined as the capacity to lead a fulfilling life, even if respondents who lack agency report being happy" (Graham 2011: 31).

CHAPTER SEVEN: EXPERIMENTS IN FAIRNESS AND DIGNITY

1. Monica DeHart (2010) presents a fascinating case in which Maya cultural politics and development economics converge and diverge.

CHAPTER EIGHT: NARCO-VIOLENCE, SECURITY, AND
DEVELOPMENT

1. See Latin American Public Opinion Project, Vanderbilt University (www.van
derbilt.edu/lapop/).

2. See Kevin O'Neill's (2010) *City of God* for more on the many ways evangelical
Christianity is shaping Guatemalan politics and urban culture.

CONCLUSION: THE GOOD LIFE AND POSITIVE ANTHROPOLOGY

1. In academic and well as popular discourse, the market itself is often portrayed
as either morally beneficial or detrimental. Adam Smith's passing mention of the
invisible hand provides the poetic basis for the argument that the market is virtuous and harmonious as a whole, no matter how selfish its constituent parts may be.
For example, market forces can discourage racism, sexism, and other "non-rational"
behaviors. The market can also foster cooperation: anonymous market transactions
may simply (if paradoxically) encourage trust and cooperation, as Jean Ensminger
(2004) and others (Henrich et al. 2004) have found. Perhaps humans have evolved
to cooperate (Silk 2005), have empathy (de Waal 2009), or to punish those who do
not cooperate (Boyd, Gintis, Bowles, and Richerson 2003). Or perhaps markets can
do all of these things.

We must take care to be attuned to pressing questions such as how to recon-
cile any virtues inherent in the market with the failures of neoliberal policies in
places like Zambia (Ferguson 1999); with how the cultural space opened up through
global capitalism squares with the hegemonic rise of transnational corporate structures and the cultural forms they proliferate (Friedman 1994); and with how the
machinery of the global pharmaceutical industry touches down in the poor, marginalized corners of the globe (Biehl 2006).

2. Deirdre McCloskey (1998, 2002) critiques the scientific aspirations of econometrics and the strategic use of numbers to purify the messiness of economic behavior. This brand of knowledge production might be seen as having a "performative"
rather than simply a documentary function. In claiming simply to describe how the
world works, science can also have a "looping" effect, yielding in the empirical world
the very modes of thought and action that are said to simply be neutral, observable
facts (Hacking 2000; Mitchell 2005).

Market models based on neo-classical economic theory have had an enormous influence in public discourse and technocratic politics. From an academic and theoretical
perspective, it makes sense for economists to simplify the world—focusing on revealed
preferences, for example—in order to model them. But translating this intellectual
endeavor into policy and practice is fraught with problems, not the least of which are
the human actors, who are predictably less predictable than their abstract academic
representations. In such models, markets are largely considered to be something apart
from society, a quasi-natural ecosystem with its own rules and Darwinian system of
rewards and punishments, ever in dynamic motion toward an elusive equilibrium.

The economics profession's assumption that individuals pursue utility maximization and their own self-interest has the effect of condoning that behavior as natural, and thus encouraging (and not just describing) it (see also Timothy Mitchell's [2005] argument regarding economics and "how a discipline makes its world"). Evidence for this exists in experiments that gauge the rationality and self-interest of students in different fields. Economics students tend to cooperate less with each other or with scholars from other disciplines and more aggressively pursue immediate self-interested maximization (Carter and Irons 1991; Frank, Gilovich, and Regan 1993; Marwell and Ames 1981).

In a free-market paradigm, competition is seen as the cure for most ills. In dominant models of price theory and following the efficient-market hypothesis (see Fama 1970; Samuelson 1965), the rationality of utility maximization is most often described in terms of monetary returns from a particular transaction, leaving little room for moral considerations, the multiple values that might be at stake in a given exchange, and enduring links between behaviors and identity formation.

While possessing the virtue of parsimony, this view, with its laser focus on utility maximization, misses something fundamental in explaining economic behavior. Common sense tells us as much. (I am hesitant to invoke common sense, given Keynes's observation that those who do are usually "slaves of some defunct economist"; but I do so not to deny the importance of theory but to point to the dangers of behavioral theories that become too removed from the behavior they seek to describe.) Any sensible person would balk at accepting the assumptions about humans as rational maximizers that one is asked to accept in introductory economics classes; but of course, what seems like a crazy leap of faith in the first semester of Econ 101 becomes, after a few short semesters, conventional wisdom, too fundamental and axiomatic to be questioned. Donald Gillies (2004) points out that Paul Samuelson's hugely influential textbook *Economics* (1948, one of the best-selling textbooks of all time) does not include a single example using real-world data.

Competition drives down prices and drives up quality; it rewards the best players and punishes the bad actors; it harnesses self-interest to produce the most efficient outcomes for all. In theory, at least. But the German examples raise interesting questions: What are the limits of competition in producing beneficial social outcomes? Are the higher prices that reduced competition allows an acceptable price to pay for the social goods of having neighborhood bookstores, more leisure time, and so on? Such questions recall the paradox of "Hotelling's duopoly" (Hotelling 1929). Hotelling's Main Street example is most often retold as a tale of two ice-cream vendors on a delimited one-mile stretch of beach with the entrance one half-mile from each end; for optimal consumer satisfaction, each vendor should position himself one quarter-mile in, in opposite directions from the entrance. Hotelling shows that competition will actually drive vendors into closer proximity to try to first expand and then not lose most customers. In such cases competition leads to lower efficiency and lower consumer satisfaction. German regulatory frameworks recognize such limits to competition and seek to balance the efficiencies produced by many forms of market competition with a broader sense of public good (see also Colloredo-Mansfeld 2011 on the commons).

3. McCloskey (2006) suggests that bourgeois commerce itself instills virtues: that capitalism nurtures not just Prudence but also Temperance, Justice, Courage, Faith, Hope, and Love. She notes that this is not the only possible list—other ethical traditions could just as well serve the purpose—but a place to begin.

4. Kelvin Knight (1998: 11) summarizes MacIntyre's argument: "Institutions ought to be organized for the sake of practices and practices for the sake of goods of excellence. For example, a university should be organized for the sake of enquiry and enquiry for the sake of truth, not profit." A number of scholars are circling the same conclusions regarding the tension between normative and relative values that MacIntyre wrestles with. Stephen White's theory of "weak ontology" recognizes the hold of deep commitments and values while allowing for the historical, cultural, and dynamic contexts in which such values emerge. These values are both deeply held and contestable; from this perspective, "one does not so much derive principles as elicit an ethos from ontological figures" (White 2000: 17). Charles Taylor (2005: 35) argues that such a perspective should be called "philosophical anthropology": engaging fundamental features of human beings and their motivations, goals, desires, and aspirations. And Yehunda Elkana (2000) has argued for a post-Enlightenment set of "negotiated universals." All seek to socially embed virtues while allowing for their absolutist claims.

5. Thanks to Jaime Kyne for this reference and discussion of these issues.

6. The notion takes off from the current fashion for "positive psychology," a booming field that ranges from scientific studies of happiness to a flurry of popularizing books. In principle, it is a compelling idea. Psychology, especially the clinical variety, is, after all, meant to improve people's lives. Yet the field is also ripe for being misconstrued and co-opted into the sort of self-help genre that speaks to notions of spiritual poverty in the face of material wealth. Those concerns notwithstanding, it seems that there is a place for a constructive sort of positive anthropology.

7. As I finished editing the page proofs for this book, I discovered the unpublished dissertation research of Juan Pablo Sarmiento Barletti, who has worked on the pursuit of the good life in an Ashaninka village in the Peruvian Amazon. Sarmiento Barletti's work, which should be forthcoming as a book, expands on several themes I touch on here.

8. For example, a 2010 study by Daniel Benjamin, Ori Heffetz, Alex Rees-Jones, and Miles Kimball asked participants if they would rather earn $80,000 and get an average of 7.5 hours' sleep a night or make $140,000 and sleep only six hours a night. About 70 percent reported they would *prefer* to earn less and sleep more. The kicker comes next: the researchers then asked this same sample what they would actually do. Depending on the question, between 17 percent and 25 percent said they would *do* what they said they would not prefer (http://www.princeton.edu/chw/events_archive /repository/Heffetz021611/Heffetz021611.pdf).

Works Cited

Akerlof, George, and Rachel Kranton. 2005. "Identity and the Economics of Organizations." *Journal of Economic Perspectives* 19 (1): 9–32.

———. 2010. *Identity Economics*. Princeton, N.J.: Princeton University Press.

Alesina, Alberto, Edward Glaeser, and Bruce Sacerdite. 2005. "Work and Leisure in the U.S. and Europe." http://papers.nber.org/papers/w11278.pdf.

Alkire, Sabina. 2002. *Valuing Freedom: Sen's Capability Approach and Poverty Reduction*. Oxford: Oxford University Press.

———. 2005. "Measuring the Freedom Aspects of Capabilities." Working paper. Harvard University: Global Equity Initiative.

———. 2008. "Concepts and Measures of Agency." OPHI Working Paper no. 9. Oxford University: Oxford Poverty and Human Development Initiative.

Alkire, Sabina, and James E. Foster. 2009. "Counting and Multidimensional Poverty Measurement." *Journal of Public Economics* 95: 476–478.

———. 2011. "Understandings and Misunderstandings of Multidimensional Poverty Measurement." OPHI Working Paper 43. Oxford: Oxford Poverty and Human Development Initiative.

Alkire, Sabina, and Emma Maria Santos. 2010. "Acute Multidimensional Poverty: A New Index for Developing Countries." OPHI Working Paper no. 38. Oxford University: Oxford Poverty and Human Development Initiative.

Alkire, Sabina, M. Qizilbash, and F. Comim. 2008. "Introduction." In *The Capability Approach: Concepts, Measures and Applications*, F. Comim, M. Qizilbash, and S. Alkire, eds., pp. 1–25. Cambridge, UK: Cambridge University Press.

Alsop, Ruth, Mette Frost Bertelsen, and Jeremy Holland. 2006. *Empowerment in Practice. From Analysis to Implementation*. Washington, D.C.: World Bank.

Alvard, Michael S. 2004. "The Ultimatum Game, Fairness, and Cooperation among Big Game Hunters." In *Foundations of Human Sociality: Economic Experiments and Ethnographic Evidence from Fifteen Small-Scale Societies*, Joseph Henrich, Robert Boyd, Samuel Bowles, Colin Camerer, Ernst Fehr, and Herbert Gintis, eds., pp. 413–35. Oxford, UK: Oxford University Press.

Appadurai, Arjun. 1986. "Introduction: Commodities and the Politics of Value." In *The Social Life of Things: Commodities in Cultural Perspective*, Arjun Appadurai, ed., pp. 3–63. Cambridge, UK: Cambridge University Press.

———. 1996. *Modernity at Large*. Minneapolis: University of Minnesota Press.

———. 2004. "The Capacity to Aspire: Culture and the Terms of Recognition." In *Culture and Public Actions*, Vijayendra Rao and Michael Walton, eds., pp. 59–84. Stanford, Calif.: Stanford University Press.

———. 2013. *The Future as Cultural Fact: Essays on the Global Condition*. London: Verso.

Appiah, Kwame A. 2008. *Experiments in Ethics*. Cambridge, Mass.: Harvard University Press.

Ariely, Dan. 2008. *Predictably Irrational: The Hidden Forces That Shape Our Decisions*. New York: HarperCollins.

———. 2010. *The Upside of Irrationality: The Unexpected Benefits of Defying Logic at Work and at Home*. New York: HarperCollins.

Ariely, Dan, and Michael Norton. 2009. "Conceptual Consumption." *Annual Review of Psychology* 60: 475–99.

Armbruster-Sandoval, Ralph. 1999. "Globalization and Cross-Border Labor Organizing: The Guatemalan Maquiladora Industry and the Phillips Van-Heusen Case." *Latin American Perspectives* 26 (2): 108–28.

Arrow, Kenneth. 1974. *The Limits of Organization*. New York: Norton.

Aspers, Patrik, and Jens Beckert. 2011. "Value in Markets." In *The Worth of Goods: Valuation and Pricing in the Economy*, Jens Beckert and Patrik Aspers, eds., pp. 3–40. Oxford, UK: Oxford University Press.

AVANCSO (Asociación para el Avance de la Ciencia Sociales en Guatemala). 1994. *Apostando al Futuro con los Cultivos Notradicionales de Exportación: Riesgos y Oportunidades en la Producción de Hortalizas en Patzún, Chimaltenango*. Guatemala City: AVANCSO.

Bacon, Christopher M., Ernesto Méndez, and Stephen R. Gliessman, eds. 2008. *Confronting the Coffee Crisis*. Boston: MIT Press.

Baran, Paul. 1957. *The Political Economy of Growth*. New York: Monthly Review Press.

Baudrillard, Jean. 1981. *For a Critique of the Political Economy of the Sign*. St. Louis, Mo.: Telos Press.

BBC News. 2004. "Internet Boom for Gift Shopping." December 14, 2004. http://news.bbc.co.uk/2/hi/technology/4091681.stm.

Becker, Gary S. 1996. *Accounting for Tastes*. Cambridge, Mass.: Harvard University Press.

Becker, Gary S., and Guity Nashat Becker. 1996. *The Economics of Life*. New York: McGraw-Hill.

Becker, Uwe. 2009. *Open Varieties of Capitalism: Continuity, Change and Performances*. New York: Palgrave Macmillan.

Beckert, Jens. 2010. "The Transcending Power of Goods: Imaginary Value in the

Economy." MPIfG Discussion Paper 10/4. Cologne: Max Planck Institut für Gesellschaftsforschung.

———. "The Transcending Power of Goods: Imaginary Value in the Economy." In *The Worth Of Goods: Valuation and Pricing in the Economy*, Jens Beckert and Patrik Aspers, eds., pp. 106–28. Oxford, UK: Oxford University Press.

Bellah, Robert N., Richard Madsen, Steven M. Tipton, William M. Sullivan, and Ann Swidler. 1992. *Good Society*. New York: Vintage.

Bemporad, Raphael, and Mitch Baranowski. 2007. "Conscious Consumers Are Changing the Rules of Marketing. Are You Ready? Highlights from the BBMG Conscious Consumer Report." www.bbmg.com.

Benson, Peter. 2012. *Tobacco Capitalism: Growers, Migrant Workers, and the Changing Face of Global Industry*. Princeton, N.J.: Princeton University Press.

Berdahl, Daphne. 1999. *Where the World Ended: Re-Unification and Identity in the German Borderland*. Berkeley: University of California Press.

Berry, Albert. 2001. "When Do Agricultural Exports Help the Rural Poor? A Political Economy Approach." *Oxford Development Studies* 29 (2): 125–44.

Bertrand, Marianne, and Sendhil.Mullainathan. 2001. "Do People Mean What They Say? Implications for Subjective Survey Data." *American Economic Review* 91: 67–72.

Bicchieri, Cristina. 1993. *Rationality and Coordination*. Cambridge, UK: Cambridge University Press.

Biehl, João. 2006. "Pharmaceutical Governance." In *Global Pharmaceuticals: Ethics, Markets, Practices*, Adriana Petryna, Andrew Lakoff, and Arthur Kleinman, eds., pp. 206–39. Durham, N.C.: Duke University Press

———. 2007.*Will to Live: AIDS Therapies and the Politics of Survival*. Princeton, N.J.: Princeton University Press.

———. 2014. "Patient Value." In *Cash on the Table: Markets, Values, and Moral Economies*, Edward F. Fischer, ed. Santa Fe, N.M.: SAR Press.

Boas, Franz. 1909. "Race Problems in America." *Science* (May 28, 1909): 839–49.

Bogin, Barry. 1999. *Patterns of Human Growth*. Cambridge, UK: Cambridge University Press.

———. 2012. "Maya in Disneyland: Child Growth as a Marker of Nutritional, Economic, and Political Ecology." In *Nutritional Anthropology: Biocultural Perspectives on Food and Nutrition*, Darna L. Dufour, Alan H. Goodman, and Gretel H. Pelto, eds., pp. 231–44. Oxford, UK: Oxford University Press.

Borneman, John. 1992. *Belonging in the Two Berlins: Kin, State, Nation*. Cambridge, UK: Cambridge University Press.

Bourdieu, Pierre. 1977. *Outline of a Theory of Practice*. Cambridge, Mass.: Harvard University Press.

———. 1984. *Distinction: A Social Critique of the Judgment of Taste*. New York: Routledge.

Boyd, Robert, Herbert Gintis, Samuel Bowles, and Peter J. Richerson. 2003. *The*

Evolution of Altruistic Punishment. Proceedings of the National Academy of Sciences 100: 3531–35.

Boyer, Dominic. 2005. *Spirit and System: Media, Intellectuals, and the Dialectic in Modern German Culture.* Chicago: University of Chicago Press.

Brickman, P., D. Coates, and R. Janoff-Bulman. 1978. "Lottery Winners and Accident Victims: Is Happiness Relative?" *Journal of Personality and Social Psychology* 36 (8): 917–27.

Brooks, Arthur C. 2012. "Why Conservatives Are Happier Than Liberals." *New York Times,* July 7, 2012.

Brown, Michael F. 2004. *Who Owns Native Culture?* Cambridge, Mass.: Harvard University Press.

———. 2010. "A Tale of Three Buildings: Certifying Virtue in the New Moral Economy." *American Ethnologist* 37 (4): 741–52.

Busch, Andreas. 2005. "Globalization and National Varieties of Capitalism: The Contested Viability of the 'German Model'." *German Politics* 14 (2): 125–39.

Calestani, Melania. 2009a. "An Anthropology of 'The Good Life' in the Bolivian Plateau." *Social Indicators Research* 90: 141–53.

———. 2009b. "'SUERTE' (Luck): Spirituality and Wellbeing in El Alto, Bolivia." *Applied Research in Quality of Life* 4: 47–75.

———. 2013. *An Anthropological Journey into Well-Being: Insights from Bolivia.* London: Springer.

Cambranes, J. C. 1985. "Coffee and Peasants in Guatemala: The Origins of the Modern Plantation Economy in Guatemala, 1853–1897." Stockholm: Stockholm University Institute of Latin American Studies.

Camerer, Colin F. 2003. *Behavioral Game Theory: Experiments in Strategic Interaction.* Princeton, N.J.: Princeton University Press.

Camerer, Colin F., and Ernst Fehr. 2004. "Measuring Social Norms and Preferences Using Experimental Games: A Guide for Social Scientists." In *Foundations of Human Sociality: Economic Experiments and Ethnographic Evidence from Fifteen Small-Scale Societies,* Joseph Henrich, Robert Boyd, Samuel Bowles, Colin Camerer, Ernst Fehr, and Hebert Gintis, eds., pp. 55–95. Oxford, UK: Oxford University Press.

Camerer, Colin F., and Richard Thaler. 1995. "Anomalies: Ultimatums, Dictators, and Manners." *Journal of Economic Perspectives* 9: 209–19.

Cameron, L. 1999. "Raising the Stakes in the Ultimatum Game: Experimental Evidence from Indonesia." *Economic Inquiry* 37 (1): 47–59.

Camfield, Laura, K.Choudhury, and J. Devine. 2009. "Wellbeing, Happiness and Why Relationships Matter: Evidence from Bangladesh." *Journal of Happiness Studies* 10: 71–91.

Cardoso, Fernando Henrique, and Enzo Falleto. 1979 [1967]. *Dependency and Development in Latin America.* Berkeley: University of California Press.

Carey, David. 2001. *Our Elders Teach Us: Maya-Kaqchikel Historical Perspectives.* Tuscaloosa: University of Alabama Press.

Carnegie, Andrew. 1988. "Wealth." *North American Review* 148 (391): 653–65.

Carrier, James G., ed. 1997. *The Meanings of the Market: The Free Market in Western Culture.* Oxford, UK: Berg.

Carrier, James G. 2010. "Protecting the Environment the Natural Way: Ethical Consumption and Commodity Fetishism." *Antipode* 42 (3): 672–89.

———. 2012."Introduction." In *Ethical Consumption: Social Value and Economic Practice.* James G. Carrier and Peter G. Luetchford, eds. Oxford, UK: Berghahn.

Carrier, James G., and Daniel Miller, eds. 1998. *Virtualism: A New Political Economy.* Oxford, UK: Berg.

Carter, J. R., and M. D. Irons. 1991. "Are Economists Different, and If So, Why?" *Journal of Economic Perspectives* 5: 171–77.

Cavanaugh, Jillian R. 2007. "Making Salami, Producing Bergamo: The Transformation of Value." *Ethnos* 72 (2): 149–72.

Chibnik, Michael. 2005. Experimental Economics in Anthropology: A Critical Assessment." *American Ethnologist* 32 (2): 198–209.

———. 2011. *Anthropology, Economics, and Choice.* Austin: University of Texas Press.

Chirkov, V. I., R. M. Ryan, Y. Kim, and U. Kaplan. 2003. "Differentiating Autonomy from Individualism and Independence: A Self-Determination Theory Perspective on Internalization of Cultural Orientations and Well-being." *Journal of Personality and Social Psychology* 84: 97–110.

CIA. 2012. *The World Factbook.* Washington, D.C.: Central Intelligence Agency.

Clark, David A. 2009. "Adaptation, Poverty and Well-Being: Some Issues and Observations with Special Reference to the Capability Approach and Development Studies." *Journal of Human Development and Capabilities* 10 (1): 21–42.

Clifford, James, and George Marcus, eds. 1986. *Anthropology as Cultural Critique: An Experimental Moment in the Human Sciences.* Chicago: University of Chicago Press.

Colloredo-Mansfeld, Rudi. 1999. *The Native Leisure Class: Consumption and Cultural Creativity in the Andes.* Chicago: University of Chicago Press.

———. 2009. *Fighting Like a Community: Andean Civil Society in an Age of Indian Uprisings.* Chicago: University of Chicago Press.

———. 2011. "Work, Cultural Resources, and Community Commodities in the Global Economy." *Anthropology of Work Review* 32: 51–62.

Comaroff, John. 2010. "The End of Anthropology, Again: On the Future of an In/discipline. *American Anthropologist* 112 (4): 524–38.

Conroy, Michael E., Douglas L. Murray, and Peter Rosset. 1996. *A Cautionary Tale: Failed U.S. Development Policy in Central America.* Boulder, Colo.: Lynne Rienner.

Corral, Margarita. 2011. "The Economics of Happiness in the Americas." *AmericasBarometer Insights* no. 58. Nashville: Latin American Public Opinion Project.

Deaton Angus. 2007. "Income, Aging, Health and Wellbeing around the World: Evidence from the Gallup World Poll." NBER Working Paper 13317. Cambridge, Mass.: National Bureau of Economic Research. http://www.nber.org/papers/w13317.

Deci, Edward L., and Richard M. Ryan. 1980. "The Empirical Exploration of Intrinsic Motivational Processes." In L. Berkowitz, ed., *Advances in Experimental Social Psychology* 13: 39–80.

DeHart, Monica. 2010. *Ethnic Entrepreneurs: Identity and Development Politics in Latin America*. Stanford, Calif.: Stanford University Press.

De Janvry, Alain. 1981. *The Agrarian Question and Reformism in Latin America*. Baltimore, Md.: Johns Hopkins University Press.

Deutsche Welle. 2009. "BMW to Link Managers' Compensation to Factory-Worker Wages." www.dw.de/p/KF8p.

De Waal, Frans. 2009. *The Age of Empathy: Nature's Lessons for a Kinder Society*. New York: Crown.

Dickins de Girón, Avery. 2011. "The Security Guard Industry in Guatemala: Rural Communities and Urban Violence." In *Securing the City: Neoliberalism, Space, and Insecurity in Postwar Guatemala*, Kevin Lewis O'Neil and Kedron Thomas, eds. Durham, N.C.: Duke University Press.

Di Tella, Rafael, and Robert MacCulloch. 2008."Happiness Adaptation to Income beyond 'Basic Needs'." NBER Working Paper 14539. Cambridge, Mass.: National Bureau of Economic Research.

Dolan, Paul, Matthew White, and Tessa Peasgood. 2008. "Do We Really Know What Makes Us Happy? A Review of the Literature on the Factors Associated with Subjective Well-Being." *Journal of Economic Psychology* 29: 94–122.

Dolan, Paul, Richard Layard, and Robert Metcalfe. 2011. "Measuring Subjective Wellbeing for Public Policy: Recommendations on Measures." Special Paper no. 23. London: Centre for Economic Performance, London School of Economics.

Dougherty, Carter. 2006. "A European Allianz Becomes Less German." *International Herald Tribune*, July 21, 2006, p. 9.

Du Bois, W. E. B. 1903. *The Souls of Black Folk*. Chicago: A. C. McClurg.

Dyson, Kenneth, and Stephen Padgett. 1995. "Introduction: Global, Rhineland or Hybrid Capitalism?" *German Politics* 14 (2): 115–24.

Easterlin, Richard A. 2001. "Income and Happiness: Towards a Unified Theory." *Economic Journal* 111: 465–84.

The Economist. 2005a. "Agent of Change: Remodeling Allianz." October 8, pp. 80–81.

———. 2005b. "Germany's Economy." August 20, pp. 54–56.

———. 2006. "Strife at the Sparkasse." May 6, pp. 77–78.

———. 2009. "A Thousand Cries of Pain." February 21, pp. 64–65.

———. 2010. "The Tyranny of Choice." December 16. p. 124.

Edelman, Marc. 1999. *Peasants against Globalization: Rural Social Movements in Costa Rica*. Stanford, Calif.: Stanford University Press.

Elkana, Yehuda. 2000. "Rethinking—Not Unthinking—the Enlightenment." Manuscript available at http://www.ceu.hu/c/document_library/get_file?folderId=22431&name=DLFE-912.pdf.

Elster, Jon. 1983. *Explaining Technical Change—A Case Study in the Philosophy of Science*. Cambridge, UK: Cambridge University Press.

Ensminger, Jean. 1996. *Making a Market: The Institutional Transformation of an African Society*. Cambridge, UK: Cambridge University Press.

———. 2002. "Experimental Economics: A Powerful New Method Tool for Theory Testing in Anthropology." In *Theory in Economic Anthropology*, Jean Ensminger, ed., pp. 59–78. Walnut Creek, Calif.: AltaMira Press.

———. 2004. "Market Integration and Fairness: Evidence from Ultimatum, Dictator, and Public Goods Experiments in East Africa." In *Foundations of Human Sociality: Economic Experiments and Ethnographic Evidence from Fifteen Small-Scale Societies*, Joseph Henrich, Robert Boyd, Samuel Bowles, Colin Camerer, Ernst Fehr, and Hebert Gintis, eds., pp. 356–81. Oxford, UK: Oxford University Press.

Escobar, Arturo. 1994. *Encountering Development: The Making and Unmaking of the Third World*. Princeton, N.J.: Princeton University Press.

Fama, Eugene. 1970. "Efficient Capital Markets: A Review of Theory and Empirical Work." *Journal of Finance* 25: 383–417.

Fatheuer, Thomas. 2011. *Buen Vivir: A Brief Introduction to Latin America's New Concepts for the Good Life and the Rights of Nature*. Berlin: Heinrich Böll Stiftung.

Fehr, Ernst, and Simon Gächter. 1995. "Reciprocity and Economics: The Economic Implications of Homo Reciprocans." *European Economic Review* 42: 845–59.

Ferguson, James. 1999. *Expectations of Modernity: Myths and Meanings of Urban Life on the Zambian Copperbelt*. Berkeley: University of California Press.

Financial Times. 2011. "VW Gives Blackberry-Wielding Workers a Silent Night." December 22.

Fischer, Edward F. 1999. "Cultural Logic and Maya Identity: Rethinking Constructivism and Essentialism." *Current Anthropology* 40 (4): 473–99.

———. 2001. *Cultural Logics and Global Economies: Maya Identity in Thought and Practice*. Austin: University of Texas Press.

———, ed. 2008. *Indigenous Peoples, Civil Society, and the Neoliberal State in Latin America*. Oxford and New York: Berghahn Books.

———, ed. 2014. *Cash on the Table: Markets, Values, and Moral Economies*. Santa Fe, N.M.: SAR Press.

Fischer, Edward F., and Peter Benson. 2006. *Broccoli and Desire: Global Connections and Maya Struggles in Postwar Guatemala*. Stanford, Calif.: Stanford University Press.

Fischer, Edward F., and Avery Dickins de Girón. 2014. "Ultimatums and Rationalities in Two Maya Towns." In *Cash on the Table: Markets, Values, and Moral Economies*, Edward F. Fischer, ed., Santa Fe, N.M.: SAR Press.

Fischer, Edward F., and Carol Hendrickson. 2002. *Tecpán Guatemala: A Modern Maya Town in Global and Local Context*. Boulder, Colo.: Westview Press.

Fischer, Edward F., and Bart Victor. 2014. "High-End Coffee and Smallholding Growers in Guatemala." *Latin American Research Review* 49 (1): 155–77.

Fischer, Edward F., and R. McKenna Brown, eds. 1996. *Maya Cultural Activism in Guatemala*. Austin: University of Texas Press.

Flood, M. 1958. "Some Experimental Games." Research memorandum 789. Santa Monica, Calif.: Rand Corporation.

Floud, Roderick, Robert W. Fogel, Bernard Harris, and Sok Cul Hong. 2001. *The Changing Body: Health, Nutrition, and Human Development in the Western World since* 1700. Cambridge, UK: Cambridge University Press.

Foster, James E. 2011. "Freedom, Opportunity, and Well-Being." In *Handbook of Social Choice and Welfare* 2: 687–728. Amsterdam: Elsevier.

Foster, James E., Suman Seth, Michael Lokshin, and Zurab Sajaia. 2013. *A Unified Approach to Measuring Poverty and Inequality: Theory and Practice*. Washington, D.C.: World Bank.

Foucault, Michel. 1979. *Discipline and Punish: The Birth of the Prison*. New York: Random House.

Fourcade, Marion, and Kieran Healy. 2007. "Moral Views of Market Society." *Annual Review of Sociology* 33: 285–311.

Frank, Andre Gunder. 1967. *Capitalism and Underdevelopment in Latin America: Historical Studies of Chile and Brazil*. New York: Monthly Review Press.

Frank, Robert H. 1988. *Passions within Reason: The Strategic Role of the Emotions*. New York: W. W. Norton.

———. 1999. *Luxury Fever: Why Money Fails to Satisfy in an Era of Excess*. New York: Free Press.

———. 2000. *Luxury Fever: Money and Happiness in an Era of Excess*. Princeton, N.J.: Princeton University Press.

———. 2010. *What Price the Moral High Ground? How to Succeed Without Selling Your Soul*. Princeton, N.J.: Princeton University Press.

———. 2011. *The Darwin Economy: Liberty, Competition, and the Common Good*. Princeton, N.J.: Princeton University Press.

Frank, Robert H., Thomas Gilovich, and Dennis T. Regan. 1993. "Do Economists Make Bad Citizens?" *Journal of Economic Perspectives* 10: 187–92.

Frank, Thomas. 1997. *The Conquest of Cool: Business Culture, Counterculture, and the Rise of Hip Consumerism*. Chicago: University of Chicago Press.

Frankfurt, Harry G. 1971. "Freedom of the Will and the Concept of a Person." *Journal of Philosophy* 68: 5–20.

Frege, Carola M. 2002. "A Critical Assessment of the Theoretical and Empirical Research on German Works Councils." *British Journal of Industrial Relations* 40 (2): 221–48.

Friedman, Jonathan. 1994. *Cultural Identity and Global Process*. Thousand Oaks, Calif.: Sage.

Fullbrook, Edward, ed. 2004. *A Guide to What's Wrong with Economics*. London: Anthem.

Galbraith, John Kenneth. 1998 [1958]. *The Affluent Society*. New York: Mariner Books.

GfK. 2005. "Price Is More Important Than Quality." www.gfk.de.

Giddens, Anthony. 1984. *The Constitution of Society: Outline of the Theory of Structuration.* Berkeley: University of California Press.

Gilbert, Daniel. 2006. *Stumbling on Happiness.* New York: Knopf.

Gillies, Donald. 2004. "Can Mathematics Be Used Successfully in Economics?" In *A Guide to What's Wrong with Economics*, Edward Fullbrook, ed., pp. 187–97. London: Anthem.

Gilmore, James H., and B. Joseph Pine. 2000. *Markets of One: Creating Customer-Unique Value through Mass Customization.* Cambridge, Mass.: Harvard Business School Press.

Gil-White, Francisco J. 2004. "Ultimatum Game with an Ethnicity Manipulation: Results from Khovdiin Bulgan Sum, Mongolia." In *Foundations of Human Sociality: Economic Experiments and Ethnographic Evidence from Fifteen Small-Scale Societies*, Joseph Henrich, Robert Boyd, Samuel Bowles, Colin Camerer, Ernst Fehr, and Hebert Gintis, eds., pp. 260–304. Oxford, UK: Oxford University Press.

Glaeser, Andreas. 1999. *Divided in Unity: Identity, Germany, and the Berlin Police.* Chicago: University of Chicago Press.

Goffman, Erving. 1974. *Frame Analysis: An Essay on the Organization of Experience.* New York: Harper & Row.

Goldín, Liliana R. 2009. *Global Maya: Work and Ideology in Rural Guatemala.* Tucson: University of Arizona Press.

Goldman, Francisco. 2007. *The Art of Political Murder: Who Killed the Bishop?* New York: Grove.

Goldstein, Daniel M. 2010. "Toward a Critical Anthropology of Security." *Current Anthropology* 51 (4): 487–517.

Goodenough, Oliver R. 2008. "Values, Mechanism Design, and Fairness." In *Moral Markets: The Critical Role of Values in the Economy*, Paul J. Zak, ed. Princeton, N.J.: Princeton University Press.

Gough, I., and A. McGregor. 2007. *Wellbeing in Developing Countries. From Theory to Research.* Cambridge, UK: Cambridge University Press.

Graeber, David. 2001. *Toward an Anthropological Theory of Value.* New York: Palgrave.

Graham, Carol. 2011. *The Pursuit of Happiness: An Economy of Well-Being.* Washington, D.C.: Brookings Institution Press.

Graham, Carol, and Lora, Eduardo. 2009. *Paradox and Perception: Measuring Quality of Life in Latin America.* Washington, D.C.: Brookings Institution Press.

Gudeman, Stephen. 2001. *The Anthropology of Economy: Community, Market, and Culture.* Oxford, UK: Blackwell.

———. 2008. *Economy's Tension: The Dialectics of Community and Market.* Oxford, UK: Berghahn.

Gudynas, Eduardo. 2011. "Buen Vivir: Today's Tomorrow." *Development* 54 (4): 441–47.

Gul, Faruk, and Wolfgang Pesendorfer. 2005. "The Case for Mindless Economics." http://www.princeton.edu/pesendor/mindless.pdf.

Gupta, Akhil. 1998. *Postcolonial Developments: Agriculture in the Making of Modern India*. Durham, N.C.: Duke University Press.

Gurven, Michael. 2004. "Does Market Exposure Affect Economic Game Behavior? The Ultimatum Game and the Public Goods Game among the Tsimane' of Bolivia." In *Foundations of Human Sociality: Economic Experiments and Ethnographic Evidence from Fifteen Small-Scale Societies*, Joseph Henrich, Robert Boyd, Samuel Bowles, Colin Camerer, Ernst Fehr, and Hebert Gintis, eds., pp. 194–231. Oxford, UK: Oxford University Press.

Güth, Wener, Rolf Schmittberger, and Bernd Schwarze. 1982. "An Experimental Analysis of Ultimatum Bargaining." *Journal of Economic Behavior and Organization* 3 (4): 367–88.

Haas, Alexander. 2009. "Liebe Leserinnen, liebe Leser." *Südstadt Magazin*, March, p. 3.

Hacking, Ian. 2000. *The Social Construction of What?* Cambridge, Mass.: Harvard University Press.

Haidt, Jonathan. 2007. "The New Synthesis in Moral Psychology." *Science* 316: 998–1002.

Hall, Crystal C., J. Zhao, and E. Shafir. 2012. "Self-Affirmation as an Intervention for Low-Income Individuals." Working paper.

Hall, Peter A., and David Soskice, eds. 2001. *Varieties of Capitalism: The Institutional Foundations of Comparative Advantage*. Oxford, UK: Oxford University Press.

Hamilton, Sarah, and Edward F. Fischer. 2003. "Non-traditional Agricultural Exports in Highland Guatemala: Understandings of Risks and Perceptions of Change." *Latin American Research Review* 38 (3): 82–110.

Hann, Chris. 2010. "Moral Economy." In *The Human Economy*, Keith Hart, Jean-Louis Laville, and Antonio David Cattani, eds., pp. 187–98. Cambridge, UK: Polity Press.

Hardin, Garrett. 1968. "The Tragedy of the Commons." *Science* 162: 1243–48.

Harris, Sam. 2010. *The Moral Landscape: How Science Can Determine Human Values*. New York: Free Press.

Hart, Keith. 2005. *The Hit Man's Dilemma: Or Business, Personal and Impersonal*. Chicago: Prickly Paradigm Press.

Hart, Keith, and Chris Hann. 2011. *Economic Anthropology: History, Ethnography, Critique*. Cambridge, UK: Polity Press.

Hart, Keith, Jean-Louis Laville, and Antonio David Cattani. 2010. "Building the Human Economy Together." In *The Human Economy*, Keith, Laville, and Cattani, eds., pp. 1–17. Cambridge, UK: Polity Press.

Hendrickson, Carol. 1995. *Weaving Identities: Construction of Dress and Self in a Highland Guatemala Town*. Austin: University of Texas Press.

Henrich, Joseph, Robert Boyd, Samuel Bowles, Colin F. Camerer, Ernst Fehr, Herbert Gintis, and Richard McElreath. 2001. "In Search of Homo economicus: Behavioral Experiments in 15 Small-Scale Societies." *AEA Papers and Proceedings* 91 (2): 73–78.

Henrich, Joseph, and Natalie Smith. 2004. "Comparative Experimental Evidence from Machiguenga, Mapuche, Huinca, and American Populations." In *Foundations of Human Sociality: Economic Experiments and Ethnographic Evidence from Fifteen Small-Scale Societies*, Joseph Henrich, Robert Boyd, Samuel Bowles, Colin Camerer, Ernst Fehr, and Hebert Gintis, eds., pp. 125–67. Oxford, UK: Oxford University Press.

Henrich, Joseph, Robert Boyd, Samuel Bowles, Colin F. Camerer, Ernst Fehr, Herbert Gintis, and Richard McElreath. 2004. "Overview and Synthesis." In *Foundations of Human Sociality: Economic Experiments and Ethnographic Evidence from Fifteen Small-Scale Societies*, Joseph Henrich, Robert Boyd, Samuel Bowles, Colin Camerer, Ernst Fehr, and Hebert Gintis, eds., pp. 8–54. Oxford, UK: Oxford University Press.

Hill, Kim, and Michael Gurven. 2004. "Economic Experiments to Examine Fairness and Cooperation among the Ache Indians of Paraguay." In *Foundations of Human Sociality: Economic Experiments and Ethnographic Evidence from Fifteen Small-Scale Societies*, Joseph Henrich, Robert Boyd, Samuel Bowles, Colin Camerer, Ernst Fehr, and Hebert Gintis, eds., pp. 382–412. Oxford, UK: Oxford University Press.

Hinton, Alexander Laban, and Kevin Lewis O'Neill, eds. 2009. *Genocide: Truth, Memory, and Representation*. Durham, N.C.: Duke University Press.

Hirschman, Albert O. 1977. *The Passions and the Interests: Political Arguments for Capitalism before Its Triumph*. Princeton, N.J.: Princeton University Press.

———. 1982. *Shifting Involvements: Private Interest and Public Action*. Princeton, N.J.: Princeton University Press.

Hiscox, Michael H., and Nicholas F. B. Smyth. n.d. "Is There Consumer Demand for Improved Labor Standards? Evidence from Field Experiments in Social Labeling." http://dev.wcfia.harvard.edu/sites/default/files/HiscoxSmythND.pdf.

Hoffman, Elizabeth, Kevin A. McCabe, K. Sachat, and Vernon L. Smith. 1994. "Preferences, Property Rights, and Anonymity in Bargaining Games." *Games and Economic Behavior* 7: 346–80.

Holmes, Bradford J., and Julie Snyder. 2007. "Retail Health Clinics: Convenience Trumps Service and Quality." http://www.forrester.com/Research/Document/Excerpt/0,7211,41216,00.html.

Höpner, Martin, and Lothar Krempel. 2003. "The Politics of the German Company Network." MPIfG Working Paper 03/9. Cologne: Max Planck Institut für Gesellschaftsforschung.

Hotelling, Harold. 1929. "Stability in Competition." *Economic Journal* 39 (1): 41–57

Ibrahim, Solava, and Sabina Alkire. 2007. "Agency and Empowerment: A Proposal for Internationally Comparable Indicators." OPHI Working Paper 4. Oxford, UK: Oxford Poverty and Human Development Initiative.

Institut für Mittelstandsforschung (Institute for Mittelstand Research). 2004. "SMEs in Germany—Facts and Figures 2004." Bonn: IfM.

International Herald Tribune. 2005. June 11–12, p. 16.

Isenhour, Cindy. 2010. "Building Sustainable Societies: A Swedish Case Study on the Limits of Reflexive Modernization." *American Ethnologist* 37 (3): 511–25.

Iyengar, Sheena S., and Mark R. Lepper. 2000. "When Choice Is Demotivating: Can One Desire Too Much of a Good Thing?" *Journal of Personality and Social Psychology* 79 (6): 995–1006.

Jackall, Robert. 1988. *Moral Mazes: The World of Corporate Managers*. Oxford, UK: Oxford University Press.

Jackson, Michael. 2011. *Life within Limits: Well-being in a World of Want*. Durham, N.C.: Duke University Press.

Jaffee, Daniel. 2007. *Brewing Justice: Fair Trade Coffee, Sustainability, and Survival*. Berkeley: University of California Press.

Jameson, Frederic. 1991. *Postmodernism, or the Cultural Logic of Late Capitalism*. Durham, N.C.: Duke University Press.

Jankowiak, William. 2009. "Well-Being, Cultural Pathology, and Personal Rejuvenation in a Chinese City, 1981–2005." In *Pursuits of Happiness: Well-Being in Anthropological Perspective*, Gordon Mathews and Carolina Izquierdo, eds., pp. 147–66. New York: Berghahn.

Jiménez, Alberto Corsín. 2007. "Well-being in Anthropological Balance: Remarks on Proportionality as Political Imagination." In *Culture and Well-Being: Anthropological Approaches to Freedom and Political Ethics*, Alberto Corsín Jiménez, ed., pp. 180–97. London: Pluto Press.

Johansson-Steman, Olof, Fredrik Carlsson, and Dinky Daruvala. 2002. "Measuring Future Grandparents' Preferences for Equality and Relative Standing." *Economic Journal* 112 (479): 362–83.

Kagel, John H., and Alvin E. Roth. 1995. *The Handbook of Experimental Economics*. Princeton, N.J.: Princeton University Press.

Kahn, Hilary. 2001. "Respecting Relationships and Día de Guadalupe." *Journal of Latin American Anthropology* 6 (1): 2–29.

Kahneman, Daniel. 2011. *Thinking, Fast and Slow*. New York: Farrar, Straus and Giroux.

Kahneman, Daniel, and Angus Deaton. 2010. "High Income Improves Evaluation of Life but Not Emotional Well-Being." *Proceedings of the National Academy of Sciences*. www.pnas.org/cgi/doi/10.1073/pnas.1011492107.

Kahneman, Daniel, and Richard H. Thaler. 1991. "Economic Analysis and the Psychology of Utility: Applications to Compensation Policy." *American Economic Review* 81 (2): 341–46.

Kearney, Michael. 1996. *Reconceptualizing the Peasantry: Anthropology in Global Perspective*. Boulder, Colo.: Westview Press.

Kimmelman, Michael. 2007. "German Border Threat: Cheap Books." *New York Times*, October 24, p. B1.

King, Arden. 1974. *Coban and the Verapaz: History and Cultural Process in Northern Guatemala*. New Orleans, La.: Tulane University, Middle American Research Institute.

Kitschelt, Herbert, and Wolfgang Streeck. 2004. "From Stability to Stagnation: Germany at the Beginning of the Twenty-First Century." In *Germany: Beyond the Stable State*, Herbert Kitschelt and Wolfgang Streeck, eds. London: Routledge.

Kleinman, Arthur. 2006. *What Really Matters: Living a Moral Life Amidst Uncertainty and Danger*. Oxford, UK: Oxford University Press

Knight, Kelvin. 1998. "Editor's Introduction." In *The MacIntyre Reader*, Kelvin Knight, ed. South Bend, Ind.: University of Notre Dame Press.

Kondo, Dorinne K. 1990. *Crafting Selves: Power, Gender, and Discourses of Identity in a Japanese Workplace*. Chicago: University of Chicago Press.

Kopytoff, Igor. 1986. "Cultural Biography of Things: Commoditization as a Process." In *The Social Life of Things*, Arjun Appadurai, ed., pp. 6–91. Cambridge, UK: Cambridge University Press.

Kotan, Murat. 2010. "Freedom or Happiness? Agency and Subjective Well-Being in the Capability Approach." *Journal of Socio-Economics* 39 (3): 369–75.

Kotthoff, Hermann. 1994. *Betriebsräte und Burgerstatus: Wandel und Kontinuität betrieblicher Interessenvertretung*. Munich: Rainer HamppVerlag.

Krueger, Alan. 2005. "For Workers, Happiness Is Next to Productivity." *International Herald Tribune*, December 14, p. 14.

———, ed. 2009. *Measuring the Subjective Well-Being of Nations: National Accounts of Times Use and Well-Being*. Chicago: University of Chicago Press.

Krugman, Paul R. 2009. *The Return of Depression Economics and the Crisis of* 2008. New York: W. W. Norton.

Laidlaw, James. 2002. "For an Anthropology of Ethics and Freedom." *Journal of the Royal Anthropological Institute* 8 (2): 311–32.

———. 2007. "The Intension and Extension of Well-Being: Transformation in Diaspora Jain Understandings of Non-Violence." In *Culture and Well-Being: Anthropological Approaches to Freedom and Political Ethics*, Alberto Corsín Jiménez, ed., pp. 156–79. London: Pluto Press

Lash, Scott, and John Urry. 1987. *The End of Organized Capitalism*. Cambridge, UK: Polity Press.

Layard, Richard. 2005. *Happiness: Lessons from a New Science*. New York: Penguin.

Levinas, Emmanuel. 1969. *Totality and Infinity: An Essay on Exteriority*. Philadelphia: Duquesne University Press.

Levitt, Steven D., and Stephen J. Dubner. 2005. *Freakonomics: A Rogue Economist Explores the Hidden Side of Everything*. New York: William Morrow.

Li, Tania M. 2007. *The Will to Improve: Governmentality, Development, and the Practice of Politics*. Durham, N.C.: Duke University Press.

Liberman, Nora, and Yaacov Trope. 1998. "The Role of Feasibility and Desirability Considerations in Near and Distant Future Decisions: A Test of Temporal Construal Theory." *Journal of Personality and Social Psychology* 75 (1): 5–18.

Lovell, W. George. 1988. "Surviving Conquest: The Maya of Guatemala in Historical Perspective." *Latin American Research Review* 23 (2): 25–57.

———. 2001. *A Beauty That Hurts: Life and Death in Guatemala*. 2nd edition. Austin: University of Texas Press.

———. 2005. *Conquest and Survival in Colonial Guatemala: A Historical Geography of the Cuchumatán Highlands, 1500–1821*. 2nd edition. Montreal: McGill Queens Press.

Luce, R. Duncan, and Howard Raiffa. 1957. *Games and Decisions: Introduction and Critical Survey*. New York: Wiley.

Lucero, José Antonio. 2008. *Struggles and Voice: The Politics of Indigenous Representation in the Andes*. Pittsburgh, Penn.: University of Pittsburgh Press.

Luttinger, Nina, and Gregory Dicum. 2006. *The Coffee Book: Anatomy of an Industry from Crop to the Last Cup*. New York: The New Press.

Luxemburg, Rosa. 1913. *Die Akkumulation des Kapitals*. Berlin: Jugendinternationale.

Lyon, Sarah. 2011. *Coffee and Community: Maya Farmers and Fair Trade Markets*. Boulder: University of Colorado Press.

MacIntyre, Alasdair. 1984. *After Virtue: A Study in Moral Theory*. South Bend, Ind.: University of Notre Dame Press.

———. 1988. *Whose Justice? Which Rationality?* South Bend, Ind.: University of Notre Dame Press.

Malinowski, Bronislaw. 1922. *Argonauts of the Western Pacific: An Account of Native Enterprise and Adventure in the Archipelagoes of Melanesian New Guinea*. London: Routledge.

Marlowe, Frank. 2004. "Dictators and Ultimatums in an Egalitarian Society of Hunter-Gatherers: The Hadza of Tanzania." In *Foundations of Human Sociality: Economic Experiments and Ethnographic Evidence from Fifteen Small-Scale Societies*, Joseph Henrich, Robert Boyd, Samuel Bowles, Colin Camerer, Ernst Fehr, and Hebert Gintis, eds., pp. 168–93. Oxford, UK: Oxford University Press.

Marmot, Michael, and Richard G. Wilkinson, eds. 2001. *Social Determinants of Health*. Oxford: Oxford University Press.

Marshall, Alfred. 1920. *Principles of Economics: An Introductory Volume*. London: Macmillan.

Martinez-Torres, Maria Elena. 2006. *Organic Coffee: Sustainable Development by Mayan Farmers*. Athens: Ohio University Press.

Marwell, G., and R. Ames. 1981. "Economists Free Ride, Does Anyone Else?" *Journal of Public Economics* 15: 295–310.

Mathews, Gordon. 2009. "Finding and Keeping a Purpose in Life: Well-Being and Ikigai in Japan and Elsewhere." In *Pursuits of Happiness: Well-Being in Anthropological Perspective*, Gordon Mathews and Carolina Izquierdo, eds., pp. 167–85. New York: Berghahn.

Mathews, Gordon, and Carolina Izquierdo, eds. 2009. *Pursuits of Happiness: Well-Being in Anthropological Perspective*. New York: Berghahn.

Mauss, Marcel. 2006 [1924]. *The Gift: The Form and Reason for Exchange in Archaic Societies*. New York: Routledge.

McCloskey, Deirdre N. 1998. *The Rhetoric of Economics*. 2nd edition. Madison: University of Wisconsin Press.

————. 2002. *The Secret Sins of Economics*. Chicago: Prickly Paradigm Press.

————. 2006. *The Bourgeois Virtues: Ethics for an Age of Commerce*. Chicago: University of Chicago Press.

McCreery, David. 1994. *Rural Guatemala: 1760–1940*. Stanford, Calif.: Stanford University Press.

McElreath, Richard. 2004. "Community Structure, Mobility, and Strength of Norms in an African Society: The Sangu of Tanzania." In *Foundations of Human Sociality: Economic Experiments and Ethnographic Evidence from Fifteen Small-Scale Societies*, Joseph Henrich, Robert Boyd, Samuel Bowles, Colin Camerer, Ernst Fehr, and Hebert Gintis, eds., pp. 335–55. Oxford, UK: Oxford University Press.

McFadden, Daniel L. 2013. "The New Science of Pleasure." NBER Working Paper 18687. Cambridge, Mass.: National Bureau of Economic Research. http://www.nber.org/papers/w18687.

McGregor, A. 2007. "Researching Wellbeing: From Concepts to Methodology." In *Wellbeing in Developing Countries. From Theory to Research*, I. Gough and A. McGregor, eds., pp. 316–50. Cambridge, UK: Cambridge University Press.

Meeks, M. Douglas. 2000. *God the Economist: The Doctrine of God and Political Economy*. Minneapolis, Minn.: Fortress Press.

Micheletti, Michele, and Andreas Follesdal. 2007. "Shopping for Human Rights." *Journal of Consumer Policy* 30: 167–75.

Miller, Daniel. 1998. *A Theory of Shopping*. Cambridge, UK: Polity Press.

Mintz, Sidney. 1985. *Sweetness and Power: The Place of Sugar in Modern History*. New York: Penguin.

Moberg, Mark. 1992. *Citrus, Strategy, and Class: The Politics of Development in Southern Belize*. Iowa City: University of Iowa Press.

Moore, Henrietta L. 2011. *Still Life: Hopes, Desires, and Satisfactions*. Cambridge, UK: Polity Press.

Müller, T. R. 2010. "Changing Resource Profiles: Aspirations among Orphans in Central Mozambique in the Context of an AIDS Mitigation Intervention." *Journal of Development Studies* 46 (2): 254–73.

Murray, Douglas L., Laura T. Raynolds, and Peter L. Taylor. 2006. "The Future of Fair Trade Coffee: Dilemmas Facing Latin Americas Small-Scale Producers." *Development in Practice* 16 (2): 179–92.

Narayan, Deepa. 2005. *Measuring Empowerment: Cross-Disciplinary Perspectives*. Washington, D.C.: World Bank.

Nash, Jr., John F. 1951. "Noncooperative Games." *Annals of Mathematics* 54: 289–95.

Nelson, Diane M. 1999. *A Finger in the Wound: Body Politics in Quincentennial Guatemala*. Durham, N.C.: Duke University Press.

————. 2009. *Reckoning: The Ends of War in Guatemala*. Durham, N.C.: Duke University Press.

————. 2013. "100 Percent Omnilife: Health, Economy, and the End/s of War." In *War by Other Means: Aftermath in Post-genocide Guatemala*, Carlota McAlister and Diane M. Nelson, eds., pp. 285–306. Durham, N.C.: Duke University Press.

Nelson, Robert H. 2001. *Economics as Religion*. University Park: State University of Pennsylvania Press.

Netting, Robert M. 1993. *Smallholders, Householders: Farm Families and the Ecology of Intensive, Sustainable Agriculture*. Stanford, Calif.: Stanford University Press.

Norenzayan, Ara, and Azim F. Shariff. 2007. "God Is Watching You: Priming God Concepts Increases Prosocial Behavior in an Anonymous Economic Game." *Psychological Science* 18 (9): 803–09.

North, Douglass C. 1990. *Institutions, Institutional Change and Economic Performance*. Cambridge, UK: Cambridge University Press.

Nozick, Robert. 1974. *Anarchy, State, and Utopia*. New York: Basic Books.

Nussbaum, Martha C. 2011. *Creating Capabilities: The Human Development Approach*. Cambridge, Mass.: Belknap Press.

Offit, Thomas. 2008. *Conquistadores de la Calle: Child Street Labor in Guatemala City*. Austin: University of Texas Press.

O'Neill, Kevin Lewis, and Alexander Laban Hinton. 2009. "Genocide, Truth, Memory, and Representation: An Introduction." In *Genocide: Truth, Memory, and Representation*, Alexander Laban Hinton and Kevin Lewis O'Neill, eds., pp. 1–27. Durham, N.C.: Duke University Press.

———. 2010. *City of God: Christian Citizenship in Postwar Guatemala*. Berkeley: University of California Press.

O'Neill, Kevin Lewis, and Benjamin Fogarty-Valenzuela. 2013. "Verticality." *Journal of the Royal Anthropological Institute* 19 (2): 378–89.

O'Neill, Kevin, Kedron Thomas, and Thomas Offit. 2011. "Securing the City: An Introduction." In *Securing the City: Neoliberalism, Space and Insecurity in Postwar Guatemala*, Kevin L. O'Neill and Kedron Thomas, eds., pp. 1–25. Durham, N.C.: Duke University Press.

Oosterbeek, Hessel, Randolph Sloof, and Gijs van de Kuilen. 2004. "Cultural Differences in Ultimatum Game Experiments: Evidence from a Meta-Analysis." *Experimental Economics* 7: 171–88.

Ostrom, Elinor. 1990. *Governing the Commons: The Evolution of Institutions for Collective Action*. Cambridge, UK: Cambridge University Press.

Paciotti, Brian, and Craig Hadley. 2003. "Ultimatum Game in Southwest Tanzania: Ethnic Variation and Institutional Scope." *Current Anthropology* 44 (3): 427–32.

Paige, Jeffrey. 1997. *Coffee and Power: Revolution and the Rise of Democracy in Central America*. Cambridge, Mass.: Harvard University Press.

Patton, John Q. 2004. "Coalition Effects on Reciprocal Fairness in the Ultimatum Game: A Case from the Ecuadorian Amazon." In *Foundations of Human Sociality: Economic Experiments and Ethnographic Evidence from Fifteen Small-Scale Societies*, Joseph Henrich, Robert Boyd, Samuel Bowles, Colin Camerer, Ernst Fehr, and Hebert Gintis, eds., pp. 96–124. Oxford, UK: Oxford University Press.

Peacock, Susan C., and Adriana Beltrán. 2003. *Hidden Powers: Illegal Armed Groups in Post-Conflict Guatemala and the Forces behind Them*. Washington, D.C.: Washington Office on Latin America.

Pendergrast, Mark. 2010. *Uncommon Grounds: The History of Coffee and How It Transformed the World*. New York: Basic Books.

Pinker, Steven. 2008. "The Moral Instinct." *New York Times Magazine*. January 13.

Polanyi, Karl. 1944. *The Great Transformation*. Boston: Beacon Press

Ponte, Stefano. 2002. "The Latte Revolution? Regulation, Markets and Consumption in the Global Coffee Chain." *World Development* 30 (7): 1099–1122.

Portes, Alejandro. 2008. "Migration and Social Change: Some Conceptual Reflections." Keynote address at the conference "Theorizing Key Migration Debates," Oxford University, July 1. www.imi.ox.ac.uk/pdfs/alejandro-portes-migration-and-social-change-some-conceptual-reflections.

Pratt, Jeff. 2007. "Food Values." *Critique of Anthropology* 27 (3): 285–300.

Ramello, Giovanni B. 2006. "What's in a Sign? Trademark Law and Economic Theory." POLIS Working Paper 73. Università' del Piemonte Orientale, Alessandria, Italy.

Ravallion, Martin. 1994. *Poverty Comparisons*. Chur, Switzerland: Harwood Academic.

Ravallion, Martin, and Dominique Van De Walle. 2008. *Land in Transition: Reform and Poverty in Rural Vietnam*. Washington, D.C.: World Bank.

Ravallion, Martin, Shaohua Chen, and PremSangraula. 2009. "Dollar a Day Revisited." *World Bank Economic Review* 23 (2): 163–84.

Rawls, John. 1971. *A Theory of Justice*. Cambridge, Mass.: Belknap Press of Harvard University Press.

Ray, Debraj. 2006. "Aspirations, Poverty and Economic Change." In *What We Have Learned about Poverty*, Abhijit Banerjee, Roland Bénabou, and DilipMookherjee, eds., pp. 409–22. Oxford, UK: Oxford University Press.

Reichman, Daniel R. 2008. "Coffee as a Global Metaphor." Occasional Paper no. 9. Nashville, Tenn.: Center for Latin American Studies, Vanderbilt University.

———. 2011. *The Broken Village: Coffee, Migration, and Globalization in Honduras*. Ithaca, N.Y.: Cornell University Press.

Renard, Marie-Christine. 1999. *Los Intersticios de la Globalización: UnLabel (Max Havelaar) para los Pequeños Productores de Café*. Mexico City: CEMCA.

Rice, Robert. 1999. "A Place Unbecoming: The Coffee Farm of Northern Latin America." *Geographical Review* 89 (4): 554–79.

———. 2003. "Coffee Production in a Time of Crisis: Social and Environmental Connections" *SAIS Review* XXIII (1): 221–45.

Rizzolatti, Giacomo, and CorradoSinigaglia.2008. *Mirrors in the Brain. How We Share Our Actions and Emotions*. Oxford, UK: Oxford University Press.

Roberts, Kevin. 2004. *Lovemarks: The Future Beyond Brands*. Brooklyn, N.Y.: powerHouse Books.

Roseberry, William. 1996. "The Rise of Yuppie Coffees and the Reimagination of Class in the United States." *American Anthropologist* 98 (4): 762–75.

Roseberry, William, Lowell Gudmundson, and Mario Samper Kutschbach, eds. 1995. *Coffee, Society, and Power in Latin America*. Baltimore, Md.: Johns Hopkins University Press.

Roth, Alvin E. 1995. "Bargaining Experiments." In *The Handbook of Experimental Economics*, J. H. Kagel and A. E. Roth, eds., pp. 253–348. Princeton, N.J.: Princeton University Press.

Roth, Alvin E., Vesna Prasnikar, MashiroOkuno-Fujiwara, and Shmuel Zamir. 1991. "Bargaining and Market Behavior in Jerusalem, Ljubljana, Pittsburgh, and Tokyo: An Experimental Study." *American Economic Review* 81 (5): 1068–95.

Ruskin, John. 1862. "Unto This Last": Four Essays on the First Principles of Political Economy." London: Collins Press. http://www.gutenberg.org/files/36541/36541-h/36541-h.htm

Ryan, Richard M., and Edward L.Deci. 2001. "On Happiness and Human Potentials: A Review of Research on Hedonic and Eudaimonic Well-Being." *Annual Review of Psychology* 52: 141–66.

Sahlins, Marshall. 1972. *Stone Age Economics*. New York: Aldine Transaction.

Samuelson, Paul A. 1938. "A Note on the Pure Theory of Consumer's Behavior." *Economica* 5, no. 17: 61–71.

———. 1948. "Consumption Theory in Terms of Revealed Preference." *Economica* 15 (60): 243–53.

———. 1950. "The Problem of Integrability in Utility Theory." *Economica* 17: 355–85.

———. 1965. "Proof That Properly Anticipated Prices Fluctuate Randomly." *Industrial Management Review* 6: 41–49.

———. 1976. *Economics*. 10th edition. New York: McGraw-Hill.

Sandel, Michael J. 2012. *What Money Can't Buy: The Moral Limits of Markets*. New York: Farrar, Straus and Giroux.

Satz, Debra. 2010. *Why Some Things Should Not Be for Sale: The Moral Limits of Markets*. New York: Oxford University Press.

Sayer, Andrew. 2000. "Moral Economy and Political Economy." *Studies in Political Economy* 61: 79–104.

———. 2004. "Moral Economy." www.lancs.ac.uk/fss/sociology/papers/sayer-moral-economy.pdf.

———. 2005. *The Moral Significance of Class*. Cambridge, UK: Cambridge University Press.

———. 2011. *Why Things Matter to People: Social Science, Values and Ethical Life*. Cambridge, UK: Cambridge University Press.

Schumann, Michael. 2005. "Mitbestimmung—ihr Beitrag für ein erfolgreiches Unternehmen." Göttingen: Soziologisches Forschungsinstitut e.V. an der Georg-August-Universität Göttingen.

Schwartz, Barry. 2004. *The Paradox of Choice: Why More Is Less*. New York: Ecco.

Schwartz, Barry, and Kenneth Sharpe. 2010. *Practical Wisdom: The Right Way to Do the Right Thing*. New York: Riverhead.

Scott, James. 1977. *The Moral Economy of the Peasant*. New Haven, Conn.: Yale University Press.

———. 1985. *Weapons of the Weak*. New Haven, Conn.: Yale University Press.

Sen, Amartya. 1979. "Rational Fools: A Critique of the Behavioral Foundations of Economic Theory." In *Scientific Models and Man*, H. Harris, ed. Oxford, UK: Oxford University Press.

———. 1982. *Choice, Welfare, and Measurement*. Oxford, UK: Blackwell.

———. 1985. "Well-Being, Agency, and Freedom." *Journal of Philosophy* 82 (4): 169–221.

———. 1997. *On Ethics and Economics*. Malden, Mass.: Blackwell.

———. 1999. *Development as Freedom*. Cambridge, Mass.: Belknap Press.

———. 2002. *Rationality and Freedom*. Cambridge, Mass.: Belknap Press.

———. 2006. *Identity and Violence: The Illusion of Destiny*. New York: W. W. Norton.

Sennett, Richard. 2008. *The Craftsmen*. New Haven, Conn.: Yale University Press.

Shiller, Robert J. 2005. "Behavioral Economics and Institutional Innovation." Discussion Paper no. 1499. New Haven, Conn.: Cowles Foundation for Research in Economics, Yale University.

Sick, Deborah. 1999. *Farmers of the Golden Bean: Costa Rican Households and the Global Coffee Economy*. DeKalb: Northern Illinois University Press.

Siebers, Hans. 1999. "'We Are Children of the Mountain': Creolization and Modernization Among the Q'eqchi'." Amsterdam: Center for Latin American Research and Documentation.

Silk, Joan B. 2005. "The Evolution of Cooperation in Primate Groups." In *Moral Sentiments and Material Interests: On the Foundations of Cooperation in Economic Life*, H. Gintis, S. Bowles, R. Boyd, and E. Fehr, eds., pp. 43–73. Cambridge, Mass.: MIT Press.

Skidelsky, Robert, and Edward Skidelsky. 2012. *How Much Is Enough? Money and the Good Life*. New York: Other Press.

Smith, Adam. 2000 [1776]. *The Wealth of Nations*. New York: Modern Library.

———. 2002 [1759]. *The Theory of Moral Sentiments*. Edited by KnudHaakonssen. Cambridge, UK: Cambridge University Press.

Smith, Julia. 2009. "Shifting Coffee Markets and Producer Responses in Costa Rica and Panama." In *Economic Development, Integration, and Morality in Asia and the Americas. Research in Economic Anthropology*, Vol. 29, Donald C. Wood, ed., pp. 201–24. Bingley, UK: Emerald Group.

Smith, Vernon L. 1999. *Bargaining and Market Behavior: Essays in Experimental Economics*. New York: Cambridge University Press.

Solnick, Sara J., and David Hemenway. 1998. "Is More Always Better? A Survey on Positional Concerns." *Journal of Economic Behavior and Organization* 37 (3): 372–83.

Der Spiegel. 2008. "Bertelsmann-studie: Die Soziale Markwirtschaft im Unfragetief." June 16. www.spiegel.de.

Statistisches Bundesamt Deutschland. 2006. http://www.destatis.de.

Stehr, Nico. 2008. *Moral Markets: How Knowledge and Affluence Change Consumers and Products*. Boulder, Colo.: Paradigm.

Steinrücken, Torsten, and Sebastian Jaenichen. 2007. "The Fair Trade Idea: Towards an Economics of Social Labels." *Journal of Consumer Policy* 30 (3): 201–17.

Stevenson, Betsey, and Justin Wolfers. 2008. "Economic Growth and Subjective Well-Being: Reassessing the Easterlin Paradox." *Brookings Papers on Economic Activity* 39: 1–102.

Stiglitz, Joseph. 1993. "Market Socialism and Neoclassical Economics." In *Market Socialism: The Current Debate*, P. Bardhan and J. Roemer, eds. pp. 21–41. Oxford, UK: Oxford University Press.

Stiglitz, Joseph E., Amartya Sen, and Jean-Paul Fitoussi. 2010. *Mismeasuring Our Lives: Why GDP Doesn't Add Up: The Report*. New York: New Press.

Stout, Lynn. 2010. *Cultivating Conscience: How Good Laws Make Good People*. Princeton, N.J.: Princeton University Press.

Strathern, Marilyn. 1988. *The Gender of the Gift*. Berkeley: University of California Press.

Streeck, Wolfgang. 1997. "German Capitalism: Does It Exist? Can It Survive?" In *Political Economy of Modern Capitalism: Mapping Convergence and Diversity*, Colin Crouch and Wolfgang Streeck, eds., pp.33–54. Thousand Oaks, Calif.: Sage.

———. 2009. *Re-Forming Capitalism: Institutional Change in the German Political Economy*. Oxford, UK: Oxford University Press.

Streeck, Wolfgang, and Kathleen Thelen. 2005. *Beyond Continuity: Institutional Change in Advanced Political Economies*. Oxford, UK: Oxford University Press.

Taylor, Charles. 1985. *Philosophical Papers*. Cambridge, UK: Cambridge University Press.

———. 2005. "The 'Weak Ontology' Thesis." *Hedgehog Review* 7 (2): 35.

Terrio, Susan J. 2000. *Crafting the History and Culture of French Chocolate*. Berkeley: University of California Press.

Thaler, Richard. 1992. *The Winner's Curse*. Princeton, N.J.: Princeton University Press.

Thaler, Richard H., and Cass R. Sunstein. 2008. *Nudge: Improving Decisions about Health, Wealth, and Happiness*. New Haven, Conn.: Yale University Press.

Thelen, Kathleen. 2001. "Varieties of Labor Politics in the Developed Democracies." In *Varieties of Capitalism: The Institutional Foundations of Comparative Advantage*, Peter A. Hall and David Soskice, eds., pp.71–103. Oxford, UK: Oxford University Press

———. 2004. *How Institutions Evolve: The Political Economy of Skills in Germany, Britain, the United States, and Japan*. Cambridge, UK: Cambridge University press.

Thelen, Kathleen, and Lowell Turner. 1997. "German Codetermination in Comparative Perspective." Report for the Project "Mitbestimmung und neue Unternehmenskulturen." Guetersloh: Verlag Bertelsmann Stiftung.

Thin, Neil. 2012. *Social Happiness: Theory into Policy and Practice*. Bristol, UK: Policy Press.

Thomas, Kedron. 2012. "Intellectual Property Laws and the Ethics of Imitation in Guatemala." *Anthropological Quarterly* 85 (3): 785–816.

Thomas, Kedron, Kevin Lewis O'Neill, and Thomas Offit. 2011. "Securing the City." In *Securing the City: Neoliberalism, Space, and Insecurity in Postwar Guatemala*. Durham, N.C.: Duke University Press.

Thompson, E. P. 1971. "Moral Economy of the English Crowd in the Eighteenth Century." *Past and Present Society* 50 (1): 76–136.

Titmuss, Richard M. 1970. *The Gift Relationship: From Human Blood to Social Policy*. London: George Allen and Unwin.

Tucker, Catherine M. 2010. *Coffee Culture: Local Experiences, Global Linkages*. Anthropology of Stuff Series. New York: Routledge Press.

Turner, Lowell. 1998. *Fighting for Partnership: Labor and Politics in Unified Germany*. Ithaca, N.Y.: Cornell University Press.

Trope, Yaacov and Nora Liberman. 2010. "Construal-Level Theory of Psychological Distance." *Psychological Review* 117 (2): 440–63.

Tsing, Anna. 2004. *Friction: An Ethnography of Global Connections*. Princeton, N.J.: Princeton University Press.

Tversky, Amos, and Daniel Kahneman. 1981. "The Framing of Decisions and the Psychology of Choice." *Science* 211: 453–58.

UNCTAD. 2002. *Coffee: An Exporter's Guide*. Geneva: International Trade Center.

UNDP. 2011. *World Development Report*. New York: United Nations Development Programme.

Urry, John. 1995. *Consuming Places*. New York: Routledge.

Vázquez, José Juan. 2013. "Happiness among the Garbage: Differences in Overall Happiness among Trash Pickers in León (Nicaragua)." *Journal of Positive Psychology* 8 (1): 1–11.

Veblen, Thorstein. 1899. *The Theory of the Leisure Class: A Economic Study of Institutions*. New York: Macmillan.

Veenhoven, Ruut. 2000. "The Four Qualities of Life: Ordering Concepts and Measures of the Good Life." *Journal of Happiness Studies* 1: 1–39.

Victor, Bart, Edward F. Fischer, Bruce Cooil, Alfredo Vergara, Abraham Mukolo, and Meridith Blevins. 2013. "Frustrated Freedom: The Effects of Agency and Wealth on Wellbeing in Rural Mozambique." *World Development* 47: 30–41.

Victor, Bart, Meridith Blevins, Ann F. Green, Elisée Ndatimana, Lázaro González-Calvo, Edward F. Fischer, Alfredo E. Vegara, Sten H. Vermund, Omo Olupona, and Troy D. Moon. 2014. "Multidimensional Poverty in Rural Mozambique: A New Metric for Evaluating Public Health Interventions." Manuscript.

Vitols, Sigurt. 2004. "Negotiated Shareholder Value: The German Variant of Anglo-American Practice." *Competition and Change* 8 (4): 357–74.

Von Neumann, John, and Oskar Morgenstern. 1944. *Theory of Games and Economic Behavior*. Princeton, N.J.: Princeton University Press.

Von Rosen, Rüdiger. 1999. "Is There an Equity Culture in Germany?" Written and expanded text of a lecture given at Brandeis University, April 26. www.dai.de/internet/dai/dai-2-0.nsf/WebAnsichtPublikationenVortraege.

Wagner, Regina. 1991. *Los Alemanes en Guatemala 1828–1944*. Guatemala: Universidad Francisco Marroquín.

———. 2003. *Historia del Café en Guatemala*. Guatemala: Villegas Asociados.

Wallerstein, Immanuel. 1974. *The Modern World System: Capitalist Agriculture and the Origins of the European World Economy in the Sixteenth Century*. New York: Academic Press.

Warren, Kay B. 1998. *Indigenous Movements and Their Critics: Pan-Maya Activism in Guatemala*. Princeton, N.J.: Princeton University Press.

Waterman, Alan S., Seth J. Schwartz, and Regina Conti. 2006. "The Implications of Two Conceptions of Happiness (Hedonic Enjoyment and Eudaimonia) for the Understanding of Intrinsic Motivation." *Journal of Happiness Studies* 9 (2008): 41–79.

Weber, Max. 1978 [1914]. *Economy and Society*. Berkeley: University of California Press.

Weissman, Michaele. 2008. *God in a Cup: The Obsessive Quest for the Perfect Coffee*. New York: Wiley.

White, Stephen. 2000. *Sustaining Affirmation: The Strengths of Weak Ontology in Political Theory*. Princeton, N.J.: Princeton University Press.

Wild, Anthony. 2004. *Coffee: A Dark History*. New York: W. W. Norton.

Wilk, Richard. 1993. "Altruism and Self-Interest: Towards an Anthropological Theory of Decision Making." *Research in Economic Anthropology* 14: 191–212.

———. 1996. *Economies and Cultures*. Boulder, Colo.: Westview Press.

———, ed. 2006. *Fast Food/Slow Food: The Cultural Economy of the Global Food System*. Lanham, Md.: AltaMira Press.

Wilkinson, John. 2007. "Fair Trade: Dynamic and Dilemmas of a Market Oriented Global Social Movement." *Journal of Consumer Policy* 30 (3): 219–39.

Wilkinson, Richard, and Kate Pickett. 2009. *The Spirit Level: Why Greater Equality Makes Societies Stronger*. New York: Bloomsbury.

Willis, Paul, and Mats Trondman. 2000. "Manifesto for Ethnography." *Ethnography* 1 (1): 5–16.

Williams, Robert. 1994. *States and Social Evolution: Coffee and the Rise of National Governments in Central America*. Chapel Hill, N.C.: University of North Carolina Press.

Wilson, Richard. 1991. "Machine Guns and Mountain Spirits: The Cultural Effects of State Repression Among the Q'eqchi' of Guatemala." *Critique of Anthropology* 11 (1): 33–61.

———. 1995. *Maya Resurgence in Guatemala: Q'eqchi' Experiences*. Norman: University of Oklahoma Press.

Witt, Ulrich. 2002. "Germany's 'Social Market Economy': Between Social Ethos and Rent Seeking." *Independent Review* VI (3): 365–75.

Wolf, Eric R. 1956. "San Jose: Subcultures of a 'Traditional' Coffee Municipality." In *The People of Puerto Rico: A Study in Social Anthropology*, Julian Steward, ed., pp. 171–264. Urbana: University of Illinois Press.

Woodward, Ralph Lee, Jr. 1990. "Changes in the Nineteenth-Century State and Its Indian Policies." In *Guatemalan Indians and the State: 1540–1988*, Carol A. Smith, ed., pp. 52–71. Austin: University of Texas Press.

Zadek, Simon, Sanjiv Lingayah, and Maya Forstater. 1998. *Social labels: Tools for Ethical Trade*. London: New Economics Foundation.

Zak, Paul J. 2008. "Values and Value: Moral Economics." In *Moral Markets: The Critical Role of Values in the Economy*, Paul J. Zak. Princeton, N.J.: Princeton University Press.

Zaloom, Caitlin. 2006. *Out of the Pits: Traders and Technology from Chicago to London*. Chicago: University of Chicago Press.

Zaloom, Caitlin, and Natasha Schüll. 2014. "Neuroeconomics and the Politics of Choice." In *Cash on the Table: Markets, Values, and Moral Economies*, Edward F. Fischer, ed. Santa Fe: SAR Press.

Index

Plates, Figures, and Tables

TABLES

Acknowledgments

The writing of this book was so thoroughly collaborative that the authorship should really read "Fischer et al." Most of the ideas presented here were worked out in conversations, emails, and collaborative writing with friends and colleagues; and my thanks will be incomplete. Know that this was a joint effort.

My wife, Mareike Sattler, provided the intellectual, emotional, and practical support that I needed to complete this work. She and our children, Johannes and Rebecca, put up with my neurotic ways and absences with aplomb and support, and I could not have done this without them. Special thanks also go to my teachers-cum-students, Pakal B'alam, Ixchel Espantzay, and Tatiana Paz. In Germany, Wolfgang Gabbert and Ute Schüren made my fieldwork not only possible but immensely enjoyable.

Over the last few years, Bart Victor and I have traveled the world together working on joint projects. Almost all that I have to say here I ran by Bart first, aided— much to his chagrin—by the enforced proximity of travel, and I have freely borrowed his ideas and tried to incorporate his critiques and comments.

Peter Benson and I have been collaborating since his days as an undergraduate at Vanderbilt, and our work together on the book *Broccoli and Desire* set the stage for the study of coffee producers that appears here. Pete and I also co-organized a seminar at the School of Advanced Research in 2009, and his ideas helped frame a number of the arguments I make here.

My tennis partner, friend, and interlocutor on human nature and economics, Jon Shayne, works hard to keep me intellectually honest, often forcing me to take a more critical look at some key assumptions. My argument has benefited from his wise advice to eschew seeing the world as a place of too-stark contrasts.

Avery Dickins de Girón and I work together daily at the Vanderbilt Center for Latin American Studies, and all of my work benefits from her intellectual and administrative support. Avery and I have done joint fieldwork, and Chapter 8 is based on collaborative research and writing.

James Foster and I have collaborated on different projects for ten years or more, and I have learned an enormous amount from him about economics, capabilities theory, and generosity of spirit. James and I have been working on a project examining the role of provenance in value. This work is reflected in Chapter 4, and what insights I offer would not have been possible without James's input.

I have the good fortune to have a group of friends and colleagues who inspire me. Arthur Demarest, another night owl and kindred spirit, always challenges me intellectually and ethically, and has been an invaluable interlocutor. Matthew Restall is a steady source of inspiration and support, and I value his friendship as well as his insights. Dan Cornfield has provided me with crucial advice and is always a willing sounding board for new ideas, offering the right blend of encouragement and critique. Brent Savoie, who claims me as a mentor, has actually taught me much more than I have taught him, and I am grateful for his friendship and for showing me parts of Guatemala I did not previously know. Carol Hendrickson introduced me to her field site of Tecpán in 1990, and has shared it with me since then. Her generosity of spirit and intellectual rigor have been invaluable.

Joseph Mella and I have spent many hours together at home and abroad, and I have learned much from him and Su Williams about what an actual good life could look like.

Special thanks for helping me think through a number of specific issues go to Michiel Baud, Jens Beckert, João Biehl, Rudi Colloredo-Mansfeld, Bob Frank, Felipe Girón, Bill Hempstead, Juliette Levy, George Lovell, Sarah Lyon, Peter Mancina, Tom Offit, Mark Pendergrast, Dan Reichman, Kedron Thomas, Jean-Marie Simon, and Tim Smith.

I benefited from the inspiration and advice of Linda Asturias, Aleksandar Boskovič, Dominic Boyer, James Carrier, Thomas Davis, Steve Gudeman, Lissa Hunter, Carlos Jauregui, Cecilia Skinner-Klée, and Luis Velázquez.

This work profited greatly from the comments of the participants in the SAR Advanced Seminar "Markets and Moralities," especially Kate Zaloom, Ana Tsing, Jim Ferguson, and Stuart Kirsch. My argument was also sharpened in the Open Anthropology Cooperative's (OAC) seminar based on this book, especially by comments from Keith Hart, John McCreey, and Huon Wardle.

At Vanderbilt, I have benefited from the work and suggestions of a number of colleagues, including Brooke Ackerly, Katherine Donato, Brian Heuser, Mitch Seligson, Liz Zechmeister, Doug Meeks, Peter Martin, Bruce Barry, Doug Knight, and Norbert Ross. Alma Paz-Sanmiguel was an enormous help in putting this book together—and generally keeping me on track.

Thanks to Tilman Sattler and Johannes Fischer for their assistance in conducting surveys and interviews. Johannes also helped put together the bibliography.

Thanks to Jens Beckert, Wolfgang Streeck, and the MPIfG staff.

Thanks to Michiel Baud and the CEDLA staff.

Thanks to Bill Hempstead, Blanca Castro, and Anacafé.

Thanks to my Fall 2013 Economic Anthropology class for very useful comments.

And thanks to Michelle Lipinski, Gigi Mark, and Janet Mowery from Stanford University Press.

Support for research and writing was provided by the Alexander von Humboldt Stiftung, the Max Planck Institut für Gesellschaftsforschung, the Centre for Latin American Research and Documentation (CEDLA), Anacafé, and Vanderbilt University. Portions of several chapters have been published in different form elsewhere. Parts of the Introduction and most of Chapter 7 are from chapters in the volume *Cash on the Table* (Fischer 2014). Much of Chapter 5 appeared in the *Latin American Research Review* (Fischer and Victor 2014). A portion of Chapter 6 is adapted from Victor, Fischer, and Cooil (2013). Part of Chapter 8 is borrowed from Fischer and Benson (2006). An abstract of the entire argument presented here appeared as OAC Working Paper No.14.